The Rise and Fall of the Incomparable Liturgy

The Alcuin Club: Promoting the Study of Liturgy

Founded in 1897, the Alcuin Club seeks to promote the study of Christian liturgy and worship in general with special reference to worship in the Anglican Communion. The Club has published a series of annual **Collections**, including *A Companion to Common Worship*, volumes 1 and 2, edited by Paul F. Bradshaw; *The Origins of Feasts, Fasts and Seasons in Early Christianity* by Paul F. Bradshaw and Maxwell E. Johnson (SPCK 2011) and, by the same authors, *The Eucharistic Liturgies: Their Evolution and Interpretation* (SPCK 2012); also *The Cross and Creation in Christian Liturgy and Art* by Christopher Irvine (SPCK 2013); *Eucharistic Epicleses, Ancient and Modern* by Anne McGowan (SPCK 2014); *Dean Dwelly of Liverpool: Liturgical Genius* by Peter Kennerley (Carnegie Publishing 2015); and *Ancient Christian Worship* by Andrew B. McGowan (Baker Academic 2016). The **Alcuin Liturgy Guides** series aims to address the theology and practice of worship, and includes *The Use of Symbols in Worship,* edited by Christopher Irvine; two volumes covering the celebration of the Christian Year: *Celebrating Christ's Appearing: Advent to Christmas* and *Celebrating Christ's Victory: Ash Wednesday to Trinity,* both by Benjamin Gordon-Taylor and Simon Jones; and, most recently, *Celebrating Christian Initiation* by Simon Jones. The Club works in partnership with the Group for the Renewal of Worship (GROW) in the publication of the **Joint Liturgical Studies** series, with two studies being published each year. In 2013, the Club also published a major new work of reference, *The Study of Liturgy and Worship: An Alcuin Guide,* edited by Juliette Day and Benjamin Gordon-Taylor (SPCK 2013).

Members of the Club receive publications of the current year free and others at a reduced rate. The President of the Club is the Rt Revd Dr Stephen Platten, its Chairman is the Revd Canon Christopher Irvine, and the Secretary is the Revd Dr Gordon Jeanes. For details of membership and the annual subscription, contact The Alcuin Club, 5 Saffron Street, Royston SG8 9TR, United Kingdom, or email: alcuinclub@gmail.com

Visit the Alcuin Club website at: **www.alcuinclub.org.uk**

The Rise and Fall of the Incomparable Liturgy

The Book of Common Prayer, 1559–1906

Bryan D. Spinks

Alcuin Club Collections 92

First published in Great Britain in 2017
Society for Promoting Christian Knowledge
36 Causton Street
London SW1P 4ST
www.spck.org.uk

British Library Cataloguing-in-Publication Data
A catalogue record for this book is available from the British Library

ISBN 978–0–281–07605–5
eBook ISBN 978–0–281–07606–2

Typeset by Manila Typesetting Company
Subsequently digitally printed in Great Britain

eBook by Manila Typesetting Company

Produced on paper from sustainable forests

*To my sons
Jeremy and Timothy*

Contents

Preface

This present work was prompted by a remark by Paul Bradshaw. In 2014 Paul was a visiting Fellow at Yale Institute of Sacred Music and he and I co-taught a class for Yale Divinity School. Paul said that he heard things in my lectures that he hadn't read or heard before, and that I should write them up while I was still alive! I have in fact previously written a number of articles, essays and books which have covered some of the material presented here. In this volume I have re-arranged, expanded and in places précised the previous work to form a single narrative. I have not been able to discover who first coined the term 'incomparable liturgy' as applied to the Book of Common Prayer, or when it first appeared in print, but it echoes the claims made for the Use of Sarum by Bishop Giles de Bridport in 1256, that 'among the churches of the whole world, the church of Sarum hath shone resplendent, like the sun in his full orb, in respect of its divine service, and its ministers'.[1] As regards the application of 'incomparable' to the Prayer Book, there was in fact little in the English language to compare it with anyway. From the 1559 edition, the mild revision of 1604, the wider revisions of 1662, and adaptations in Scotland, Ireland and the USA, the sixteenth-century forms by and large held a monopoly in the Anglican churches until the serious scholarly-based and pastorally motivated revisions of the twentieth century. This study concludes at the beginning of the end of the hegemony of the 'incomparable liturgy', signalled by the 1906 Report of the Royal Commission on Ecclesiastical Discipline. I have drawn on my own previously published material used in the following books and articles, which are acknowledged here, though I have also added new material.

---

1 Cited in Archdale A. King, *Liturgies of the Past* (London: Longmans 1959), p. 286.

Chapters 1–3

'Anglicans and Dissenters' in Geoffrey Wainwright and Karen B. Westerfield Tucker (eds), *The Oxford History of Christian Worship* (Oxford: Oxford University Press 2006), pp. 492–533.

'From Elizabeth I to Charles II' in Charles Hefling and Cynthia Shattuck (eds), *The Oxford Guide to the Book of Common Prayer: A Worldwide Survey* (New York: Oxford University Press 2006), pp. 44–55.

'On the Wrong Side of History? Reimagining William Whittingham, Dean of Durham, 1563–1579' in Teresa Berger and Bryan D. Spinks (eds), *Liturgy's Imagined Past/s: Methodologies and Material in the Writing of Liturgical History Today* (Collegeville, MN: Liturgical Press 2016), pp. 205–29.

Sacraments, Ceremonies and the Stuart Divines: Sacramental Theology and Liturgy in England and Scotland 1603–1662 (Collegeville, MN and Ashgate: Aldershot 2002).

'Brief and Perspicuous Text; Plain and Pertinent Doctrine: Behind "Of the Preaching of the Word" in the Westminster Directory' in Martin Dudley (ed.), *Like a Two-Edged Sword* (Norwich: Canterbury Press 1995), pp. 91–111.

'Durham House and the Chapels Royal: Their Liturgical Impact on the Church of Scotland', *Scottish Journal of Theology* 67 (2014), pp. 379–99.

'Liturgy and Worship' in Jeremy Gregory (ed.), *Oxford History of Anglicanism: Reformation and Identity 1520–1662* (Oxford: Oxford University Press, forthcoming).

Chapter 4

Bryan D. Spinks, *Liturgy in the Age of Reason: Worship and Sacraments in England and Scotland 1662–c.1800* (Farnham: Ashgate 2008).

'Liturgy and Worship' in Jeremy Gregory (ed.), *Oxford History of Anglicanism: Establishment and Empire 1662–1829* (Oxford: Oxford University Press, forthcoming).

Chapter 5

'The Transition from "Excellent Liturgy" to being "Too Narrow for the Religious Life of the Present Generation": The Book of Common Prayer in the Nineteenth Century' in Stephen Platten and Christopher Woods (eds), *Comfortable Words: Piety and the Book of Common Prayer* (London: SCM 2012), pp. 98–120.

'Not So Common Prayer: The Third Service' in Michael Perham (ed.), *The Renewal of Common Prayer: Unity and Diversity in Church of England Worship* (London: SPCK 1993), pp. 55–67.

My thanks to Dr Juliette Day for comments on Chapter 1, and I owe a great debt of gratitude to my research assistant, the Revd Stephen McCarthy, who has worked tirelessly to check and correct quotations and typos while at the same time managing his own workload for the Yale Master of Sacred Theology degree.

BRYAN D. SPINKS
Epiphany season 2017

Introduction

For very obvious reasons, most histories of the Church of England's Book of Common Prayer begin with the circumstances and making of the first Prayer Book of 1549, and then its more explicitly Protestant second edition of 1552, both under the firm guidance and mostly the penmanship of Archbishop Thomas Cranmer. Textually and theologically this is logical, and it is these two texts which indicate to us the sources Cranmer used, and the shift to a more explicit Protestant theology.[1] However, the shelf life of these two Prayer Books was extremely short. Introduced with an Act of Uniformity on Whitsunday, 9 June 1549, the first Prayer Book was itself displaced by the second edition with another Act of Uniformity on 1 November 1552. With the accession of Queen Mary in July 1553, the Prayer Book quickly fell into abeyance as the Latin services were reintroduced. The 1552 book continued to be used in certain clandestine meetings, and it was used in some parishes in Scotland, and in modified versions by exiles on the Continent. Realistically, as important as the 1549 and 1552 books are for establishing the basic text of the Book of Common Prayer, their cumulative lifespan was at maximum three and a half years. Mary's reign of five years reintroduced the long-established Latin rites and saw five editions of the Missal, eight of the Processional, six of the Manual, eight of the Breviary, and 34 editions of the Primer.[2] As Eamon Duffy and

---

1 F. E. Brightman, *The English Rite*, 2 vols (London: Rivingtons 1915), is still important. For Cranmer's theology, see Gordon Jeanes, *Signs of God's Promise: Thomas Cranmer's Sacramental Theology and the Book of Common Prayer* (London: T & T Clark 2008); Bryan D. Spinks, 'Treasures Old and New: A Look at Some of Thomas Cranmer's Methods of Liturgical Compilation' in P. Ayris and D. Selwyn (eds), *Thomas Cranmer: Churchman and Scholar* (Woodbridge: Boydell and Brewer Ltd 1993), pp. 175–88; *Reformation and Modern Rituals and Theologies of Baptism: From Luther to Contemporary Practices* (Aldershot: Ashgate 2006); *Do This in Remembrance of Me: The Eucharist from the Early Church to the Present Day* (London: SCM Press 2013).
2 Eamon Duffy, *Fires of Faith: Catholic England under Mary Tudor* (New Haven, CT: Yale University Press 2009), p. 59.

others have shown, the re-establishment of the 'old religion' in England was carefully and thoroughly applied and, but for the untimely death of Mary and other circumstances, might have endured. It did not. Duffy notes:

> It was the wholly unexpected double demise of cardinal as well as Queen, and not any gradual loss of direction or waning of determination, that halted the Marian project, and the Marian burnings, in their tracks . . . The Marian project was over, apparently as dead as the unhappy Mary and her cousin the Cardinal.[3]

It was with the Elizabethan Settlement and the relatively long and stable reign of Elizabeth that the Church of England as a reformed episcopal church with a Book of Common Prayer became firmly established and its liturgy became part of the national identity. For this reason, this study of the Book of Common Prayer begins with the introduction of what was the third edition/recension, namely that of 1559 by Queen Elizabeth I. It concludes with the Report of the Royal Commission on Ecclesiastical Discipline (1906), which in many ways set the scene in England for the eventual move towards alternative forms for worship other than the Book of Common Prayer.

---

3 Duffy, *Fires of Faith*, pp. 187 and 188.

Chapter I

The 1559 Book of Common Prayer and worship in the Elizabethan Church

ELIZABETHAN LITURGICAL PROVISIONS

The official or authorized liturgical provisions of the Elizabethan Church may be divided into three categories. First, provision was made for regular public worship and comprised the Litany and Suffrages, the Book of Common Prayer (1559) and the Latin versions of the Book of Common Prayer for the collegiate chapels of Oxford, Cambridge, Eton and Winchester of 1560 and 1571/72. Next were the official primers and collections of prayers for private use which were issued at various dates from 1559 to 1590. This category consisted of several distinct collections of devotional material. Both the forms for public worship and several examples of these primers and manuals of prayer were edited in the mid-nineteenth century by William Clay.[1] According to Clay's introduction, those private devotional forms, set forth by authority (though the nature of the authority is debatable), fall into four groups.

1 The Primer, published in 1559, and another version in 1566, and a second edition in 1575. These are quite distinct from the reprints in 1560 and 1568 of the Edwardian Primer (1553).
2 The *Orarium*, or Hours in Latin, published in 1560 and 1573.
3 The Latin *Preces Privatae* of 1564, 1568, 1573 and 1574.

---

1 William K. Clay (ed.), *Liturgies and Occasional Forms of Prayer Set Forth in the Reign of Queen Elizabeth* (Cambridge: Cambridge University Press 1847); *Private Prayers Put Forth by Authority during the Reign of Queen Elizabeth* (Cambridge: Cambridge University Press 1851).

4 Significantly different from the Primers, *The Book of Christian Prayers*, 1569, 1578, 1581 and 1590. These contained traditional Catholic and contemporary Protestant devotional material.

A third category was forms of worship for occasional use, such as for days of special celebration or fasting.[2] These latter were expected to be used in all cathedrals and churches, thus maintaining uniformity, but nevertheless departed in content from the usual Book of Common Prayer services. These various liturgical compilations, as well as articles and injunctions, replaced the worship texts and ceremonies of the Marian Church. However, the process and the apparent contradictions that these cumulatively present witness to a somewhat complex and layered religious settlement.

THE PROCESS

In his study of Parliament and the settlement of religion of 1559, Norman Jones noted that Elizabeth the politician and Elizabeth the person can never be disentangled.[3] In matters of religion she was Protestant. Although it is difficult to tell exactly which brand of Protestantism (John Booty's designation of Protestant-humanist is a fair description),[4] it is obvious that Elizabeth would not tolerate a Church independent from the State – particularly a Church under a Roman pontiff who regarded the new queen as illegitimate and not a rightful heir to the English throne. Thus royal supremacy was at the very centre of both her political and religious policy. The emergence of the 1559 Book of Common Prayer and the various subsequent liturgical provisions are therefore intricately bound to the political manoeuvres of the first months which secured Elizabeth as undisputed monarch of England.

Within the first weeks of her succession, Elizabeth received documents, four of which have survived, giving her advice on future policies. Sir Nicholas Throckmorton sent a letter in which he advised a discreet beginning and suggested advisers, some of whom were conservative Catholics, and others known for Protestant sympathies. Armagill Waad

---

2 Natalie Mears, Alasdair Raffe, Stephen Taylor and Philip Williamson (with Lucy Bates) (eds), *National Prayers: Special Worship Since the Reformation. Vol. 1: Special Prayers, Fasts and Thanksgivings in the British Isles 1533–1688* (Woodbridge: The Church of England Record Society and the Boydell Press 2013).

3 See Norman Jones, *Faith by Statute: Parliament and the Settlement of Religion 1559* (London: Royal Historical Society 1968) for fuller details, and also William P. Haugaard, *Elizabeth and the English Reformation* (Cambridge: Cambridge University Press 1968).

4 John E. Booty, *The Book of Common Prayer 1559* (Charlottesville, VA: University of Virginia 2005, reprint), p. 332.

addressed a document entitled 'Distresses of the Commonwealth with the Remedy Therin', which set out the nation's problems, and advised caution. Richard Goodrich, a seasoned lawyer, compiled 'Divers Points of Religion Contrary to the Church of Rome', which listed the legal precedents for limiting and curtailing papal authority in the nation. However, it is the anonymous document, 'Device for the Alteration of Religion', which has been mainly regarded as pertinent to the 1559 Book of Common Prayer. This document, generally acknowledged to have been written in 1558 by someone highly placed within the Church, called for a committee of divines to draw up reforms for the Church. The extent to which this advice was consciously adopted and used as a blueprint is disputed, but it certainly foreshadowed what was to unfold in the following months. What did begin to emerge, however, was a national need to make a settlement which would ensure no invasion by either Spain or France, and a desire to be free of papal authority. On matters of religion, the nation was more divided, and an independent Catholic Church, as in the days of Henry, was probably what many anticipated. However, Thomas Thirlby, Bishop of Ely, informed one of the secretaries of Cardinal de Granville that he had no friends in the new council, and predicted the fall of the 'old religion' in England.

Already by 17 December 1558 (a month to the day after the deaths of Mary and Pole) there were rumours that Elizabeth was using an English Litany in her Chapel Royal. That Christmas she requested the Bishop of Carlisle not to elevate the host at Mass. He declined so to do, and the Queen retired after the singing of the Gospel. A Royal Proclamation was sent to the Lord Mayor of London on 28 December. It was concerned with unlicensed preaching, but declared that preaching should be confined to the Epistle and Gospel of the day and the Ten Commandments in the vulgar tongue 'without exposition'. However, it also allowed the Litany 'used at this present in her majesty's own chapel' and the Lord's Prayer and Creed in English. Nothing new was to be done 'until consultation may be had by parliament, by her majesty'. Richard Jugge hurriedly printed 'the letanye, used in the Quenes Maiestie chappel' to allow those with a Protestant taste to take advantage of this permission.

Some controversy surrounds the precise liturgical details of the coronation on 15 January 1559. There are three contemporary accounts: a fragmentary herald's account in College of Arms, volume W.Y. fol. 198; an English eyewitness account known as *The Ceremonies of the Coronacͨon of the moost excellent Queen Elysabeth*; and a letter from the Mantuan envoy Il Schifanoya to the Castellan of Mantua of 23 January 1559. Elizabeth chose to be escorted into Westminster Abbey by the choir of the Chapel Royal singing the English litany rather than be accompanied by the monks with torches. The accounts are in conflict over whether the host was elevated at the Mass, whether it was administered in two kinds, and whether Elizabeth communicated, though she was apparently anointed from the same oil used by her half-sister, procured from the Bishop of Arras, Antoine Perrenot de Granville.[5] Certainly by Easter Elizabeth was receiving Communion in two kinds, rather than just the host as was the Catholic practice. The preachers selected for Lent to preach before Elizabeth tended to be those named in the anonymous 'Device', and were clearly Protestant in sympathy.

As already noted, Elizabeth and her advisers were concerned to proceed within the legal system. The first step was for Parliament to pass a new Act of Supremacy, removing the English Church from papal control. A bill to this purpose was introduced into the Commons on 9 February 1559. It is uncertain as to whether this bill also included reform of the liturgy. However, a second, new bill of supremacy was introduced on 21 February and did incorporate provision for ordering services and a prayer book. On 23 February it passed after a stormy debate. According to Il Schifanoya:

> a book passed by the Commons forbidding the Mass to be said or the Communion to be administered except at the table in the manner of Edward VI; nor were the Divine offices to be performed in Church; priests likewise being allowed to marry, and the Christian religion and the sacraments being absolutely abolished; adding thereto many extraordinary penalties against delinquents. By a majority of votes they have decided that the aforesaid things shall be expunged from the book, and that the Masses, Sacrament, and the rest of the divine offices shall be performed as hitherto; but some persons say that this decision cannot last long, the catholics insisting at any rate on retaining the Mass, the Offices, and the rest of the Sacraments, and the Protestants insisting on the contrary.[6]

The clergy of the Convocation of Canterbury drew up a protestation of faith, reaffirming the real presence in the Eucharist, transubstantiation,

---

5 Dale Hoak, 'The Coronations of Edward VI, Mary I, and Elizabeth I, and the Transformation of the Tudor Monarchy' in C. S. Knighton and Richard Mortimer (eds), *Westminster Abbey Reformed 1540–1640* (Aldershot: Ashgate 2003), pp. 136–7.

6 Venetian papers, no. 45, 21 March 1558–9, cited in H. N. Birt, *The Elizabethan Religious Settlement: A Study of Contemporary Documents* (London: George Bell and Sons 1907), p. 77.

the sacrifice of the Mass and papal supremacy, and insisted that it was the Church, not the State, which defined matters of dogma. The Bishop of London delivered these on 3 March to the Lord Keeper, Nicholas Bacon, who apparently did nothing further with them. The bill passed to the Lords and was read on 28 February, where it met with stiff opposition. On 13 March the bill was given to a committee of Lords. The committee appears to have been quite conservative as regards the religious intentions of the bill, and reduced it to a skeleton; the supremacy was acceptable, but not the Protestant proposals. The much-altered bill came for its third reading on 18 March. The Commons was in a quandary, since to reject the bill would mean that the Pope was still head of the English Church; to pass it would be to have supremacy of the Queen with Catholic services. A proposal to allow the Edwardian services as an alternative came to nothing. The bill as amended by the Lords passed on 22 March, and Elizabeth was named Supreme Governor of the Church of England.

A proclamation printed on 22 March, but never issued, suggests that provision was to be made to use something similar to the Order of the Communion issued in 1548, which was an English vernacular devotion inserted in the Latin Mass. However, as Parliament recessed for Easter, events seem to have gathered speed. A disputation was arranged between the bishops and other Catholic representatives and carefully selected Protestant divines. As with most disputations in this era, it was already weighted to a Protestant victory. The dispute never got past the second day. The bishops refused to follow the agenda prescribed by the moderator, Lord Keeper Bacon, and later that day all the Catholic disputants were arrested. This severely weakened the numerical opposition in the Lords, and weakened conservative morale. A new supremacy bill was introduced in the Commons on 10 April 1559 and was completed by 29 April. This new bill styled the monarch 'supreme governor' of the Church, rather than 'supreme head'. On 18 April a new Act of Uniformity was read in the Commons, and concluded in the Lords on 28 April. Henry Machyn recorded in his diary that on 12 May services in English began in the Queen's chapel.[7]

AMBIGUOUS SETTLEMENT

The Prayer Book enacted by the bill was that of 1552, but with some significant, even if not totally explicable, alterations.

---

7 John Gough Nichols (ed.), *The Diary of Henry Machyn: Citizen and Merchant-Taylor of London, From AD 1550–AD 1563* (London: Camden Society 1848), p. 197.

1 The rubric concerning the position of the officiant at Morning and Evening Prayer was altered from that of 1552 to now read:

The Morning and Evening Prayer shall be used in the accustomed place of the church, chapel, or chancel, except it shall be otherwise determined by the ordinary of the place; and the chancels shall remain as they have done in times past.

2 The so-called ornaments rubric was placed before Morning Prayer and seems to have sanctioned Mass vestments as well as candles and altars, though it was never so invoked until the nineteenth century. It read:

And here is to be noted that the minister at the time of the Communion, and at all other times in his ministration, shall use such ornaments in the church as were in use by authority of Parliament in the second year of the reign of King Edward the Sixth according to the Act of Parliament set in the beginning of this book.

3 The 'Black Rubric' of the 1552 Communion service which explained the injunction to kneel for receiving Communion was removed.
4 In the Communion service the words of delivery at Communion from the 1549 Prayer Book were introduced and combined with those of 1552:

The bodie of our lord Jesu Christ, which was geven for thee, preserve thy body and soule into everlastinge life: and take and eate this in remembraunce that Christ died for thee, feede on him in thine heart by faith, with thankesgevynge.

The bloude of our lorde Jesu Christ, which was shedd for the, preserve thy body and soule into everlasting life: and drinke this in remembraunce that Christes bloude was shedde for thee, and be thankeful.

5 In the Litany and in the Ordination rites deprecations of the Bishop of Rome were removed. The Ordinal received no mention in the Act of Uniformity, and the legality of its use was challenged by Bishop Bonner in 1564. It was authorized by Parliament in 1566.
6 In 1561, 57 saints' days reappeared in the calendar.

Elizabeth's own vision for the English Church is shrouded by a certain ambiguity. On the one hand she seems to have wanted to retain rood screens and the roods themselves, but in fact the latter were ultimately removed and destroyed. Some have thought she would have preferred the 1549 Book of Common Prayer. Roger Bowers suggests that the instructions given to her chapel composers demonstrate that she expected such restoration of Edwardian forms to be based on the Book of Common Prayer not of 1552 but of 1549.[8] He notes that William Mundy's First Service, which on stylistic grounds cannot be earlier than 1558, uses the 1549 texts. Similarly the First Service of Robert Parsons, which uses the text of 1549; in the years 1549–52 Parsons was in his early teens, and on stylistic grounds the work is early Elizabethan. The free-standing setting of the Te Deum of Thomas Tallis uses the 1549 text, but all informed opinion dates it on stylistic grounds to the first years of Elizabeth's reign at the earliest. Since by 23 March 1559, and no later than 18 April, it was clear that it would be the 1552 Prayer Book that prevailed, they were probably composed before that time.[9] So Bowers concluded:

> It is clear, therefore, that by a date which can hardly have been later than around the beginning of December 1558 instructions were being given to the Chapel Royal composers to begin to write new music in preparation for a return to vernacular liturgy that was considered to be imminent. Such instruction can have originated only with the monarch herself . . . their existence indicates strongly that the liturgy whose restoration the queen envisaged as her reign began was that of the Prayer Book of 1549.[10]

Diarmaid MacCulloch, though, has argued that Bower's case is flawed by his misreading of the date of John Sheppard's death, and the music was written prior to 1553.[11]

Yet even if this be the case, there are other ambiguities that point to a practical conservatism. Section 13 of the Elizabethan Act of Uniformity had given the Queen authority 'to ordeyne and publishe suche further Ceremonies or rites as maye bee most meet for the advancement of Goddes Glorye, the edifying of his church and the due Reverence of Christes holye mistries and Sacraments'. Under this section the

---

8 Roger Bowers, 'The Chapel Royal, the first Edwardian Prayer Book, and Elizabeth's Settlement of Religion, 1559', *The Historical Journal* 43.2 (2000), pp. 317–44, p. 320.
9 Bowers, 'The Chapel Royal', pp. 329–30.
10 Bowers, 'The Chapel Royal', p. 330.
11 D. MacCulloch, 'Putting the English Reformation on the Map', *Transactions of the Royal Historical Society* 15 (2005), pp. 75–95, p. 88, n. 29.

Queen authorized by letters patent of 6 April 1560 the *Liber Precum Publicarum*, a Latin edition of the Book of Common Prayer for use in the chapels of Oxford, Cambridge, Eton and Winchester. However, the translator, thought to be Walter Haddon, drew on the Latin version of the 1549 Book of Common Prayer. Among its differences from the 1559 English Book was provision for an epistler and gospeller, vested in copes at the Communion, reservation of the sacrament, a fuller calendar of saints, a service commemorating college benefactors, and provision for a requiem Communion. Protestant scholars were not slow to note the differences, and it was reported that most Cambridge colleges refused to use it. The Primer that was published in 1559 was a reissue of the 1551 edition of Henry's 1545 Primer. Whereas the Prayer Book provided two offices of Morning and Evening Prayer, the Primer gave English versions of the more traditional eight offices, suggesting a more conservative Catholic trend. In 1560 the *Orarium* was published, giving the eight offices in Latin, and it included Latin hymns. It is these elements that suggest an ambiguity about Elizabeth's ideal for her Church.

Services in another category – those issued as occasion arose for special services, such as the Accession Service and fasts – have been usefully collected together and edited recently. The editors noted two distinct forms: first, the *Short fourme of thankesgeuyng* for the end of the plague was issued in 1564 and set a pattern for special forms that was still followed in the nineteenth century; the second, issued for use during the plague of 1563, and which was used periodically until 1665, provided services for different days of the week. Based on Morning and Evening Prayer, these forms used special collects, readings and psalms, including cento psalmody.[12]

Commissioners toured the dioceses collecting and confiscating the traditional Mass vestments, but Elizabeth's intention was to have copes worn over the surplice at Communion. Ultimately it was difficult enough to insist on the surplice, and copes were enforced only in the cathedrals. The ambiguity of the religious settlement was reflected in the varied performance of the prescribed rites. In a manuscript of 1564, which John Strype transcribed, we learn:

> Some say the Service and Prayers in the Chancel; others in the Body of the Church. Some say the same in a Seat made in the Church; some in the Pulpit, with their Faces to the People. Some keep precisely the

---

12 Mears et al. (eds), *National Prayers*, p. lxxviii.

Order of the Book; Others intermeddle Psalms in metre. Some say with a Surplice; others without a Surplice.

The Table standeth in the Body of the Church in some Places; in others it standeth in the Chancel. In some Places the Table standeth Altarwise, distant from the Wall Yard. In some Places in the middle of the Chancel, North and South. In some Places the Table is Joined: In others it standeth upon Tressels. In some the Table hath a Carpet, in others it hath none.

Some with Surplice and Cap; some with Surplice alone, others with none. Some with Chalice, some with a Communion Cup; others a common Cup. Some with Unleavened bread, and some with Leavened.

Some Receive Kneeling, others Standing, others Sitting.

Some Baptize in a Font, some in a Basin. Some Sign with the Sign of the Cross; others Sign not. Some Minister in a Surplice, others without.

Some with a Square Cap; some with a Round Cap; some with a Button Cap; some with a Hat; Some in Scholar's Cloathes, some in others.[13]

The liturgical style much depended upon the incumbent and his own theological leanings. Many priests tried to celebrate the Communion as much like the Mass as possible, whereas the more reformed did the exact opposite. Sir Christopher Trychay of Morebath went on calling the Sunday evening service 'Second evening prayer', which was a hangover from the observance of First and Second Vespers of the Latin rite, and referred to the Communion table as the 'auter' or 'hye auter'.[14] In the 1560s Christ Church Cathedral, Dublin, apparently still observed St Katherine, Our Lady Day (8 December), Christmas Day to 1 January, Epiphany, St Bride's Day, St Patrick, St Peter, St Laurence, the Assumption, St Bartholomew, St Michan, St Matthew, Michaelmas and Nativity of our Lady, at least as holidays from work. At Christmas, many candles were set out on every side of the choir and rood loft according to the usual custom.[15] In many parish churches Communion became limited to a monthly, quarterly or tri-annual celebration and the main

---

13 John Strype, *The Life and Acts of Matthew Parker* (London: printed for John Wyat 1711), Book II, p. 152.
14 Eamon Duffy, *The Voices of Morebath: Reformation and Rebellion in an English Village* (New Haven, CT: Yale University Press 2001), p. 178.
15 James Mills, 'The Journal of Sir Peter Lewys, 1564–1565', *Royal Society of Antiquities of Ireland* 6 (1896), pp. 136–41, pp. 138 and 139.

Sunday services of the Elizabethan Church were Morning Prayer, the Litany, and the first part of the Communion Service with a sermon, and Evening Prayer with catechism. A contemporary account was given by the historians Raphael Holinshed and William Harrison:

There is nothing read in our churches but the canonicall scriptures, whereby it commeth to passe that the psalter is said ouer once in thirtie daies, the new testament foure times, and the old testament once in the yeare. And herevnto if the curat be adiudged by the bishop or his deputies, sufficientlie instructed in the holie scriptures, and therewithall able to teach, he permitteth him to make some exposition or exhortation in his parish, vnto amendment of life. And for so much as our churches and vniuersities haue béene so spoiled in time of errour, as there cannot yet be had such number of able pastours as may suffice for euerie parish to haue one: there are (beside foure sermons appointed by publike order in the yeare) certeine sermons or homilies (deuised by sundrie learned men, confirmed for sound doctrine by consent of the diuines, and publike authoritie of the prince) and those appointed to be read by the curats of meane vnderstanding (which homilies doo comprehend the principall parts of christian doctrine, as of originall sinne, of iustification by faith, of charitie, and such like) vpon the sabbaoth daies, vnto the congregation. And after a certeine number of psalmes read, which are limited according to the daies of the month, for morning and euening praier, we haue two lessons, wherof the first is taken out of the old testament, the second out of the new, and of these latter that in the morning is out of the gospels, the other in the after noone out of some one of the epistles. After morning praier also we haue the letanie and suffrages, an inuocation in mine opinion not deuised without the great assistance of the spirit of God, although manie curious mindsicke persons vtterlie condemne it as superstitious and sauoring of coniuration and sorcerie.

This being doone, we procéed vnto the communion, if anie communicants be to receiue the eucharist, if not we read the decalog, epistle and gospell with the Nicene créed (of some in derision called the drie communion) and then procéed vnto an homilie or sermon, which hath a psalme before and after it, and finallie vnto the baptisme of such infants as on euerie saboth daie (if occasion so require) are brought vnto the churches: and thus is the forenoone bestowed. In the after noone likewise we méet againe, and after the psalmes and lessons ended we haue commonlie a sermon, or at the leastwise our youth catechised by the space of an houre. And thus doo we spend the sabaoth daie in good and godlie exercises, all doone in our vulgar toong, that each one present may heare and vnderstand the same, which also in cathedrall and collegiat churches is so ordered, that the psalmes onelie are soong by note, the rest being read (as in common parish churches) by the minister with a lowd voice, sauing that in the administration of the communion the quier singeth the answers, the créed, and sundrie other things appointed, but in so plaine, I saie, and distinct maner, that each one present may understand what they sing, euerie word hauing but one note, though the whole harmonie consist of manie parts, and those verie cunninglie set by the skilfull in that science.[16]

The Church of England became the sole Protestant Church to base its main Sunday Service on the old divine office, and thus the priest's desk or stall became more important than the altar table as the main locus of worship. In Morebath, a priest's desk had been constructed 'at the quire dore' before the dismantling of the rood.[17] Holinshed and Harrison explained:

As for our churches themselues, belles, and times of morning and euening praier, remaine as in times past, sauing that all images, shrines, tabernacles, roodlofts, and monuments of idolatrie are remooued, taken downe, and defaced; onelie the stories in glasse windowes excepted, which for want of sufficient store of new stuffe, and by reason of extreame charge that should grow by the alteration of the same into white panes throughout the realme, are not altogither abolished in most places at once, but by little and little suffered to decaie, that white glasse may be prouided and set vp in their roomes. Finalie, whereas there was woont to be a great partition betwéene the quire and the bodie of the church; now it is either verie small or none at all: and to saie the truth altogither needlesse, sith the minister saith his seruice commonlie in the bodie of the church, with his face toward the people, in a little tabernacle of wainscot prouided for the purpose: by which means the ignorant doo not onelie learne diuerse of the psalmes and vsuall praiers by heart, but also such as can read, doo praie togither with him: so that the whole congregation at one

---

16 Raphael Holinshed, *The Chronicles of England, Ireland and Scotland* (London: Johnson et al. 1807), p. 232.
17 Duffy, *Voices*, p. 178.

instant powere out their petitions vnto the liuing God, for the whole
estate of his church in most earnest and feruent manner.[18]

In addition, as George Yule observed, once sermons and Bible readings
became central elements in the services, pews and benches became a
necessity, though these also became markers of hierarchy in the local
community.[19]

THE CHAPEL ROYAL

In the Chapel Royal, though, things were rather different. Elizabeth
insisted that in her chapel the table would be set altarwise, and would
be furnished like an altar with cross and candles. Bishop John Jewel, in a
letter of 16 November 1559 to Peter Martyr Vermigli, had commented:

> The doctrine is every where most pure; but as to ceremonies and
> maskings, there is a little too much foolery. That little silver cross,
> of ill-omened origin, still maintains its place in the queen's chapel.
> Wretched me! this thing will soon be drawn into a precedent.[20]

Henry Machyn recorded for 1560: 'The vj of Marche dyd pryche at
the court doctur Byll dene of Westmynster that day in the quen('s)
chapell, the crosse and ij candylles bornyng and the tabulles standyng
auter-wyse.'[21] Strype recorded that on 24 March 1560, Midlent Sunday:

> The same day, in the afternoon, bishop Barlow, one of King Edward's
> bishops, now bishop of Chichester, preached in his habit before the
> queen. His sermon ended at five of the clock: and presently after her
> chapel went to evening song: the cross, as before, standing on the
> altar, and two candlesticks, and two tapers burning in them: and,
> service concluded, a good anthem was sung.[22]

---

18 Holinshed, *The Chronicles of England*, p. 279.
19 George Yule, 'James VI and I: Furnishing the Churches in His Two Kingdoms' in
Anthony Fletcher and Peter Roberts (eds), *Religion, Culture and Society in Early Modern
Britain* (Cambridge: Cambridge University Press 2006), pp. 182–208, p. 191; C. Marsh,
'"Common Prayer" in England 1560–1640: The View from the Pew', *Past and Present*
171 (2001), pp. 66–94; 'Sacred Space in England, 1560–1640', *Journal of Ecclesiastical
History* 53 (2002), pp. 286–311.
20 *The Zurich Letters, Comprising the Correspondence of Several English Bishops and
Others* (Cambridge: Parker Society 1842), p. 55.
21 Nichols (ed.), *The Diary of Henry Machyn*, p. 226.
22 John Strype, *Annals of the Reformation* (Oxford: 1824), Vol. 1, Part 1, pp. 298–9.

The Old Cheque-book of the Chapel Royal contains an account of Communion on Easter Day 1593:

> Her Majestie entred her travess moste devoutly, there knyelinge: after some prayers she came princely before the Table, and there humbly knielinge did offer the golden obeysant, the Bishop the hon. Father of Worcester holding the golden bason, the Subdean and the Epistler in riche coaps assistante to the sayd Bushop (*sic*) . . . her Majestie . . . [received] the most blessed Sacramente of Christes bodye and blood, in the kinds of bread and wyne, accordinge to the laws established by her Majestie and Godly laws in Parliament. The bread beinge wafer bread of some thicker substance, which her Majestie in most reverend manner toke of the Lord Bushop in her naked right hand . . . and likewise her Majestie received the cuppe, having a moste princely lynned clothe layd on her cushion pillowe and borne at the four ends by the noble Erle of Herefford, the Erle of Essex, the Erle of Worcester, and the Erle of Oxford: the side of the sayd clothe her Majiestie took up in her hande, and therewith toke the ffoote of the golden and nowe sacred cuppe.[23]

This may be conservatism, but it was also royal pride, not wishing to have the ceremonial and etiquette of the English Court compromised by bare liturgical ceremonial. Bernadette Nelson has shown that the ceremonial and music for the Spanish Royal Chapel, 1559–61 (and now one of England's enemies and rivals), was sumptuous, concluding that the 'diverse ceremonies' described in *La Orden* were extremely elaborate and protracted affairs in which ritual, ceremony and musical performance were linked within a coherent and highly programmed structure.[24] John Adamson noted that despite the Reformation, most of the major elements of court ceremonial continued until the accession of the Hanoverians. Some feast days such as Corpus Christi disappeared, but otherwise the pre-Reformation calendar remained virtually

23 Edward Francis Rimbault (ed.), *The Old Cheque-book, or Book of remembrance, of the Chapel Royal, from 1561–1744* (London: Camden Society 1872), pp. 150–1. For a more accurate rendering of the original spellings, see Andrew Ashbee and John Harley (eds), *The Cheque Books of the Chapel Royal*, 2 vols (Aldershot: Ashgate 2000), Vol. 1, pp. 54–5.
24 Bernadette Nelson, 'Ritual and Ceremony in the Spanish Royal Chapel, c.1559–c.1561', *Early Music History* 19 (2000), pp. 105–200, p. 168. See also Michael Noone, *Music and Musicians in the Escorial Liturgy under the Hapsburgs, 1563–1700* (Woodbridge: University of Rochester Press 1998).

unchanged, with 12 major court days forming an annual cycle from Michaelmas to St John the Baptist. The great Sunday processions and holy-day processions remained unaltered, and when the monarch received Communion it was under a little canopy or pavilion erected on one side of the Chapel Royal, in imitation of the Castilian court.[25] Elizabeth might not get her way in parish churches, but she was not going to tolerate paltry and mean worship in her presence. Court etiquette and royal grandeur meant that the ceremonial and music of the English Chapels Royal and other royal ecclesiastical establishments differed from that found in most English parish churches. Machyn frequently noted the copes and combination of ecclesiastical and court ceremonial on the feast of St George.[26] In 1575 a report compiled by Venetian visitors to Windsor reported:

> After remaining three days in London we went to Windsor where the Queen was then residing, and on being conducted to the palace were introduced to what is called the Presence Chamber, at the hour when her Majesty was to pass through on her way to Chapel. The apartment was very crowded, and the nobility assembled there greeted us cordially, and with every mark of honour. After some short talk and a joke or two . . . Elizabeth moved towards the Chapel, where she remained about twenty minutes until the service was ended. The service consisted first of all, of certain psalms chanted in English by a double chorus of some thirty singers. A single voice then chanted the Epistle, and after this another the Gospel, and all the voices then sang the Creed. This concluded the service, and we with the rest then returned to the Presence Chamber to see the Queen once more, and to pay due homage as she passed.[27]

Elizabeth's hope may have been that the Chapels Royal would set an example for cathedrals and parish churches, though in fact they became the exception. Jewel's fears, though, were to prove prophetic. Westminster Abbey was a Royal Peculiar. J. F. Merritt has pointed out that Gabriel Goodman was Dean of the Abbey from 1561 until

25 John Adamson, 'The Kingdom of England and Great Britain: The Tudor and Stuart Courts 1509–1714' in John Adamson (ed.), *The Princely Courts of Europe: Ritual, Politics and Culture Under the Ancien Régime 1500–1750* (London: Weidenfeld and Nicolson 1999), pp. 95–117, pp. 100, 102, 104.
26 Nichols (ed.), *The Diary of Henry Machyn*, pp. 232, 257, 258.
27 R. Brown and G. C. Bentinck, *Calendar of State Papers Venetian VII (1558-80)* (London: Her Majesty's Stationery Office 1890), p. 525.

his death in 1601, during which 'under his lengthy and sober tenure, Westminster Abbey, experienced a remarkable period of stability, which enshrined the most conservative aspects of the Elizabethan period'.[28] An inventory of the Abbey in the seventeenth century lists a number of old copes and canopies that appear to be pre-Reformation survivals, and that included the depictions of Christ dead in the arms of God the Father and the death of the Virgin Mary. This conservatism was built upon by his successors Lancelot Andrewes and Richard Neile in their attention to the choir, the fabric and ornamentation, and it was Neile who installed a new organ, a programme of music-copying and additional funding for the choir. Andrewes, and later William Laud, were Deans of the Chapel Royal. John Overall had been a royal chaplain, as had John Buckeridge, who had also been a canon of Windsor. The furnishings and ceremonial of the English Chapels Royal, as well as of episcopal private chapels such as Andrewes', became for these later 'Laudian' churchmen the standard to which cathedrals, collegiate churches and, ultimately in their minds, also parish churches should aspire. The style was derived from Elizabeth's Chapels Royal.

CATHEDRAL AND PARISH CHURCH MUSIC

Diarmaid MacCulloch has suggested that the cathedrals were forces of conservatism and a cuckoo in the nest.[29] More recently Jonathan Willis has suggested that the situation was in fact more complex and that at least with regard to music they were institutions that embraced change and adapted themselves to a Protestant settlement. The continuity was with daily choral services.[30]

The Royal Injunctions of 1559 made clear that the choral foundations in cathedrals, collegiate churches and some parish churches were to continue, and that

> there be a modest and distinct song so used in all parts of the common prayers in the church, that the same may be as plainly understanded, as if it were read without singing; and yet nevertheless for the comforting of such that delight in music, it may be permitted,

---

28 J. F. Merritt, 'The Cradle of Laudianism? Westminster Abbey, 1558–1630', *The Journal of Ecclesiastical History* 52 (2001), pp. 623–46, p. 627.
29 D. MacCulloch, *The Later Reformation in England, 1547–1603* (Basingstoke: Palgrave 2001), p. 29.
30 Jonathan Willis, *Church Music and Protestantism in Post-Reformation England: Discourses, Sites and Identities* (Farnham: Ashgate 2010), pp. 133–59.

that in the beginning, or in the end of common prayers, either at morning or evening, there may be sung an hymn, or suchlike song to the praise of Almighty God, in the best sort of melody and music that may be conveniently devised, having respect that the sentence of the hymn may be understood and perceived.[31]

In the cathedrals, collegiate churches and chapels and certain parishes where there was provision for choirs, a fine repertoire of music developed to accompany Morning and Evening Prayer, the Litany, the Communion service and other offices such as burial. Thomas Tallis and William Byrd remain the more widely known of the Elizabethan church musicians who provided music for the new English services. From 1563 until 1572 Byrd was organist at Lincoln Cathedral, and in 1570 he was appointed one of the Gentlemen of the Chapel Royal. Byrd remained a Catholic and composed music for the Latin services, but also is associated with the compositions for the Prayer Book services in D minor.[32] Other leading composers included Robert Parsons, Robert White, William Mundy, Thomas Morley and John Bull.[33] At Durham Cathedral Dean William Whittingham encouraged music, was a musician himself, and obtained music from the Chapel Royal for use in the cathedral. He himself wrote of his work in the cathedral:

First, in the Morning at Six of the Clock the Grammar Schoole and Song Schole with all the Servants of the House, resort to Prayers into the Church. Which Exercise continueth almost half an Houre. At nyne of the Clock we have our ordinary Service; and likewise at three after none. The Wednesdays and Fridays are appointed to a general Fast with Prayers, and Preaching of God's Word. The Sundaies and Holydays before none we have Sermons; and at after none the Catechisme is expounded.

Because we lak an able Scholemaster I bestow daily three or Four Hours in teaching the Youth, till God provide us of some that may better suffice.[34]

31 Henry Gee, *The Elizabethan Clergy and the Settlement of Religion* (Oxford: Clarendon Press 1898), p. 60.

32 John S. Bumpus, *A History of English Cathedral Music 1549–1889* (Westmead: Gregg International Reprint 1972), p. 64.

33 Bumpus, *A History of English Cathedral Music 1549–1889*, pp. 68, 73. Peter Phillips, *English Sacred Music 1549–1649* (Oxford: Gimell 1991), pp. 44–55.

34 Strype, *Matthew Parker*, p. 135.

This contrasted with Robert Horne, Bishop of Winchester, who disapproved of the use of organs and tried to restrict the repertoire of the cathedral choir.[35]

A number of parish churches had organs and choirs, though this seems to have declined from the 1570s, possibly because of a dearth of organ repairers and inflation.[36] According to the study of A. Smith, at Ludlow Latin motets were still in use in the 1570s, illustrating the conservative nature of some parishes.[37] A verse anthem became commonplace at cathedral Evening Prayer, apparently being a Protestant adaptation of the Marian devotion sung at Vespers.[38]

Surveying the evidence for the choral tradition of the Elizabethan parish churches, Johnathan Willis concluded that there was not a single pattern of religio-musical activity, but a range of paradigms and possibilities which itself was a result of the vagueness of the Elizabethan Injunctions.[39] A good number had organs and singers, and owned pricking books (copied vocal music). However, over time in many parish churches music came to be confined to the metrical psalms of Sternhold and Hopkins of 1562.[40]

Metrical psalmody has a complex history and in the English-speaking world the lead was taken by Miles Coverdale and Thomas Sternhold.[41] Sternhold, a mid-level civil servant, published 19 metrical psalms in 1547/48 under the title *Certayne Psalmes*. He died in 1549, but 18 more of his compositions were posthumously published, together with the original 19 by Edward Whitchurch under the title *Al such psalms*

35 Peter Le Huray, *Music and Reformation in England 1549–1660* (London: Herbert Jenkins Ltd 1967), pp. 37–8; Nicholas Temperley, *The Music of the English Parish Church*, Vol. 1 (Cambridge: Cambridge University Press 1979), p. 42.

36 Temperley, *Music*, p. 43.

37 Alan Smith, 'Elizabethan Church Music at Ludlow', *Music and Letters* 49.2 (1968), pp. 108–21.

38 Robin A. Leaver, 'Liturgical Music as Homily and Hermeneutic' in Robin A. Leaver and Joyce Ann Zimmerman, *Liturgy and Music: Lifetime Learning* (Collegeville, MN: Liturgical Press 1998), pp. 340–59, p. 343.

39 Jonathan Willis, *Church Music and Protestantism in Post-Reformation England: Discourses, Sites and Identities* (Farnham: Ashgate 2010), p. 131.

40 Peter Phillips, *English Sacred Music 1549–1649* (Oxford: Gimell 1991); Beth Quitslund, *The Reformation in Rhyme: Sternhold, Hopkins and the English Metrical Psalter, 1547–1603* (Aldershot: Ashgate 2008).

41 Robin A. Leaver, *Goostly Psalmes and Spirituall Songes: English and Dutch Metrical Psalms from Coverdale to Utenhove 1535–1566* (Oxford: Oxford University Press 1991); Quitslund, *The Reformation in Rhyme*; Timothy Duguid, 'Sing a New Song: English and Scottish Metrical Psalmody from 1549–1640', PhD thesis, University of Edinburgh, 2011; *Metrical Psalmody in Print and Practice: English 'Singing Psalmes' and Scottish 'psalm Buiks' c.1547–1640* (Farnham: Ashgate 2014).

of David as Thomas Sternehold late grome of [the] kings Maiesties Robes,
didde in his life time draw into English Metre. This book included a
further seven psalms by John Hopkins. Both these psalters were probably intended for private use rather than public worship, though public
worship would become their destiny. With the death of Edward VI
and the accession of Queen Mary, English metrical psalmody was on
hold in England, but began to take on a more prominent role in the
worship of the English groups that fled to the Continent. New compositions were made in Wesel, but it was from those in Frankfurt that
a wider and more lasting contribution came. 'The Troubles Begun at
Frankford' record that when the English exiles had been granted the
use of the church used by the French Reformer Valerand Poullain, in
their worship the people were to 'sing a Psalm in metre in a plain tune;
as was and as is accustomed in the French, Dutch, Italian, Spanish and
Scottish Churches'.[42] Though initially *Al such psalms* was probably used,
William Whittingham, later to become Dean of Durham, revised the
poetry and added new compositions of his own. He was an accom-
plished linguist and he also knew Hebrew. The fruits of his skills were
included in the 1556 *Form of Prayers*, which was the liturgy used by the
English congregation in Geneva. There were now 51 psalms and also a
metrical version of the Ten Commandments. Whittingham contributed
versions of Psalms 23, 51, 114, 115, 130, 133 and 137. In the 1558
edition, Whittingham contributed further additions: Psalms 37, 50, 67,
71, 119, 121, 124, 127 and 129. With reference to the 1556 edition,
Quitslund notes the following:

> The primary prose source of all the psalms is the Great Bible, as it was
> for both Sternhold and Hopkins. Each of the new texts shows verbal
> traces, however, of the French metrical psalms by Clémont Marot
> and Theodore Beza, most likely from the 1551 version, *Pseames*
> *octante trois de Dauid mis en rime Françoise.* The Ten Commandments
> amounts, in fact, to a loose translation of Marot's version, though
> influenced by the language of the Great Bible.[43]

Robin Leaver has suggested that since initially the Frankfurt exiles had
agreed to use forms similar to the French, a versification of the Ten
Commandments was required, and Whittingham composed them to

---

42 E. Arber (ed.), *A Brieff Discours of the Troubles at Frankfort 1554–1558 A.D.* (London:
Elliot Stock 1908), p. 25.
43 Quitslund, *The Reformation in Rhyme*, p. 144.

fill this need.[44] Timothy Duguid notes how Whittingham's translations were guided by the current situation of the exiles.[45] Thus verses 3 and 4 of Psalm 137:

> Then they to whome we prisoners were
> said to vs tauntinglie,
> nowe let vs heare your hebrewe songes
> and pleasaunte melodie.
> Alas sayde we, who can once frame
> his sorrowfull hart to synge:
> the praises of our louyng god,
> thus vnder a strange kynge?

Whittingham also rewrote some of Sternhold's and Hopkins' verses.

The Anglo-Genevan Psalter did not incorporate the whole 150 psalms; 1556 provided 51 psalms, and 1558 contained 67. It was expanded again in 1560 with 25 further psalms by William Kethe. In England the printer John Day published editions of these partial metrical psalters, and, as a step towards a full psalter, in 1562 he published a collection entitled *The residue of all Davids Psalmes in metre, made by John Hopkins and others*. Among the others were psalms by Thomas Norton. In that same year, Day also published a full psalter under the title *The whole booke of Psalmes, collected into Englysh metre by T. Starnhold I. Hopkins, & others*. Though some of Whittingham's compositions were replaced by those of John Hopkins, and *The whole booke of Psalmes* is regarded as having a more Edwardian and London flavour than the Geneva Psalter, nevertheless Day kept Whittingham's revisions of the original Sternhold versions.

Day's edition included some hymns and canticles in metre, but perhaps most important is the third section of this metrical psalter, which Quitslund believes demonstrates the continuities between Day's finished metrical psalter and the aspirations of the Marian exile communities. This last section contained prayers for use in the home, but nearly all were selected from the *Form of Prayers*. Day used the household prayers as found in the 1561 edition of the *Form of Prayers*, which had already been adapted to make them suitable for Elizabethan England. Two prayers from the Public Sunday liturgy had been incorporated into these household forms. Day reproduced them. In considering a

---

44 Leaver, *Goostly Psalmes*, p. 220.
45 Duguid, *Metrical Psalmody*, p. 34.

description of the book as 'a model of selfhood based upon the struggle to achieve confessional purity' Quitslund has aptly commented on Day's psalter: 'Though in support of the Elizabethan Church, the materials with which it sought to create such a selfhood were in large part those that had been created to sustain the godly during the Marian diaspora.'[46]

The 1559 Injunction relating to music was interpreted by most as allowing the metrical psalmody. John Craig has commented: 'Congregations exceeded this permission and incorporated metrical psalms, not just one but several, and sung by the whole congregation, both morning and evening, in their weekly services.'[47] In many parishes it also became the custom for the parish clerk (a lay appointment but a survival from the medieval minor orders) to read out or sing every line, which was then repeated by the congregation.[48] Archbishop Grindal issued the following injunction for the Province of York in 1571:

> That no parish Clerk be appointed against the goodwill or without the consent of the parson, vicar, or curate of any parish, and that he be obedient to the parson, vicar, and curate, specially in the time of celebration of the divine service or sacraments, or in any preparation thereunto; and that he be able also to read the first lesson, the epistle, and the psalms, with answers to the suffrages as is used; and that he keep the books and ornaments of the church fair and clean and cause the church and choir, the Communion table, the pulpit, and the font to be kept decent and made clean against service time, the Communion, sermon, and baptism, and also that he endeavor himself to teach young children to read, if he be able so to do.[49]

The parish clerk thus became the right-hand man in smaller parishes and the surrogate liturgical voice of the congregation.

46 Quitslund, *The Reformation in Rhyme*, p. 235.

47 John Craig, 'Psalms, Groans and Dogwhippers: The Soundscape of Worship in the English Parish Church, 1547–1642' in Will Coster and Andrew Spicer (eds), *Sacred Space in Early Modern Europe* (Cambridge: Cambridge University Press 2005), pp. 104–23, pp. 106–7.

48 For the varied duties of parish clerks, see James Christie, *Some Account of Parish Clerks* (private printing 1893); P. H. Ditchfield, *The Parish Clerk* (Createspace Independent Publishing Platform, USA, 2014).

49 *The Remains of Edmund Grindal* (Cambridge: Parker Society/Cambridge University Press 1843), p. 142.

OBJECTIONS TO THE 1559 BOOK

If the majority of clergy and laity accepted the 1559 Book of Common Prayer as authorized, certain more Protestant divines found fault with the Book and agitated for further reform. Some of these 'puritans' or 'godly' may have been behind certain editions of the Book of Common Prayer which omitted some of the terms that they objected to (see further below). However, a good number of godly churchmen felt that the Prayer Book was too close to its Roman parent, and they looked forward to and agitated for a more Protestant reform. Some of these 'puritans' were extremely hostile to the liturgy. Some objected to the surplice and wore only a black gown. Some omitted pieces of the liturgy they did not like. The liturgical complaints of the more radical puritans were presented in *An Admonition to the Parliament* (1572), authored by John Field and Thomas Wilcox. Comparing their understanding of the early Church with the Elizabethan Settlement, they objected to copes, surplices, the use of the cross in baptism and the mandatory use of a ring in the marriage rite.[50] The authors complained of the services:

> We must nedes say as foloweth, that this boke is an unperfecte booke, culled & picked out of that popishe dunghil, the Masse booke full of all abhominations. For some, & many of the contents therin, be suche as are againste the woord of God, as by his grace shall be proved unto you. And by the way, we can not but much marvel at the craftie wilynesse of those men whose partes it had ben fyrst to have proved eche and every content therin, to be agreable to the worde of God, seing that they enforce men by subscription to consent unto it, or else send them packing from their callings.

> I. They shoulde first prove, that a reading service by the woorde of God going before, and with the administration of the sacraments, is according to the woorde of God, that private Communion, private baptisme, baptisme ministred by women, holydayes ascribed to sainctes, prescript services for them, kneeling at communion, wafer cakes for their breade when they minister it, surplesse and coape to do it in; churching of women, coming in vails, abusing the psalm to her, I have lifted up mine eyes unto the hilles, etc, and suche other

---

50 W. H. Frere and C. E. Douglas, *Puritan Manifestoes* (London: SPCK 1907), pp. 14, 29–30.

foolishe things, are agreeable to the written woorde of the almightie. But their crafte is plaine.[51]

The authors wanted only elements in worship that were commanded in Scripture and a form of worship that showed no affinities with Catholic antecedents. A Bill of 1572 proposed allowing clergy to omit parts of the Book of Common Prayer and also to allow use of the liturgies of the 'Stranger' Churches – the Dutch and French Protestant groups who had found asylum in England. The latter respectively used liturgies of Petrus Datheen (1564) and Valerand Poullain's edition of Calvin's liturgy for Strasbourg.[52] There are also so-called 'puritan' editions of the Book of Common Prayer where the word 'minister' is substituted for 'priest', and references to celebrating at the North side were omitted, though Ian Green has argued that these are simply the abbreviation of printers and more to do with sales than doctrine.[53] Other godly ministers and groups used prayers from the 1556 *Form of Prayers*, the later household prayers of which were contained in editions of the Sternhold and Hopkins metrical psalter used in most parish churches. This liturgy had been compiled for the English exiles in Geneva by John Foxe, William Whittingham, John Knox and Anthony Gilby, and in 1562, and re-affirmed in 1564, it was recommended for use in the Church of Scotland.[54] Twice in Elizabeth's reign there were attempts in Parliament to enact editions of this liturgy in place of the Book of Common Prayer, under the title *A Book of the Form of Common Prayers, administration of the sacraments: &c. agreeable to God's Word, and the use of the reformed churches.* These two editions, the Waldegrave Book of 1584 and the Middleburg Book of 1586, were presented respectively in Bills of 1584, introduced by Dr Peter Turner, and in 1587, introduced by Peter Wentworth and Anthony Cope. In keeping with the Reformed tradition,

---

51 Frere and Douglas, *Puritan Manifestoes*, p. 21.

52 Bryan D. Spinks, *From the Lord and 'The Best Reformed Churches': A Study of the Eucharistic Liturgy in the English Puritan and Separatist Traditions 1550–1633* (Rome: CLV Edizioni Liturgiche 1984).

53 A. E. Peaston, *The Prayer Book Tradition in the Free Churches* (London: James Clarke 1964), pp. 31–2; Ian Green, '"Puritan Prayer Books" and "Geneva Bibles": An Episode in Elizabethan Publishing', *Transactions of the Cambridge Bibliographical Society* 11 (1998), pp. 313–49.

54 See Spinks, *From the Lord*. I have argued that, given his literary abilities, most of the work was done by William Whittingham. Bryan D. Spinks, 'On the Wrong Side of History? Reimagining William Whittingham, Dean of Durham, 1563–1579' in Teresa Berger and Bryan D. Spinks (eds), *Liturgy's Imagined Past/s: Methodologies and Material in the Writing of Liturgical History Today* (Collegeville, MN: Liturgical Press 2016), pp. 205–29.

there were no versicles and responses. The main Sunday morning service consisted of a greeting, confession of sins, a psalm, a prayer for illumination, Lord's Prayer, Scripture reading, sermon, a prayer for the Church, Apostles Creed, Decalogue, Lord's Prayer, psalm and blessing. When there was a Communion, the words of institution were read after the final psalm, followed by an exhortation, a Eucharistic Prayer (derived in part from a liturgy that Knox drew up for Berwick on Tweed), Communion, followed by a thanksgiving, a psalm and the blessing. Both attempts were quashed by royal intervention. Elizabeth insisted that her bishops enforce conformity, and those more extreme 'nonconformist' Puritans were often deprived of their livings or had their licences revoked. No doubt some ministers made their own ad hoc emendations and omissions, but no official further reforms were authorized.

Rather different were the extreme separatists such as Henry Barrow and John Greenwood. They rejected the idea of a national Church, however reformed it might be, and they rejected what they termed 'stinted' liturgy; that is, any set forms of prayer, be it the Book of Common Prayer or the *Form of Prayers*. Since these groups did not write prayers, we have little information about their worship other than passing remarks in their polemical theological writings. A deposition before a magistrate outlined the Lord's Supper as celebrated by a Barrowist congregation in London:

> Beinge further demaunded the manner of the Lord's Supper administred emongst them, he saith that five whight loves or more were sett vppon the table and that the pastor did breake the bread and then delivered yt unto some of them, and the deacons delivered to the rest, some of the said congregacion sittinge and some standing aboute the table and that the pastor delivered the cupp unto one and he an other, and soe from one to another till they had all dronken, usinge the words at the deliverye therof according as it is sett downe in the eleventh of the Corinthes the xxiiiith verse.[55]

Barrow and Greenwood refused to conform or repent and were executed for sedition.

If the authors of the *Admonition to the Parliament* and the Separatists rejected the Elizabethan liturgical forms, a stout defence of the 1559 Prayer Book was mounted by Richard Hooker. Though in his day

---

55 Leland H. Carlson (ed.), *The Writings of John Greenwood and Henry Barrow 1592–1593* (London: George Allen and Unwin Ltd 1970), p. 307.

Hooker was by no means a typical representative of the theological thought of the English Church, his *Lawes of Ecclesiastical Polity* were a massive apologia for the Elizabethan Church Settlement and in later Anglican history have been taken as its normative expression.[56] In Book V, Hooker defended the use of set prayer and the services of the Prayer Book, arguing:

> A great part of the cause, wherefore religious minds are so inflamed with the love of public devotion, is that virtue, force, efficacy, which by experience they find that the very form and reverend solemnity of common prayer duly ordered hath, to help that imbecility and weakness in us, by means whereof we are otherwise of ourselves the less apt to perform unto God so heavenly a service, with such affection of heart, and disposition in the power of our souls as is requisite. To this end therefore all things hereunto appertaining have been ever thought convenient to be done with the most solemnity and majesty that the wisest could devise. It is not with public as with private prayers. In this rather secrecy is commended than outward show, whereas that being the public act of a whole society, requireth accordingly more care to be had of external appearance. The very assembling of men therefore unto this service hath been ever solemn.[57]

Though at the beginning of Elizabeth's reign there were many who were theologically and devotionally attached to the traditional Latin rites, Judith Maltby has shown how by the last decades of Elizabeth's reign most English people had become devoted to the new English Prayer Book and had absorbed its spirituality.[58] Daniel Swift has illustrated how its prose is reflected in Shakespeare's plays, and Sophie Read has noted some of its direct and indirect influence on the poetic imagination in early modern England.[59] Diarmaid MacCulloch remarked

---

56 Bryan D. Spinks, *Two Faces of Elizabethan Anglican Theology: Sacraments and Salvation in the Thought of William Perkins and Richard Hooker* (Lanham, MD: Scarecrow Press 1999); D. MacCulloch, 'Richard Hooker's Reputation', *English Historical Review* 117 (2002), pp. 773–812.

57 Richard Hooker, *Lawes of Ecclesiastical Polity*, Book V, Ch. xxv.1 (Oxford: Clarendon Press 1865, Keeble edition), p. 118.

58 Judith Maltby, *Prayer Book and People in Elizabethan and Early Stuart England* (Cambridge: Cambridge University Press 1998).

59 Daniel Swift, *Shakespeare's Common Prayers: The Book of Common Prayer and the Elizabethan Age* (New York: Oxford University Press 2013); Sophie Read, *Eucharist and the Poetic Imagination in Early Modern England* (Cambridge: Cambridge University Press 2013).

that Elizabeth established a version of the Edwardian Church which proved to be a snapshot, frozen in time, of the Church as it had been in September 1552.[60] In fact, through the Chapel Royal, her first Latin version of the Prayer Book and the Primers, she actually turned the clock back a few minutes. The resulting ambiguity would be a Trojan horse in a Church that regarded itself as thoroughly Protestant.

---

60 D. MacCulloch, *Thomas Cranmer: A Life* (New Haven, CT: Yale University Press 1996), p. 620.

Chapter 2

The Jacobean religious settlement: the 1604 Book of Common Prayer

JAMES VI AND I

Since Elizabeth had no direct heir, on her death on 24 March 1603 the throne passed to James VI of Scotland. During his progress south in April 1603 James was presented with the 'Millenary Petition'. Claiming to have been signed by over a thousand 'godly' ministers, the petition requested that a number of 'offences' be removed, amended or qualified, which in effect would further the reform of the Church of England's structuring, discipline and liturgy. Most pertinent to the Book of Common Prayer was the very first of the 'offences':

> In the Church service: that the cross in baptism, interrogatories ministered to infants, confirmation, as superfluous, may be taken away; baptism not to be ministered by women, and so explained; the cap and surplice not urged; that examination may go before the communion; that it be ministered with a sermon; that divers terms of priests, and absolution, and some other used, with the ring in marriage, and other such like in the book, may be corrected; the longsomeness of service abridged, Church songs and music moderated to better edification; that the Lord's Day be not profaned; the rest upon holy days not so strictly urged; that there may be a uniformity of doctrine prescribed; no popish opinion to be any more taught or defended; no ministers charged to teach their people to bow at the name of Jesus; that the canonical Scriptures only be read in the Church.[1]

---

1 Text in H. Gee and W. J. Hardy, *Documents Illustrative of English Church History* (London: Macmillan 1896), pp. 508–11, which, with other documents and commentary, is reproduced in Colin Buchanan, *The Hampton Court Conference and the 1604*

Since James VI presided over a Reformed Church in Scotland, the godly hoped that he would conform the Church of England to be more like the more Reformed Church of Scotland. In this they were to be disappointed and perhaps misinformed. Whether because he was known to be the heir to the English throne, or because he was himself theologically informed and had his own views, he had in fact begun to 'Anglicize' the Church of Scotland, and had already reintroduced bishops into the Scottish Presbyterian structure. Furthermore, like Elizabeth, on important Scottish royal occasions, liturgical ceremony and symbol were elevated beyond the normal customs of Scottish Reformed parish worship. James had the Chapel Royal at Stirling constructed for the baptism of his son Henry, and the plan followed Solomon's Temple in its proportions – 3.5 to 1.[2] Of its decoration, MacKechnie wrote:

> James loved and used symbolism. For him, rapid completion of the chapel was so important that not only had he 'the supply of the greatest number of artificer's in the whole country, convened there of all craftes for that service', but he personally undertook the function of 'dayly overseer, with large and liberall payment'. The interior was lavish, with cloth of gold and tapestries; the sense of drama was heightened by partitioning, and James's throne was at the north-east end.[3]

William Fowler, secretary to James's wife, Queen Anne, described Henry's baptism in 1594 thus:

> In the middest of the Chappell Royall within the partition, where the Kings Maiestie, the Ambassadors, and Prince with his conuoy were placed, there was a newe pulpite erected: The same was richly hung with cloth of gold: All the pauement within this partition, was Prince-like laide with fine tapestrie.
> Under the Pulpit was another deske, wherein sate in the middest, M. David Cuninghame, Bishop of Abirdene, M. Dauid Lindesay, Minister of Leyth, and Iohn Duncanson, one of the ordinary

Book of Common Prayer with Related Documents, Introduction and Annotation, Alcuin/ GROW Liturgical Study 68 (Norwich: Hymns Ancient and Modern 2009), pp. 15–17.
2 Aonghus MacKechnie, 'James VI's Architects and their Architecture' in Julian Goodare and Michael Lynch (eds), _The Reign of James VI_ (Edinburgh: Birlinn Ltd 2008), pp. 154–69.
3 MacKechnie, 'James VI's Architects and their Architecture', p. 164, citing 'A true reportarie of the baptisme of the Prince of Scotland' (see following footnote).

ministers to the Kings Maiestie: before whom was set a table, couered with yealowe veluote . . .

Then the Trumpets sounding melodiously before the Prince and his conuoy, went forwarde: LYON King of Armes, and the Heraulds his brethren with their coat-armors, in goodly order following.

Next followed the Princes Honors, borne by these Noble men: The Lorde Sempill carrying a Lavar of water, the Lord Seton, a fair Basen: The Lord Leuingston a Towell, and the Lorde Home a low Crowne competent for a Duke, rich lie set with Diamonds, Saphires, Rubies, Emerauldes: who approching neere the Pulpit, where these Honors were receaued from them, by the maister of the Ceremonies, and by him placed on the Table before the pulpite: the Noble men retyring back to their appointed places . . .

Without the patition, were ornate fourmes, all couered with greene, whereupon were placed the Gentlemen of England, Denmarke, Almaine, Flanders, and Scotland. And as all men wer thus competentlie placed, and vuniuersall silence made, entered M. Patrik Galloway, one of his Maiesties ordinarie Preachers into the Pulpite, who learnedlie and godlie, entreated vpon the text of the 21 of Genesis. Which being done, the Bishop of Aberdene, stood vp in his seate, and taught vpon the Sacrament of Baptisme, firste, in the vulgar tongue, and next in the Latine, to the end, all men might generallie vunderstand. That done, the Provost, and Prebends of the Chappell Royall, did sing the 21. Psalme of Dauid, according to the art of Musique, to the great delectation of the noble Auditorie.

They then proceeded to the action. The King arose, and came towards the Pulpit. The Ambassadours followed in their order. The Barons that carried the Pale aboue the Prince, mooued towards the Pulpit: The Duke of Lennox, receaued the Prince from the Countesse of Mar, and deliuered him to the hands of the Erll of Sussex, Ambassadour for England: Where he was named by all their consents, FREDERIK HENRIE, HENRIE FREDERIK, and so baptised, In the name of the Father, Sonne, and holie Ghost, by the said names. (*washing of hands of the Ambassador followed*)

This being done, the Bishop ascended to the Pulpite, where, after that hee had deliuered in verse, a certaine praise and commendation of the Prince, then hee converted the rest of his Latine Oration, in prose to the Ambassadours, euery one in particular, beginning at the Ambassadour of England, and so continuing with the rest: Wherein he made mention of the Chronology of e[a]ch of these Princes: & recited the proximitie, and neernesse of blood that they had with

Scotland. Concluding his Oration, with exhortation & thanksgiuing to God for that good occasion, and prosperous assemblie.

In conclusion, the blessing being giuen Lyon King of Armes, cryed with a loud voice, God saue FREDERIK HENRIE, and HENRIE FREDERIK, by the grace of God, Prince of Scotland. The rest of the Herauldes, proclaymed the same at an open window of the Chappell Royall, with sound of Trumpet.[4]

Rick Bowers has aptly commented that this High Church pageantry, which was beyond the stern literalism expected of a Calvinist Scottish baptism in 1594, represents the rejection of religious extremes epitomized in James's advice to Henry, 'as well as ye represse the vaine Puritane, so suffer not proude Papall Bishops'.[5] As attentive as James might be to Scripture, on the question of ceremonies he had little time for the 'vaine Puritane'. He came south with a mission to unite his two kingdoms politically, and probably in religion too.[6] Rather than conform the Church of England to that of Scotland, James made various attempts to bring the Church of Scotland more in line with his English Church.

THE HAMPTON COURT CONFERENCE

In response to the Millenary Petition, James arranged for a conference – or series of interviews – between a few of those representing the views of the petitioners, and a select number of bishops and deans representing the status quo. Daniel Swift has usefully commented:

The Hampton Court Conference may now seem a minor episode in the great sweep of British history, and is perhaps most famous as the occasion at which the new King James Version of the Bible was commissioned. This was completed in 1611, now a little more

---

4 'A True Reportarie of the Most Triumphant, and Royal Accomplishment of the Baptisme of the most Excellent, right High, and mightie Prince, FREDERIK HENRY; By the grace of God, Prince of Scotland. Solemnized the 30. Day of August. 1594' in Henry W. Meikle (ed.), *The Works of William Fowler*, Vol. 2 (Edinburgh: Blackwood 1936), pp. 169–95, pp. 180–3.

5 Rick Bowers, 'James VI, Prince Henry, and *A True Reportarie* of Baptism at Stirling 1594', *Renaissance and Reformation* 29 (2005), pp. 3–21, p. 12. The quote of James is in James Craigie (ed.), *Basilicon Doron* (Edinburgh: Blackwood 1944), p. 81.

6 See the details in Lori Anne Ferrell, *Government by Polemic: James I, the King's Preachers, and the Rhetorics of Conformity, 1603–1625* (Palo Alto, CA: Stanford University Press 1998), ch. 2.

than four hundred years ago. But the conference was a great affair, much-discussed, much-anticipated, and its consequences ran wide.[7]

As Swift explains in some detail, the clerical visitors to Hampton Court finally met on Saturday 14 January 1604, and their conference followed the larger festivities at Hampton Court, which had brought together a number of theatre companies, including Shakespeare and his company for fun, festivities and revels for the twelve days of Christmas.[8] The clerical conference had been planned for 1 November 1603 but was postponed because of an outbreak of the plague. Even with its rescheduling, Swift notes that it began like a Shakespeare play, in confusion and rumour. The bishops and deans assembled on 12 January, and after presenting themselves to the King, were told to return on Sunday 14 January.[9] Meetings were held on 14, 16 and concluded on 18 January.

There are a number of contemporary accounts of the conference: a letter of King James; an account by Toby Matthew, Bishop of Durham, written for the Archbishop of York; an account of William Barlow, Dean of Chester, which is regarded as representing the episcopal status quo reading of the conference; a letter by James's Scottish chaplain, Patrick Galloway; an 'anonymous' account; and an unpublished account by one of the 'godly' attendees, Laurence Chaderton.[10] Whereas the account by Barlow suggests that the King sided with the bishops, the anonymous account and that of Chaderton suggest that on a number of issues, James was on the side of the godly. According to a remark in a letter of Sir John Harrington on the conference, 'the spirit was rather foul-mouthed'.[11]

The two principal movers of the Millenary Petition, Arthur Hildersham and Stephen Egerton, were not invited to participate.[12] Instead, the signatories were represented by Laurence Chaderton of

---

7 Daniel Swift, *Shakespeare's Common Prayers: The Book of Common Prayer and the Elizabethan Age* (Oxford: Oxford University Press 2013), p. 3.

8 Swift, *Shakespeare's Common Prayers*, pp. 4–13.

9 Swift, *Shakespeare's Common Prayers*, pp. 15–16.

10 Buchanan, *The Hampton Court Conference*; Roland G. Usher, *The Reconstruction of the English Church*, 2 vols (London: D. Appleton and Co. 1910), Vol. 2, Appendix III; Arnold Hunt, 'Laurence Chaderton and the Hampton Court Conference' in Susan Wabuda and Caroline Litzenberger (eds), *Belief and Practice in Reformation England* (Aldershot: Ashgate 1998), pp. 207–28.

11 Melville of Halhill, *Memoirs of his Own Life*, ed. T. Thompson (Edinburgh: Bannatyne Club 1827), p. 262.

12 For Hildersham, see Lesley A. Rowe, *The Life and Times of Arthur Hildersham, Prince among the Puritans* (Grand Rapids, MI: Reformation Heritage Books 2013).

Cambridge, John Rainholds of Oxford, John Knewstubbs, Rector of Cockfield, Suffolk, and Dr Thomas Sparkes, Rector of Bletchley, who were regarded as less extreme than Hildersham and Egerton. The episcopal status quo party was represented by Archbishop Whitgift and Bishop Bancroft of London, together with seven other bishops and seven cathedral deans.

According to Toby Matthew's account, on the first day the King outlined the contentions regarding liturgy and church government, and those relating to liturgy were the form of absolution after the public confession of sins, the manner of confirmation of children, and the toleration of private baptism administered by laymen and -women. On the Monday, James met with the 'godly' party, and Matthew wrote:

> The doctors named divers abuses, but insisted chiefly upon the *confirmation*, the *cross* in baptism, the *surplice, private baptism, kneeling* at the communion, reading of the *Apocrypha*, subscriptions to the Book of Common Prayer and Articles; one only translation of the Bible to be authentical, and read in the church: the censure of *excommunication* for so small causes: the *corruptions* in the bishops' and archdeacon's courts, committed by their chancellors, commissaries, officials, registers, and such like officers; together with their immoderate exactions and fees, to be reformed. Of all which, also concerning the oath (upon many and sundry catching articles unto the preachers) *ex officio*, to entangle them: which one of them compared to the Spanish Inquisition.[13]

The outcome was outlined in the King's Commission issued after the conference, ordering certain changes to the text of the Prayer Book. These included a change in the rubric before absolution, renaming it 'Absolution or Remission of Sins'; a change in the rubric at baptism, excluding lay baptism; some changes to the rubrics at confirmation; the removal of some readings from the Apocrypha; and some additional prayers. Additionally, the catechism was expanded to include teaching on the sacraments, and new canons were issued in 1604 which also had a bearing on liturgical celebration. Of particular note was the subtitle at private baptism: 'Of them that are to be baptized in private houses in time of necessitie, by the Minister of the Parish, or any other lawfull Minister, that can be procured.' This effectively excluded midwives, which was a major concern of the 'godly'. Confirmation was titled 'The

---

13 Buchanan, *The Hampton Court Conference*, p. 19.

Order of Confirmation, or laying on of hands upon children baptized, and able to render an account of their faith, according to the Catechisme following'. Prayers for rain, fair weather, thanksgiving for plenty, for peace and victory and deliverance from the plague were provided. The addition to the catechism was made by John Overall, Dean of St Paul's and later Bishop of Coventry and Lichfield, and then Norwich, and it was based on the catechism of Alexander Nowell.

The 1604 canons ordered:

> The Common Prayer shall be said or sung distinctly and reverently upon such days as are appointed to be kept holy by the Book of Common Prayer, and their Eves, and at convenient and usual times of those days, and in such place of every Church as the Bishop of the diocese, or Ecclesiastical Ordinary of the place shall think meet . . . without either diminishing in regard of preaching, or in any other respect, or adding any thing in the matter or form thereof.[14]

The canons reinforced the wearing of the surplice, and for graduates their degree hood, and in cathedrals copes were to be worn for Communion. Communion was to be received three times a year, and canon 21 stated: 'Furthermore, no Bread or Wine newly brought shall be used; but first the words of institution shall be rehearsed, when the said Bread and Wine be present upon the Communion-table.' This may have been in response to the case of Robert Johnson in 1573.[15] During Communion the wine gave out, and Johnson, who was often in trouble with authority, sent for more, and immediately poured it into the cup and continued giving Communion. He was prosecuted on the grounds that he should have recited the words of consecration over the new wine. His defence was that there was no rubric that required this. He was found guilty and sent to prison, where he subsequently died. It is difficult to know how widely the case was known, and no rubric was added at the time. Although there was still no rubric in the liturgical text, 'reconsecration' was now required by canon law. Canon 30 gave a lengthy defence of the use of the cross in the baptismal rite.

After the dust of the Hampton Court conference had settled, ecclesial life seemed to continue much as it had under Elizabeth. As in Elizabeth's

---

14 Conveniently listed in Buchanan, *The Hampton Court Conference*, pp. 53–60; here p. 50.
15 E. C. Ratcliff, 'The English Usage of Eucharistic Consecration 1548–1662 – II', *Theology* 60 (1957), pp. 273–80; Richard Buxton, *Eucharist and Institution Narrative* (London: SPCK 1976), pp. 89–92.

reign, occasional services were issued: for example, thanksgiving for the decline of the plague, prayers during the pregnancy of Queen Anne, and thanksgiving for Prince Charles's return from Spain.[16] By far the most enduring was the annual service for deliverance from the Gunpowder Plot. England already adopted the Scottish thanksgiving for James's deliverance from the Gowrie plot, and prayers were issued in November 1605 after the discovery of the Gunpowder Plot, and in 1606 it became an annual celebration. Mears et al. comment:

> This was the most popular of the anniversary commemorations, perhaps not least because it became a focus both for the expression of English protestant identity and for partisan appropriation and re-appropriation, and it has continued as a day of secular celebration long after the abolition of the religious thanksgiving in 1859.[17]

As with many other special services, it was an emended form of Morning Prayer, with cento psalmody, special suffrages and special collects.[18]

Royal occasions displayed much ecclesiastical ceremonial. At the baptism of Princess Mary at Greenwich in May 1605 the Cheque-Book of the Chapel Royal recorded:

> At the tyme when the Royall Infant should be brought to the Chappell, the gentlemen of that place (after many companies goinge before) went out of the Chappell two and two in their surplesses unto the nurcerie doore, there following them the Deane of the Chappell, next after came the Arch Bishop of Canterbury, bothe in rich copes of Needellworke . . . When the Royall Infant was thus brought unto the lower Chappell doore, there did the Archbishop and the Deane of the Chappell receave the Babe and came next before it into the higher Chappell. At the same instant did the Organest begine and continew playing aloude until the Child was placed in the Traverse . . .

---

16 Natalie Mears, Alasdair Raffe, Stephen Taylor and Philip Williamson (with Lucy Bates) (eds), *National Prayers: Special Worship Since the Reformation. Vol. 1: Special Prayers, Fasts and Thanksgivings in the British Isles 1533–1688* (Woodbridge: The Church of England Record Society and the Boydell Press 2013), pp. 253–74.

17 Mears et al., *National Prayers*, p. lxxxi. Continuing as Bonfire Night or Firework Night, an effigy of Guido (Guy) Fawkes is burnt in place of effigies of the pope. See also David Cressy, *Bonfires and Bells: National Memory and the Protestant Calendar in Elizabethan and Stuart England* (Berkeley, CA: University of California Press 1989), ch. 9.

18 Mears et al., *National Prayers*, p. 253, gives the immediate form issued by Bancroft. For the later service see <www.lewesbonfirecelebrations.com/article/thanks-giving-fifth-november> (accessed September 2016).

When all were placed, then begane an Antheme, shewinge the dedication of the Royall Infant unto Almightie God by baptisme (the Chorus whereof was filled with the help of musicall instrumentes): the which Antheme beinge endid the child was brought from the Traverce to the Font, whome the Arch Bishop baptized with great reverence (beinge still in his rich cope), who was assisted in the administracōn of the Sacrament by the Deane of the Chappell (he also beinge in his cope) . . . And the Baptisme beinge ended, an other Antheme was songe of thanksgeevinge to God for the ingraffinge of the Blessed Infant into Christ his Holy Church by Baptisme . . . Then began the offertorye to be played, in which tyme the noble baptized Infant was brought to the Holye Table and there it offered, by the person of the Lord Treasurer. Then the God Father and God Mothers did severallye offer also, beinge fett [fetched] from ther seates by the Lord Chamberlaine, the Deane of the Chappell receavinge ther offerings at the Communion Table in his cope. Then followed a full Anthem (Singe joyfullye), in the singing wherof the Gosipp's great giftes weare brought out of the vestrie (by certaine Knightes) and placed uppon the Communion Table, at thend of which Antheme the Collect for the Kinge was read, and therwith the service ended.[19]

Copes were worn for the royal weddings and for the service of swearing in of new ambassadors, when the oaths were sworn on the Latin Vulgate Bible.[20] In cathedrals the cope appears to have been worn on the occasions of the Communion, but in parish churches the same mixed conformity of Elizabeth's reign seems to have continued. Laurence Chaderton argued that the surplice was a scholastic or academic habit, and could be lawfully worn in a university setting, and he agreed to wear it in Emmanuel College, though he did not think that others outside a university setting had the same duty.[21] Chaderton seems to have had misgivings over the sign of the cross in baptism, but perhaps did not have to administer baptisms himself. Samuel Hieron, writing in 1605, claimed that bishops were flexible, 'accepting of some the use of the crosse, and surplice onely; of others the use of the surplice alone; of others a promise to use them onely; and of some the profession of their

19 Edward F. Rimbault (ed.), *The Old Cheque-book or Book of Remembrance of The Chapel Royal from 1561 to 1744* (London: Camden Society 1872; reprint, New York: De Capo Press 1966), pp. 167–9.
20 *The Old Cheque-book*, pp. 152, 165.
21 Hunt, 'Laurence Chaderton and the Hampton Court Conference', p. 216, citing Lambeth Palace Library, MS 2550, fol. 58r.

judgment onely that they may be used, without pressing them to the use of them, at all'.[22] A list of complaints about the popish ceremonies was presented to James by some clergy of the Lincoln diocese in 1605, and a further list of complaints was published in 1606, both renewing the old complaints of the Elizabethan 'godly'.[23] Kenneth Fincham calculated that between 73 and 83 ministers lost their benefices for nonconformity between 1604 and 1609.[24] Some bishops made a distinction between hardline 'godly' and the more moderate, and some tolerated occasional conformity among the latter. In 1613 the Rector of Shalbourne was presented for sometimes omitting the use of the surplice, and he was ordered to wear it *most* Sundays and holy days.[25] Richard Bernard claimed that Bishop Lake excused him from wearing his graduate hood for services.[26] Others did not receive such permissions. In 1618 Jeremiah Holliday was cited for failure to wear a surplice and for omitting the sign of the cross in baptism.[27] In 1624 Anthony Hilton of Chichester diocese was accused of failing to wear the surplice, of administering Communion to some who refused to kneel, of not insisting women wear veils for churching, of failing to announce saints days and of truncating the burial service.[28] On 5 April 1618 Nicholas Assheton recorded in his diary concerning the Easter Day service: 'After dinner some argument abt. Mr. Leigh's ministering ye Sacrament witht the Cirploise, betw. my bro. Sherbourne and my father.'[29] It seems that laypeople too had conflicting views on the matter of conformity.

THE RISE OF THE AVANT-GARDE OR PATRISTIC REFORMED CHURCHMEN

The 'godly' wanted further reform of the Church of England and its liturgy. However, a more conservative group of churchmen, many

---

22 Samuel Hieron, *A short dialogue proving that the ceremonies and some other corruptions now in question, are defended, by none other arguments then such as the Papists have heretofore used* (London: 1605), p. A4v.
23 *An Abridgment of that Booke which the Ministers of the Lincolne Diocese Delivered to his Majestie upon the first of December 1605* (London: 1617); *A Survey of the Book of Common Prayer By way of 197 Quares grounded upon 58 places* (London: 1610).
24 Kenneth Fincham, *Prelate as Pastor: The Episcopate of James I* (Oxford: Clarendon Press 1990), pp. 214–15.
25 Fincham, *Prelate as Pastor*, p. 229.
26 Fincham, *Prelate as Pastor*, p. 229.
27 Paul S. Seaver, *The Puritan Lectureships: The Politics of Religious Dissent, 1560–1662* (Palo Alto, CA: Stanford University Press 1970), p. 227.
28 Fincham, *Prelate as Pastor*, p. 197, citing West Sussex Record office papers.
29 F. R. Raines (ed.), *The Journal of Nicholas Assheton*, Chetham Society Publication, vol. 14 (1848), pp. 87–8.

associated with the Chapels Royal, were concerned to conserve what was in place, to enforce the Elizabethan Injunctions and the new canons, and even enrich the liturgy. They were more concerned with patristic authorities than Reformation authorities, and seemed (perhaps like Queen Elizabeth) to have had a preference for the 1549 Book of Common Prayer. They found their inspiration in Bishops Lancelot Andrewes, John Overall and John Buckeridge. Overall wrote little and is a somewhat shadowy figure.[30] With Andrewes, though, we have a clearer picture.

Andrewes was educated at Cambridge, first at Pembroke Hall, and in 1576 was elected a fellow at Pembroke College, and was catechist. In 1589 he was given the St Pancras prebend's stall at St Paul's Cathedral. Prior to the Reformation this stall had been attached to the role of penitentiary. Andrewes took this tradition seriously, and during Lent he made himself available in the cathedral for those seeking spiritual counsel. In 1597 he was appointed a prebend of Westminster Abbey, and its dean in 1601. He preached at Court before Elizabeth, and then became a favourite preacher of King James. He was one of the translators/revisers of the King James Bible. In 1600 he had preached a sermon on absolution that caused a stir at Court, some perhaps smelling a whiff of popery. His collected sermons show that he regarded sacraments as conduit pipes, which convey grace. He distanced himself from the Lambeth Articles of 1595 concerning predestination. More importantly, as Bishop of Ely, he furnished his London chapel in a manner after the Chapel Royal, with the table in altarwise position, with candles; he supplemented or enriched the Book of Common Prayer service of Communion in his own chapel and had special vessels crafted for Communion. He also burnt incense in a small bowl in his chapel.[31] It should be noted that his additions to the Prayer Book were technically as 'nonconformist' as the omissions and alterations made by the 'godly'.

Andrewes believed very much in the need for order and decency in worship and, contrary to what he perceived to be the 'godly' belief, he argued that the sermon was not the key element in worship. In a sermon commemorating the foiling of the Gunpowder Plot, he said:

---

30 For Overall, see Anthony Milton, '"Anglicanism" by Stealth: The Career and Influence of John Overall' in Kenneth Fincham and Peter Lake (eds), *Religious Politics in Post-Reformation England* (Woodbridge: Boydell Press 2006), pp. 159–76.
31 See Peter McCullough, 'Absent Presence: Lancelot Andrewes and 1662' in Stephen Platten and Christopher Woods (eds), *Comfortable Words: Polity, Piety and the Book of Common Prayer* (London: SCM Press 2012), pp. 49–68.

The word is holy, I know, and I wish it all the honour that may be; but God forbid we should think that *in hoc uno sunt omnia*. All our 'holiness' is in hearing, all our service ear-service: that were in effect as much as to say all the body were an ear.

An error it is, to shut up His service into any one part, which it diffused through all; another, so to do, into this one. It is well known that all the time of the Primitive Church, the sermon was ever done, before the service begun.[32]

Earlier in the same sermon Andrewes had expressed concern about irreverence in worship:

'The table of the Lord is not regarded.' That Sacrament that ever hath been counted of all holies the most holy, the highest and most solemn service of God, (where are delivered to us the holy symbols, the precious memorials of our greatest delivery of all;) why, of all others they speed worst. How are they in many places denied any reverence at all, even that which prayer, which other parts have? No service then, no servants there; but bidden guests, hail fellows, homely and familiar, as one neighbour with another. And not only *de facto* none they have; but *de jure* it is holden, none they ought to have. And that so holden as rather than they shall any, some will suffer for it, or rather for their own proud folly, in refusing it.[33]

Andrewes also wrote some notes on the Book of Common Prayer, which were in fact on what he called the 'Great Service' – Morning Prayer, Litany and Communion.[34] He argued that Evening Prayer should be kept on Saturdays, and that vigils and fasting should be kept before saints' days. These 'notes' suggested some additional Scripture sentences at the beginning of Morning Prayer, and gave detailed rubrics for the singing of the Litany from a faldstool, which was his practice in his chapel. An Introit was to be sung after the Litany, and then the sermon preached. Peter McCullough observed:

Music ('an Introit is sung') should not surprise us; anthems sandwiching the sermon (to cover the progress to and from the pulpit)

---

32 'A Sermon before the King's Majesty at Whitehall, 5 November 1617' in *Ninety-Six Sermons by the Right Honourable and Reverend Father in God, Lancelot Andrewes*, Vol. IV (Oxford: John Henry Parker 1841), p. 377.

33 Andrewes, 'A Sermon', pp. 375–6.

34 Lancelot Andrewes, *Works*, Vol. VI (Oxford: John Henry Parker 1854), pp. 141–58.

was common cathedral and royal chapel practice, here achieved by an introit sung from the 'music table' while the preacher processed to the pulpit. What is surprising here, though, is Andrewes's placement of the sermon after the Litany, and not after the Creed within the Holy Communion.[35]

The reason for this may have been Andrewes' reading of the Eastern dismissal of the catechumens prior to Communion, which he alluded to in the same 1617 Gunpowder Plot sermon. If this was his practice in his chapel, then this was once more an example of his own 'nonconformity'. After the sermon, Andrewes refers to three adorations made towards the altar and assumes that there will be at least one other minister. They take positions at either end of the altar table, representing the two cherubim either side of the mercy seat described in the Old Testament. The Ten Commandments were to be read at 'the door of the septum', which seems to mean at the chancel step of his chapel. He also gave intricate details for the preparation of the bread and wine, including mixing water with the wine. He had a special vessel made so that the wine gushed out from it into the cup looking like blood gushing. Another vessel held water for the mixed chalice. McCullough thought that the rubrics made it extremely unlikely that the celebrant could stand at the north side as the Prayer Book directed.[36] It is possible that Andrewes followed the practice of Bishop John Overall, which was to use the first thanksgiving prayer after Communion immediately after the prayer with the words of institution – in other words, following the 1549 structuring.

A similar concern for holiness and decorum in worship was expressed by Bishop John Buckeridge in a sermon of 1617. He criticized those who

> turne Oratories into Auditories, and Temples into scholes, and all adoration and worship into hearing of a Sermon . . . Hearing indeed is a good part of Christianitie, but it is but a part: and faith comes by hearing, but faith, hope and charitie, Iustice, and Religion, are not hearing, but the fruits of hearing: and therefore no man may thinke that he hath giuen God his due worship if hee haue heard God speake by his Minister.[37]

---

35 See McCullough, 'Absent Presence', p. 57.

36 McCullough, 'Absent Presence', pp. 66–7.

37 John Buckeridge, *A Sermon preached before his Maiestie at Whitehall, March 22 1617* (London: 1618), pp. 10–11.

These views would be shared by those associated with Durham House, the London residence of the Bishop of Durham. One of Andrewes' protégés, Richard Neile, was appointed Bishop of Durham in 1617 and surrounded himself with younger protégés including such figures as John Cosin, Francis White, William Laud, Gabriel Clarke, Francis Burgoyne, Robert Newell, Augustine Lindsell, Eleazar Duncon, Richard Montague and Marmaduke Blakiston. Meeting at Neile's London residence, they became known as the Durham House group. Victoria Raymer has remarked:

> Like the members of other seventeenth-century associations for concerted action, the individuals entertained at Durham House did not publicize their joint activities and tried to obliterate evidence that might make them appear to others as fomenters of faction or conspiracy.[38]

Among their concerns, which subsequently have come to be termed 'Laudianism', were a high regard for royal authority, for episcopacy, for sacraments and the beauty of holiness in worship, and the sacredness of church buildings. They questioned the prevailing double predestination, preferring the wiggle room of Arminius, and gave greater weight to the Fathers than to the foundational sixteenth-century Reformers. Of this Durham House group, Robert Newell, Augustine Lindsell, Gabriel Clarke, Francis Burgoyne, Marmaduke Blakiston, John Cosin and Eleazar Duncon were all appointed to prebend stalls at Durham and the cathedral became the showcase of Durham House or 'Laudian' piety and worship. Most had associations with the Chapels Royal.

Kenneth Fincham and Nicholas Tyacke draw attention to the fact that from the turn of the century there was a growing movement nationally for the re-edification and indeed beautification of churches, involving in a minority of cases the reintroduction of images and revival of organ music.[39] According to Edmund Howes, at least 16 London churches underwent repair work by 1608.[40] In circa 1613 new windows

38 Victoria Raymer, 'Durham House and the Emergence of Laudian Piety', PhD dissertation, Harvard University 1981, p. 62; Peter Lake, 'The Laudian Style: Order, Uniformity and the Pursuit of the Beauty of Holiness in the 1630s' in Kenneth Fincham, *The Early Stuart Church, 1604–1642* (Palo Alto, CA: Stanford University Press 1993), pp. 161–85; see also Calvin Lane, *The Laudians and the Elizabethan Church* (London: Pickering and Chatto 2013).
39 Kenneth Fincham and Nicholas Tyacke, *Altars Restored: The Changing Face of English Religious Worship, 1547–c.1700* (Oxford: Oxford University Press 2007), p. 74.
40 Howes, cited in Fincham and Tyacke, *Altars Restored*, p. 93.

were erected at St Stephen, Walbrook, containing 'personages in colored glasse'.[41] At St Dunstan-in-the-East in 1611 the vestry voted to keep the organs when many churches were removing organs. Several churches erected rails around the Communion table, though this did not usually change the east–west orientation of the table for Communion. However, in 1617 the new Dean of Gloucester and one of the Durham House group, William Laud, ordered the Communion table to be moved to the east end of the cathedral, and that the prebends bow to the east during divine service. Laud claimed – rightly – that he was following the practice of the Chapel Royal. In the same year, just prior to Neile being appointed to Durham, the Communion table was moved to the east end, almost certainly on the authority of Francis Burgoyne, a royal chaplain. In 1620 the new Dean of Durham, Richard Hunt, installed a new altar made of stone. Changes in taste regarding church furnishings went hand in hand with the developing liturgical ideals of the Durham House group.

REVERSE LITURGICAL OSMOSIS

The godly hoped that James would conform the English Church to that of Scotland. However, the 'Anglicanization' that some detected even before James's succession to the English throne continued, and particularly around his first and only visit back to Scotland, in 1617. The ideals of Andrewes, Neile, Buckeridge and Overall as practised in the English Chapels Royal, some of which seem to have been shared by King James's sense of royal pomp and ceremony, had an influence and parallel in Scotland.[42] In 1606, when James summoned a number of Scottish Presbyterians to London to be lectured on Royal authority, Andrewes and Buckeridge were among the four episcopal preachers. Bishops in Scotland had been restored as civil servants to safeguard the royal interests in appointments and property. In 1610 James summoned the Archbishop of Glasgow and the Bishops of Brechin and Galloway to London, where they were consecrated by the Bishops of London, Bath and Wells, and Ely – that is, James Montague (Dean of the Chapel Royal, 1603–19), George Abbot and Lancelot Andrewes. The Scottish bishops returned north to consecrate their fellow bishops according to

---

41 Fincham and Tyacke, *Altars Restored*, p. 100.

42 See the descriptions of services during James's reign, from the swearing in of the Spanish ambassador (with Latin oaths and a Latin Bible) to the baptism of Princess Mary and the 'churching' of Anne of Denmark – whereon each occasion rich copes were worn and elaborate anthems sung. *The Old Cheque-book*, pp. 151–2, 167–8, 170.

the English rite. It is perhaps no accident that during King James's visit to Scotland in 1617 he was accompanied by Bishops Lancelot Andrewes (Lord High Almoner), Richard Neile and James Montague (Dean of the Chapel Royal), as well as one of James's royal chaplains, Dr William Laud. Concerning the King's Progress we are told, 'On the 20th of April, it being Easter Sunday, Bishop Andrews, who was accompanying the King on the Progress, delivered before him in Durham Cathedral, a Sermon on Matth. xii.39,40.'[43] In Edinburgh it was recorded: 'On the 8th June, being Whitsunday, Bishop Andrews preached before the King in "Halyrud House", on Luke, vi.18,19.'[44]

Of this visit in 1617, we are told that King James desired some greater conformity between the English and Scottish Churches, and towards this end 'his Majesty hath set up his Chapel here [i.e. Holyrood House] in like manner of service as it is in England, which is yet frequented well by the people of the country'.[45] Indeed, in a letter to Sir Dudley Carlton of 7 December 1616, it was reported that a pair of organs had been sent, as well as all manner of furniture for a chapel, which Inigo Jones had charge of, together with pictures of the apostles, Faith, Hope and Charity, and such other religious representations 'which how welcome they will be thither God knows'.[46] Charles Rogers, in his *History of the Chapel Royal in Scotland*, observed:

> The existing furniture was to be taken out, and all traces of Presbyterian worship obliterated. Not only so, but an altar was to be constructed, which, richly decorated, was to support elegantly sculptured candlesticks and other ornaments. The stalls of the prebendaries and choristers were to be adorned with carved and gilded figures of the apostles and evangelists.[47]

According to the treasurer's accounts, the work was finished by March 1617. Payments were also made to a Mr Dalam, an organ-maker, as well as to some musicians for furnishing everyone 'a suit of apperrell'.[48]

43 John Nichols, *The Progresses, Processions, and Magnificent Festivities, of King James the First* (London: J. B. Nichols 1828), Vol. 3, p. 279.

44 Nichols, *The Progresses*, p. 336. For discussions of both sermons, see Kenneth Stevenson, *Liturgy and Interpretation* (London: SCM Press 2011), pp. 173–205.

45 Nichols, *The Progresses*, p. 336.

46 Nichols, *The Progresses*, p. 230.

47 Charles Rogers, *History of the Chapel Royal in Scotland* (Edinburgh: The Grampian Club 1882), p. cxxii.

48 Rogers, *History of the Chapel Royal in Scotland*, p. cxxv.

Choral services were established, but the Dean of the Chapel Royal, Bishop William Cowper, did manage to persuade James against the installation of 'images'.[49]

Refurbishing the Chapel Royal and establishing singers and choral services was a clear statement of the royal wish for some uniformity between the two Churches. The Scottish bishops were encouraged to repair and refurbish their cathedral churches. A eulogy to Bishop Patrick Forbes of Aberdeen noted:

> His first and foremost care, was for the House of God; and especiallie of the cathedral Church where he did reside, aedifying, and repairing the ruines thereof, and furnishing it with ornamentes convenient; and which had lyen waste and desolate since the Reformation.[50]

Additional uniformity with England was attempted through the Five Articles of Perth, and the revision of the liturgy. The former included kneeling for Communion, the observance of Christmas, Good Friday, Easter, Ascension and Whitsunday, episcopal confirmation, and private baptism and Communion. All of these proved troublesome. Pressure from James led to them being passed by a General Assembly at Perth in 1618 and a parliament held in 1621, but they were ignored by many ministers and were impossible to enforce.

Revision of the liturgy had been signalled by James in 1615, and a draft Morning Service exists that was mainly the work of Peter Howat. Two further drafts, which Donaldson dated 1616–17 and 1618–19, were the work of the Dean of the Scottish Chapel Royal, Bishop William Cowper. Cowper seems to have been a moderate bishop, though for those of Andrew Melville's persuasion there could be no such thing. Cowper himself had once compared bishops to stinking candle snuff, but his submission to royal will allowed him to see episcopacy as not incompatible with presbytery. He studied at St Andrews and then spent some years in England studying divinity. At age 19 he returned to Edinburgh, continued his studies and was ordained.[51] In his response to the Five Articles, Cowper found kneeling for Communion the hardest, and he himself had declined to receive kneeling at Holyrood House in

49 Rogers, *History of the Chapel Royal in Scotland*, p. cxxiv.
50 *Funerals of a Right reverend father in God. Patrick Forbes of Corse, Bishop of Aberdene*, ed. David Lindsay (Aberdeen: 1635), pp. 64–5.
51 The Life and Death of William Cowper, Bishop of Galloway, in *The Workes of William Cowper* (London: 1623), pp. 3–6.

1617.[52] As Dean of the Chapel Royal, he preached at the King's arrival at Holyrood House, and at Dumfries at his departure for England. Both sermons extolled the office of king. His sermon at the translation of Archbishop Spottiswoode in 1615 was not excessively in praise of episcopacy, but concentrated on the duties of pastors. The second draft liturgy – and the first by Cowper – represented an interesting rewriting and updating of the *Form of Prayers* and its sacramental theology was thoroughly Reformed in tone.[53] The baptismal rite spoke of the sacrament as 'the seale of the covenant of grace', which showed the influence of the terminology developed by the German Reformed theologians Ursinus and Olevianus and mediated to England by Dudley Fenner. The prayer after the baptism was a clear expression of the Bullinger line, which Brian Gerrish has described as symbolic parallelism,[54] where a distinction is made between the ecclesial rite in water and baptism with the Holy Spirit:

> We have in thy name baptised them with water, bot, O Lord, baptise thou them with the holie Spirit that so this baptisme may become to them the laver of regeneration and they, through thy grace renuncing the devil, the world and the flesh, may serve Thee all their daies in holiness of lyfe.[55]

In his *Workes*, Cowper had picked up the two crucial terms used by Bucer and Calvin (but rejected by Bullinger), that sacraments are 'instruments' that 'exhibit'.[56] A favourite term in Cowper's *Workes* is 'exhibiting instrument'. In his Communion rite, Cowper, after taking the bread and cup, the minister asked:

> Lord blesse it that it may be unto us ane effectual exhibiting instrument of the Lord Jesus, for we come here to seeke the Phisician of

52 'The Bishop of Galloway, his answeres to such as desire a resolution of their scruples against the Acts of the last Assembly holden at Perth, in the Moneth of August. 1618', *Workes*, pp. 7–10.

53 Text in Gordon Donaldson, 'A Scottish Liturgy of the Reign of James VI' in *Miscellany of the Scottish History Society* 10 (1965), pp. 89–117.

54 Brian Gerrish, 'The Lord's Supper in the Reformed Confessions' in Donald K. McKim (ed.), *Major Themes in the Reformed Tradition* (Grand Rapids, MI: Eerdmans 1992), pp. 245–58.

55 Donaldson, 'A Scottish Liturgy', p. 104.

56 See the discussion in Bryan D. Spinks, *Sacraments, Ceremonies and the Stuart Divines: Sacramental Theology and Liturgy in England and Scotland 1603–1662* (Aldershot: Ashgate 2004).

our soules and to celebrat with thanksgeving the remembrance of his death and passion untill his coming againe.[57]

Though rather inelegant, it was Reformed theology, and only a hint here of Church of England terminology. The third draft of 1618–19 (Cowper's second draft) used more phraseology from the English Book of Common Prayer. The Lord's Supper reused more material from the *Form of Prayers*, but also drew more heavily on the 1604 Prayer Book. However, although emended, it retained the distinctive Cowperian rendering of Calvin's terminology: 'Send doune o Lord thy blissing upon this Sacrament, that it may be unto us the effectual exhibitive instrument of the Lord Jesus.'[58]

The Articles of Perth caused such an uproar that all thoughts of introducing a new liturgy evaporated. The redecoration of the Chapel Royal, the Articles and this concern for updating and enriching the liturgy seem to be a Scottish symptom of that movement in England stemming from the English Chapels Royal and led by patristic Reformed churchmen, such as Andrewes, who served them. The 'upgrading' of the Scottish Chapels Royal and the repair of the cathedrals were, however, dependent upon royal patronage. A smouldering problem was that many ministers in the Church of Scotland found this liturgical osmosis thoroughly objectionable.

JACOBEAN WORSHIP

The pattern of services established in Elizabeth's reign continued: Morning Prayer, Litany and the first part of the Communion service, and Evening Prayer, with most parish churches having Communion three or four times a year. Church music in England also continued the same course as under Elizabeth. The lead in new composition centred on the Chapel Royal and the cathedrals. John Bull was the organist of Hereford Cathedral and in 1591 had been appointed organist of the Chapel Royal, though only one anthem, for Epiphany, 'O Lord, my God, I will exalt you', has survived.[59] Thomas Tomkins, who was appointed to the Chapel Royal in 1621, was a pupil of Byrd. Orlando Gibbons was a chorister at King's College, Cambridge, and in 1604 was

57 Donaldson, 'A Scottish Liturgy', p. 109.
58 G. W. Sprott, *Scottish Liturgies of the Reign of James VI* (Edinburgh and London: Blackwood 1901), p. 93. For a discussion on Calvin's terminology, see Spinks, *Sacraments, Ceremonies and the Stuart Divines*, pp. 5–8.
59 John S. Bumpus, *A History of English Cathedral Music 1549–1889* (Westmead: Gregg International reprint 1972), p. 73.

appointed organist at the Chapel Royal. It was during Gibbons's time at King's College that an organ was restored to the Chapel in 1605.[60] His celebrated Service in F and a second Service in D were published posthumously. Adrian Batten of St Paul's, London, was also a notable Jacobean church musician, as was John Amner of Ely and Thomas Ravenscroft of Christ's Hospital.[61]

Metrical psalmody was the staple diet in most parish churches, whereas larger churches with singers had a slightly richer repertoire. Sternhold and Hopkins remained unchallenged, partly because of James's belief that he himself might provide a new psalter, and partly because of the monopoly held by the Stationer's Company to print psalmody. The most popular harmonized version was that of Thomas East, first published in 1592, and reprinted in James's reign. Another harmonized version was published by Thomas Ravenscroft in 1621, which introduced some new tunes, few of which were adopted.[62] Joseph Hall published nine metrical psalms in his *Holy Observations* (1607). George Wither also prepared a psalter in 1620, though it was not published until 1632. However, Wither is notable for his attempt, with royal encouragement, to compose hymns for worship, and he compiled *Hymns and Songs of the Church* (1623), with music by Orlando Gibbons. James Doelman commented on its fate:

> The patent given to Wither by James for this work, along with the injunction that it be appended to the Psalter, would seem to have bode well for Wither. However, at this stage of his reign, James' support could have limited effect, and Wither's hymns found no place in the congregational worship of the church, either in his own or later times. Ultimately the Stationer's Company's resistance proved superior. The fate of Wither's hymns also stemmed from the unassailable position of the Psalter as the basis of congregational worship; freely composed hymns were not to figure largely in English worship until the introduction of Watt's hymns in the early eighteenth century.[63]

60 See Roger Bowers, 'Chapel and Choir, Liturgy and Music' in Jean Michel Massing and Nicolette Zeeman (eds), *King's College, Chapel 1515–2015* (London: Harvey Miller Publishers 2014), pp. 259–83, p. 277.
61 See further, Peter Le Huray, *Music and the Reformation in England 1549–1660* (New York: Oxford University Press 1967), ch. 9.
62 Nicholas Temperley, *The Music of the English Parish Church*, Vol. 1 (Cambridge: Cambridge University Press 1979), pp. 71–3.
63 James Doelman, *King James I and the Religious Culture of England* (Cambridge: D. S. Brewer 2000), p. 145.

James died on Sunday 27 March 1625. The Old Cheque-book of the Chapel Royal records:

> At Denmark House the hall there was made a chappell for the tyme, where the Confessor read morninge prayer daylie, and uppon Sondayes one of the Chaplaines preched: the deske was covered with black cothe.
>
> Two dayes before the daye of the funeralls the corps were brought into the sayd Chappell in great solemnitie with an Anthem, and sett under an hearse of velvett, and the Gentlemen of the Chappell from that tyme wayted there, and performed solemne service with the Organs brought thither for that purpose; they also wayted with the corps by course night and day: by night, first Decany syde, and next Cantoris syde, and twise in the night, viz. at nine of the clock and at midnight, they had prayers with a first and second Chapters, and ended with an Anthem.[64]

This would be the Jacobean quiet before an approaching Caroline liturgical storm.

---

64 *The Old Cheque-book*, p. 154.

Chapter 3

Charles I and the Prayer Book: ceremonial adornment, Scottish revision and parliamentary proscription

THE CORONATION OF CHARLES I

The coronation of Charles I took place on Candlemas 1626. The Old Cheque-book of the Chapel Royal records that the members of the Chapel met with the choir of Westminster Abbey and 'they putt on surplesses and copes and went into Westminster Hall'.[1] The first anthem was from Psalm 122, and the fourth anthem during the anointing of the sovereign was 'Zadok the Priest'. The music for the occasion was by Thomas Tomkins (1572–1656), a senior colleague of Orlando Gibbons, though the music has not survived. During the Communion service the Nicene Creed was sung by the choir. The Old Cheque-book records:

> After all the ceremonie in the Church was ended, the Kinge returned back againe into Westminster Hall in the same manner as he went, the Chappell goeinge in their former order, and singinge all the waye till they came to Westminster Hall dore and their they stayed, makinge a lane for the Kinge and all the Lordes to passe betwixt them, and continued singinge till the Kinge was within the Hall: and from thence they returned back into the Church, where in the vestry they putt of their copes and surplusses, and cam to White hall, wher they had some allowance of diett for their suppers.[2]

---

1 Edward Francis Rimbault (ed.), *The Old Cheque-book, or Book of remembrance, of the Chapel Royal, from 1561–1744* (London: Camden Society 1872), p. 157.
2 *The Old Cheque-book*, pp. 159–60.

No revised edition of the Book of Common Prayer was issued other than alterations to the prayers for the King and royal family. Prior to his coronation, Charles had issued by royal proclamation on 3 July 1625 an order for a 'publike, general, and solemn Fast' to be held on Wednesday 20 July and every Wednesday during the plague, which reached a peak in 1625 and 1626. The fast was initiated in Parliament, and the order covered all three kingdoms. Like previous orders, it was composed of cento psalmody and based on Morning and Evening Prayer of the Book of Common Prayer. Of some significance though was the inclusion of a rubric after the Litany:

> The Priest standing at the North side of the Lord's Table, shall say [The Lord's Prayer, followed by the communion service from the BCP until and including the prayer for the king, 'Almighty God, whose kingdom is everlasting'].[3]

The Ante-Communion was a normal part of the Sunday service even when there was no Communion. However, whatever the rubric in the Book of Common Prayer, the position of the minister during its reading varied. The avant-garde preferred a move to the Communion table as per the rubric, whereas many ministers preferred to remain in the reading stall where they had read the 'First Service' (Morning Prayer and Litany). The rubric in this service of the fast reiterated the Prayer Book rubric and privileged the avant-garde churchmen. Since the order was drawn up not only by George Abbot the Archbishop of Canterbury but also by Durham House figures such Richard Neile, Lancelot Andrewes, William Laud and John Buckeridge, it was no surprise.

THE BEAUTY OF HOLINESS

Although there was no new Book of Common Prayer, Charles's reign was characterized by a struggle about how the services were to be celebrated, and the arrangement and adornment of their architectural setting. The Chapel Royal became the blueprint for cathedrals and, in turn, cathedrals became the paradigm for parish churches, and the Durham House divines also appealed to the Elizabethan Injunctions,

---

3 Natalie Mears, Alasdair Raffe, Stephen Taylor and Philip Williamson (with Lucy Bates) (eds), *National Prayers: Special Worship Since the Reformation. Vol. 1: Special Prayers, Fasts and Thanksgivings in the British Isles 1533–1688* (Woodbridge: The Church of England Record Society and the Boydell Press 2013), p. 281.

giving them their own interpretation.[4] The Durham House members regarded the church building as sacred and the space requiring order, decency and the beauty of holiness. In a sermon preached on 22 March 1617, John Buckeridge, the Bishop of Rochester, took as his text the Venite, and expounded the implications for posture, particularly 'kneeling to him that bare our sinnes on the Crosse, and us as lost sheepe on his shoulders'.[5] Buckeridge argued that in worship engagement must be with all the senses, and eyes must see God's beauty.[6] The sacraments are 'chanels and conduits, wherein Gods mercies and graces doe runne'; they are 'part of Gods worship: not as reading or meditation is: but as prayer, and the like, which properly offer divine adoration to God'.[7] Likening Christian worship to Moses and the presence of God in the burning bush, Buckeridge asked of the Communion, 'Is not this sacred mystery as holy, if not more holy then this burning bush?'[8] He continued:

And if holinesse doe become *Domum Dei*, the house of God forever, much more doth holines become *Deum Bethel*, the God of *Bethel*, the God of that house. If holinesse become the materiall house, or Temple, much more doth it become the spirituall house, and table of the Lord, in which wee offer our soules and bodies, to be spirituall Temples to the Lord.[9]

Of course, his emphasis here is the temple of our bodies, but that is in addition to the holiness of the house and the table. In a sermon of 1627 on the text of fearing God and honouring the King, Bishop Matthew Wren asserted:

That's true, we have a great deale of Religion in our Eares too. But yet higher or lower though we have none, None upon our Heads, for a due Reverence before him; None in our Knees, to bow at his blessed Name; None for our Bodies, to cast them downe and *worship*.

Especially not in his house, in the most Sacred presence of our God; No, the lesse a doe there, the better, the lesse Superstition.

---

4 Calvin Lane, *The Laudians and the Elizabethan Church* (London: Pickering and Chatto 2013).

5 John Buckeridge, *A Sermon Preached before His Maiestie at Whitehall, March 22. 1617 . . . To which is added a Discourse concerning kneeling at the Communion* (London: 1618), p. 2.

6 Buckeridge, *A Sermon*, p. 6.

7 Buckeridge, *A Sermon*, pp. 29, 40.

8 Buckeridge, *A Sermon*, p. 114.

9 Buckeridge, *A Sermon*, p. 115.

Doe but come in confidently, and without any more stirre, sit downe, and be covered, and *heare*; and who dare say, that we *feare* not *God*? Whatsoever is more than this, for Adoration or any Beautie of Holines, talke K. David what he will of it, yet it is but δεισιδαιμονία, a Superstitious overfearing of God with many of us: for where requires he any of these Expressions and Externall operations in his *worship*?[10]

There is a difference, argued Wren, between ordinary places and the Table of the Lord, the House of the Lord and the Presence of the Lord, which requires reverence and worship. Wren returned to the theme again later in the sermon. The text shows, said Wren,

> that the *Feare* of the Lord requires the *Worship* of him, and that the due *worship* of him requires so much Beauty and Reverence, that all our saucy and carelesse demeanour before him, all negligent and perfunctorie performance of our Religion, all slight and unawful Expressions in it, as in Gods presence, are the foulest Scorn and Abasement that may be; Ungodding him no lesse in true construction, then does rash and unadvised blasphemie.[11]

The ideals for a holy house and table were set forth by 'R. T.' in *De Templis: A Treatise of Temples, wherin is discovered the Ancient Manner of Building, Consecrating and Adorning of Churches* (1638). The anonymous author wrote:

> The roof if it be vaulted, is more agreeable to antiquitie, than if flat, it makes the voyce more audible; you may adorn it with an azure colour, and gilded stars and then as in figure, so in colour it resembles the Hemisphear of the Heavens.[12]

He continued:

> The Chancel, as it has alwayes beene divided from the Church, so may the roof of it be of a different height, and more richly adorned, and the windoores of a differing fashion from the Church: That

---

10 Matthew Wren, *A Sermon Preached before the Kings Maiestie On Sunday the seventeenth of February last, at White-Hall* (Cambridge: 1627), p. 16.
11 Wren, *A Sermon Preached*, p. 33.
12 R. T., *De Templis: A Treatise of Temples, wherin is discovered the Ancient Manner of Building, Consecrating and Adorning of Churches* (London: R. Bisho 1638), p. 198.

when we shall enter into this place, more holy & divine thoughts may possesse our minds, occasioned by the differing structure, and more glorious ornaments.

But of all parts of the Chancell, that where the Communion Table stands, has ever beene accounted most sacred; in adorning that, no cost ought to be thought too much. There we behold the mystery of our Redemption lively expressed.[13]

'R.T.' explained that the altar is sacred because Christ is present there in the celebration of the blessed sacrament, and so 'Hither bring your stateliest hangings, and adorne the wals; hither your richest carpets, and bespred the ground; hither the most glorious silks and finest linnen, to cover the holy Table.'[14]

The practical implications are summarized perfectly by Graham Parry:

Choirs and chancels would be clad in new panelling; the roof of the chancel might be glorified with carved or painted stars, or sunbursts. The altar would be moved eastwards, and honoured by being raised on several steps, so that it had to be approached in reverent humility. The altar would be railed off, and a handsome chair provided for the use of the priest. Sometimes a reredos or decorated screen would be set behind the altar, or a canopy erected above it. Embroidered altar cloths would be made. The bible that was often placed on the altar would be given an embroidered binding or cover. Cherubs would appear on the panelling, on pulpits and on tombs, descendants of those that had hovered over the ceremonies in the temple of Solomon (I Kings 6:21–32). Many chancels would be freshly paved as part of the restructuring of the interior, with black and white marble slabs laid diaper-wise, the preferred fashion. A chancel screen might be erected, to mark the division between the semi-circular space of the nave and the more holy space beyond.[15]

The concern for 'holiness' of church buildings translated into the use of consecration services with considerable ceremony. An order for the consecration of churches had been drawn up by Lancelot Andrewes, and this form served as the basis for the consecration of St Katherine

---

13 *De Templis*, pp. 199–200.
14 *De Templis*, p. 201.
15 Graham Parry, *The Arts of the Anglican Counter-Reformation: Glory, Laud and Honour* (Woodbridge: The Boydell Press 2006), pp. 21–2.

Cree, London, in 1631. Laud, as Bishop of London, consecrated it in January 1631 with such ceremonial that William Prynne was able to use it as ammunition against Laud at his trial. Shortly afterwards Laud consecrated St Giles Church, London. It had been rebuilt between 1623 and 1625, but the then Bishop of London did not consider it necessary to reconsecrate the building. Laud did, and closed the building until he consecrated it.[16]

In his attack on William Laud for 'popery', William Prynne described how at the consecration of St Giles, Laud engaged in excessive bowing.[17] Bowing at the name of Jesus was mandated in canon 18 of 1604, and the 'Laudian' divines encouraged and attempted to enforce this, as well as other bowings and gestures. John Young, the Dean of Winchester, recorded in his diary for 26 November 1629 how he had charged Robert Moore, one of the Prebendaries, with preaching against the bowing at the name of Jesus, and 'against standing at the *gloria patri*, and bowing ore crouching as he called it, towards the Communion table'.[18] Young himself apparently did not practise bowing to the altar, though Laud's Vicar General advised Young and the Chapter 'to stand at all the Creeds, Apostles, Nicene, Athanasian & only at the Gospel'.[19] Young wrote:

> I professed to do so, protesting how much I honoured the Church of England, I only wishing ane uniformitie, for now we stood at the Te Deum, Magnificat etc. The Dr Lewes, Lany, Halsey, pressed me for not bowing to the altare. I saide that I dide not disalow those that dide it, nay in the Kings chappel & in the church of Wells dide practise it, & hier also at the administrating of the Comunion bet dide forbeare at other times till I hade ane order from superioures into the which I would submit, the rather becaus I hade been so traduced & publikly in pulpit for innovations wtout direction etc.[20]

Young was thus a moderate ceremonialist, but sensitive to 'puritan' accusations of innovation. In a sermon published in 1630, Giles Widdowes had attacked 'Schysmatical Puritans' for not bowing at the name of Jesus, and the 'Laudian' argument was set out by Widdowes in *A Treatise of Justiffication of Bowing at the Name of Jesus* (1631).

---

16 Parry, *The Arts of the Anglican Counter-Reformation*, p. 34.
17 William Prynne, *Canterburies Doom* (London: 1646).
18 Florence Remington Goodman (ed.), *The Diary of John Young S.T.P. Dean of Winchester 1616 to the Commonwealth* (London: SPCK 1928), p. 84.
19 Goodman, *Diary*, June 1635, p. 108.
20 Goodman, *Diary*, pp. 108–9.

Probably the most contentious issue was the railing of the Communion table. The Elizabethan practice was that when not in use the Communion table was to stand where the old altar had stood, but when in use the practice was to move it into the chancel or even the nave, and to position it so that the longest sides were on the north and south. Some parishes left the table in this position. The 'Laudian' ideal was to have the table where the old altar had stood and to put rails around it. This served two purposes. First, it made moving the table more difficult and thus more likely that it would remain 'altarwise' during Communion. Second, in some parishes, such as the three parish churches in Nottingham, Communion was received in the pews, and the erection of Communion rails gave less reason for anyone to receive other than kneeling around or at the table.[21] Laud and other bishops such as Wren and Neile enforced the railing in the altars throughout their dioceses and (Laud and Neile) their Provinces. Julian Davies questioned how far this was Laud's hobby horse and how far he was simply following the royal policy of Charles. Indeed, he placed the 'Laudians' in five categories according to how consistent and vigorous they were in enforcing railing in of the Holy Table, Communion at the rail, and east–west orientation of the table, placing Laud in a more moderate category.[22] However, Kenneth Fincham revisited the diocesan and parish records, and concluded that Neile and Laud were the central figures in this reordering of the table. Neile led the way, imposing altar rails in the northern province in 1633, and his example was followed, after the hearing of St Gregory's Church, London, in November 1633, by bishops in the southern province. Laud followed belatedly, but wholeheartedly.[23] The one episcopal opponent of this reordering was Bishop Williams of Lincoln, and he defended the older Elizabethan and Jacobean custom in *The Holy Table, Name and Thing* (1637).

Through preferment the members of the Durham House group attained places of power and were able to pursue their ideals about liturgical worship, though not without opposition and protest. The opposition by some parishes and the use of the ecclesiastical courts to enforce the 'Laudian' policies have been carefully documented by Fincham and

---

21 For Nottingham, see Kenneth Fincham and Nicholas Tyacke, *Altars Restored: The Changing Face of English Religious Worship, 1547–c.1700* (Oxford: Oxford University Press 2007), p. 213.
22 Julian Davies, *The Caroline Captivity of the Church: Charles I and the Remoulding of Anglicanism* (Oxford: Clarendon Press 1992), p. 218.
23 Kenneth Fincham, 'The Restoration of Altars in the 1630s', *Historical Journal* 44 (2001), pp. 919–40.

Tyacke, and Parry.[24] The policy may be best illustrated here by certain case studies.

JOHN COSIN AT DURHAM CATHEDRAL AND PETERHOUSE, CAMBRIDGE

John Cosin typifies the ideals of the Durham House group in his work both at Durham Cathedral and at Peterhouse Chapel, Cambridge. Cosin had been secretary to Bishop John Overall and at the latter's death he became chaplain to Bishop Richard Neile, who had been translated to Durham in 1617. As noted in the previous chapter, Neile surrounded himself with younger protégés, including such figures as John Cosin, Francis White, William Laud, Gabriel Clarke, Francis Burgoyne, Robert Newell, Augustine Lindsell, Eleazar Duncon, Richard Montague and Marmaduke Blakiston. Of this Durham House group, Robert Newell, Augustine Lindsell, Gabriel Clarke, Francis Burgoyne, Marmaduke Blakiston, John Cosin and Eleazar Duncon were all appointed to prebend stalls at Durham and the cathedral became the showcase of Durham House or 'Laudian' piety and worship.

At Morning Prayer on Sunday 7 July 1628 (though some editions give it as 27 July),[25] Peter Smart, the second most senior prebendary of Durham Cathedral, mounted the pulpit of the cathedral and launched a vitriolic attack on his fellow prebend John Cosin. His text was Psalm 31.7, 'I have hated them that hold of superstitious vanities.' Smart's affiliation with the cathedral dated from 1597 when he was headmaster of the grammar school. He was appointed holder of the sixth prebend's stall in 1609, and then holder of the fourth stall from 1614. He had thus served under the deanship first of William James, who was later appointed Bishop of Durham, then under Adam Newton and, from 1620, under Dean Richard Hunt. Smart no doubt had been aware of some changes in worship during his long tenure, but his outburst was prompted by what he regarded as drastic popish innovations which had

---

24 Fincham and Tyacke, *Altars Restored*; and Parry, *The Arts of the Anglican Counter-Reformation*.
25 Peter Smart, *A Sermon Preached in the Cathedrall Church of Durham, July 7 1628* (printed 1640). Some editions date the sermon as 27 July. Gabriel Sewell, Head of Collections at Durham Cathedral, writes: 'Was the 27 July imprint a way of concealing the book's true origins? The 27 July is only used in the title pages of the editions printed in London but with a false Edinburgh imprint. Using a false imprint was a way of avoiding censorship etc. The first London edition of 1628 gives the date of the sermon of 7 July; the two editions also of 1628 with the false imprints of "Edenborough" both have 27 July. By the 1640 editions, it is back to the 7 July.' Email 5 March 2014.

been introduced by Cosin, who had been appointed to the tenth stall in 1624. Smart asserted:

> For before wee had Ministers, as the Scripture calls them, we had Communion tables, wee had Sacraments; but now wee have Priests, and Sacrifices and Altars, with much Altar-furniture, and many Massing implements. Nay what want we? Have not all Religion againe[?]
>
> For if Religion consist in Altar-ducking, Cope-wearing, Organ playing, piping and singing, crossing of Cushions, and kissing of Clouts, oft starting up, and squatting downe, nodding of heads, and whirling about, till their noses stand Eastward:
>
> Setting Basons on the Altar, Candlesticks and Crucifixes; burning Waxe-candles, in excessive number, when and where there is no use of Lights.[26]

Earlier in this sermon Smart had complained about the prebends putting on and off the cope during the service, reading the Epistle, Gospel and Ten Commandments at the altar, and singing the Nicene Creed at the altar. And, he claimed:

> Lastly, why forbid they singing of Psalmes in such tune, as all the people may sing with them, and praise God together, before and after Sermons, as by authority is allowed, and heretofore hath been practised both here in all reformed Churches
>
> How dare they in stead of Psalmes, appoint Anthems, (little better then prophane Ballads some of them) I say, so many Anthems to be sung, which none of the people understand, nor all the singers themselves.[27]

Smart added that this change was done out of spite 'they beare to *Geneva*, which all papists hate'.[28] Referring to John Cosin as 'our young Apollo', Smart accused him of setting out the choir 'with strange Babylonish ornaments', and 'the hallowed Priests dance about the altar, making pretty sport, and fine pastime, with trippings, and turnings, and crossings and crouchings'.[29] He accused Cosin of wearing 'Babylonish robes' and standing where he might 'heare a delicate noise of singers, with

26 Smart, *Sermon*, p. 23.
27 Smart, *Sermon*, pp. 19–20.
28 Smart, *Sermon*, p. 20.
29 Smart, *Sermon*, p. 24.

Shakebuts, and Cornets, and Organs, and if it were possible, all kinde of Musicke, used at the dedication of *Nabuchodonosors* golden Image'.[30]

The sermon landed Smart in court and then in prison. Some of what he complained of he had in fact, as a member of the cathedral chapter, agreed to, or at least not dissented from. From the Elizabethan Settlement onwards, copes were supposed to be worn for Communion in cathedrals, and had been at Durham, leading Dean William Whittingham (1563–79) to cease celebrating Communion in the cathedral. Smart's complaint seems to have been about their more frequent use and the use of ornamented copes rather than the use of copes per se. Furthermore, it was prior to Cosin's arrival that a stone altar had been installed by Dean Hunt (*c.* 1620), who had also purchased a new Communion plate and a new organ.[31] However, Smart was certainly correct that there had been changes in the ceremonial in the cathedral. Richard Hutchinson, a singing-man and organist of Durham, corroborated much of this in a statement made on 16 March 1629. Among his 17 listed changes, he recorded:

> 6 Then for our ten a clock Service we were commanded to begin with the ten Commandments, and with the Epistle and Gospel, Creed and Anthem, with the Collects after, and so an end, for Munday, Tuesday, Thursday, and Saterday.
> 7 On Wednesday, Friday, and Sunday, to begin with the Letany, the ten Commandments, the Epistle and Gospel, Creed.
> 8 Then the Sermon, and after an Anthem, the Collect, and an end.
> 9 So that before and after Sermons and Lectures we have had of late no Psalmes but all Anthems, and many of the ditties neither in the Bible nor Communion book.
> 11 (*sic*) And every Sunday two or three Copes worne.[32]

Smart had declared:

> *The Kings Chappell, say they, hath an Altar, and all furniture belonging thereunto; 'Dare you disallow in ours, what the King hath in his? It is little better then treason,* as one said.

---

30 Smart, *Sermon*, p. 22.

31 Fincham and Tyacke, *Altars Restored*, p. 117.

32 Cited in Brian Crosby, "'The Sacrament it selfe is turned well neare into a theatricall stage play': Liturgical Innovations and Reactions in the 1620s' in *Conflict and Disaster at Durham: Four Talks delivered to the Friends of Durham Cathedral 2001–02* (Durham: Friends of Durham Cathedral 2003), pp. 15–34, pp. 29–30.

I answer, It was never out of the Kings Chappel (at least the name of an Altar) since the first reformation in King *Edwards* time, if it had, I suppose it had never come in againe in his religious successors raigne.[33]

Here at least Smart was accurate in tracing the ceremonial back to the Chapel Royal. Left unsaid, though, was the fear of the influence of the other Chapel Royal – the Roman Catholic chapel at the palace of St James for the use of the Queen, Henrietta Maria, of France. According to John Evelyn, it was the fact that the French ladies at Court had Books of Hours that led John Cosin to compile *A Collection of Private Devotions* (1627), for use by English ladies at Court.[34] It represented a new version of the Primers issued in the early years of Elizabeth's reign and in this sense had good precedent. However, as a popular devotional form it had faded from the Church of England psyche and so to many seemed less a revival than a 'popish' innovation, and brought forth not only remarks by Smart but a scathing attack from Henry Burton and William Prynne.[35]

Cosin weathered the Durham storm and went on to succeed Matthew Wren as Master of Peterhouse, Cambridge, in 1635. The chapel was begun by Wren in 1628 with the clearing of the ground for the foundations, and the foundation was laid on 30 June 1628. According to Willis and Clark, one George Thompson was the freemason, but there is no record of the person who made the design.[36] The masonry of the windows was paid for in November 1629 but they were not glazed until 1632. The roof took between 1629 and 1631 to complete. The seats and altar furniture were provided in 1632, and it was on 17 March 1632 that Bishop Francis White consecrated the chapel. The service is recorded in the college archives. After several Latin speeches, instructions and prayers, the service prayed:

We are now here assembled to put thy name upon this place, & the memorials of it, to make it thy house, to devote, & dedicate it for

---

33 Smart, *Sermon*, p. 32.
34 Evelyn Diary III, 45–6, cited in P. G. Stanwood (ed.), *John Cosin: A Collection of Private Devotions* (Oxford: Oxford University Press 1967), p. xxxiv.
35 *A briefe Survey and censure of Mr. Cozens His Couzening Devotions* (1628). See Bryan D. Spinks, 'What was Wrong with Mr. Cosin's Couzening Devotions? Deconstructing an Episode in Seventeenth-Century Anglican "Liturgical Hagiography"', *Worship* 74 (2000), pp. 308–29.
36 Robert Willis and John Willis Clark, *The Architectural History of the University of Cambridge*, Vol. 1 (Cambridge: Cambridge University Press [1886] 1988), p. 41. For the chapel details I am dependent upon this source.

ever unto the, utterly separating it from all former uses common, & profane & wholly & only to consecrate it to the invocation of thy blessed name, wherein supplications, prayers, intercessions may be made for all men, Thy sacred Word may be read, preched, & heard, the holy Sacraments may be administered; thy pryses celebrated, & sounded forth; thy people blessed by putting thy name upon them.[37]

The chapel was 64 feet long by 26 feet wide. Subscriptions totalled £2,365, including £300 from the previous Master, Leonard Mawe. The walls were constructed of rough brickwork, presumably awaiting a further benefaction. In a hostile pamphlet, perhaps written by William Prynne, entitled *Wren's Anatomy. Discovering His notorious pranks, and shamfull wickednesse; with some of his most lewd facts, and infamous deeds; both in his government of Peter-house Colledge, and domineering in three Bishopricks, to his perpetuall shame and infamy* (1641), under 'Prank' or 'shameful wickedness', item three, we read:

This wicked *Wren*, being Master of *Peter-house* Colledge, and Clerke of the Kings Closet, besides other preferments, being intimately familiar with *Canterbury*, and being a quick-sighted bird, and of an active spirit, perceived the times drive so hard after Popery, he smelt the way to a Bishoprick, and studied nothing more to please the Papists, and *Canterbury*; and among other devises, he was noted to be either the first or one of them who brought in use againe, Latine service in his Colledge; thinking that young Students being trained up therein, and used thereto, would be an introduction to Latin service in Churches; which when he should come to be Archbishop, might be effected: and in the meane time, thought it would be excusable if any question should arise, because the Rubrick of the Service book, doth allow private prayers in any tongue that they themselves doe understand, (perhaps intending forrainers and strangers Churches here in *England*) which words be spied, and wrested to his own advantage, and so brought up Latine Service in *Peter-house*; and by his example, some other Colledges did the like.[38]

In the accounts of the chapel between 1632 and 1633, the following payments are listed: 'et de xxijs.xd pro 8 libris Liturgiae Latinae; et de

---

37 Peterhouse MS, Consecration of St. Pet. Collg Chap. AD 1632.
38 *Wren's Anatomy. Discovering His notorious pranks, and shamfull wickednesse; with some of his most lewd facts, and infamous deeds; both in his government of Peter-house Colledge, and domineering in three Bishopricks, to his perpetuall shame and infamy* (1641), p. 3.

xxiiijs.iiijd pro 4 aliis libris Anglicanis, Bibliis scil. duobus et duobus Liturgiis vernaculis constringendis et ornandis in usum Sacelli'.[39] Exactly how widely in the College Chapels and for how long the Latin forms continued in use is far from clear. Christ Church, Oxford, had Latin editions printed in 1615. Clay notes that this edition, entitled *Liber Precum Publicarum in usum Ecclesiae Cathedralis Christ, Oxon*, contained only Morning Prayer, the Athanasian Creed, Evening Prayer, the Litany, Collects and Psalter, with some prayers and graces.[40] The English Short Title Catalogue also lists a 1639 edition for Christ Church. Corpus Christi, Oxford, paid 1 shilling for 'A Latin Psalter for the Chappell' in 1630/31 and in January 1632 the college paid 4s 4d to a Mr White 'for a latine prayer booke and a Lat.testament and for binding them together with the singing psalmes'.[41] The President of Corpus at this time was Thomas Jackson and the Visitor was Bishop Richard Neile. St John's College, Oxford, purchased a new service book in Hilary Term 1632 and another in Michaelmas 1634.[42] No language is specified, but given that Laud had been President of the College and was now Chancellor of the University, they indeed may have been Latin. In a letter to the Vice-Chancellor dated 26 November 1636, Laud insisted that the University Church and the college chapels should begin each term with the service of Morning Prayer and Litany, and Communion be in Latin, as well as the sermon. He further instructed: 'And that such as are not furnished, may the better provide themselves of service books in Latin, so soon as conveniently they can, you shall do well to make it so much the sooner known to the heads.'[43]

At Cambridge, in addition to Peterhouse, we know that when William Beale was Master of Jesus College, nine Latin service books were purchased in 1632/33.[44] It would appear, given the date of the Prayer Book that contains Latin Morning and Evening Prayer, and from the date of the college accounts, that Wren at least provided for the possibility of some services in Latin in the newly built chapel.

---

39 Willis and Clark, *Architectural History*, Appendix 5, pp. 75–6.
40 William K. Clay (ed.), *Liturgies and Occasional Forms of Prayer Set Forth in the Reign of Queen Elizabeth* (Cambridge: Cambridge University Press 1847), p. xxxii.
41 Corpus Christi College Oxford C/1/1/9. This volume is not foliated or paginated. I am grateful to Julian Reid, archivist at CCCO, for providing these details.
42 St John's College Archive 1.A.16 f 22r; 1.A. 19 f. 21v. I am grateful to Michael Riordan, college archivist, for supplying these references.
43 *The Works of the Most Reverend Father in God, William Laud, DD* (Oxford: John Henry Parker 1853), Vol. 5, Part 1, p. 156.
44 Jesus College Archives A/C 1.3, In Capella.

John Cosin was appointed Master of Peterhouse on 8 February 1635. It was under his mastership that the interior of the chapel was completed, and his wife Frances paid for the pavement. Though perhaps exaggerated, William Prynne gave a description of the liturgical ceremonial and furnishings of Peterhouse in his 1646 *Canterburies Doom*:

> that in Peter House Chappell there was a glorious new *Altar* set up, and mounted on steps, to which the Master, Fellowes, Schollers bowed, and were enjoyned to bow by Doctor Cosens the Master, who set it up; that there were Basons, candlesticks, Tapers standing on it, and a great Crucifix hanging over it . . . That in S.John's and Peter House Chappells there were pictures of the Holy Ghost in form of a Dove; that in Peter House there was likewise a carved cross at the end of every seat, and on the Altar a Pot, which they usually called the incense-pot: that the Masters, fellows, and Schollers of that house at their entering into, & going out of the Chappell, made a low obeisance to the Altar, being enjoyned by Doctor Cosens under a penalty (as they reported it) to doe it; and none of them might turne their backs towards the Altar going in nor out of the Chappell: That divers Scholars of other houses usually resorted thither, some out of curiosity only to behold, others to learn and practice the Popish ceremonies and orders used in that chappell: and the common report, both among the Schollers of that house and others, was, that none might approach the Altar in Peter house but in Sandalls and that there was a special consecrated Knife there kept upon the Altar, to cut the sacramental bread that was to be consecrated.[45]

A bill given to Cosin for plate and other chapel requirements in 1638 lists candlesticks, a flagon and a 'Sencor', making a new case for the 'Sencor', which seems to confirm the ceremonial use of incense. Prynne later accused Cosin of introducing the hours of his *Private Devotions* into the chapel, and that the container for the incense was that once belonging to Lancelot Andrewes.[46]

WILLIAM LAUD'S REORDERING OF ST PAUL'S CATHEDRAL AND OTHER CHAPELS

Archbishop William Laud became the epitome of the Durham House agenda and bore the brunt of Puritan resentment and hatred. His

45 Prynne, *Canterburies Doom*, pp. 73–4.
46 Prynne, *Canterburies Doom*, pp. 208, 123.

insistence on the use of Latin in the Oxford colleges and university has already been noted, as also his insistence on consecrating new and rebuilt churches. When Bishop of London, and with royal patronage, he raised money for the repair and refurbishing of St Paul's Cathedral. Gordon Higgott writes:

> The architect of the restoration, in the broadest sense, was William Laud, the high churchman whom Charles appointed bishop of London in 1628 and elevated to the archbishopric of Canterbury in 1633 . . . He established a mechanism by which funds for the repair of the cathedral could be obtained by a commission of 5 January 1631 'for inquiring into the execution of the laws for relief of the poor and supervising of the administration of gifts for pious uses'. This was followed on 10 April 1631 by the king's royal commission for the repair of the cathedral.[47]

Work on repairing the choir screen and refitting the choir was paid for by Sir Paul Pinder. The contemporary writer William Dugdale gave some details of the restoration that Pinder financed:

> [He] repaired the decays of that goodly partition, made at the West end of the Quire; adorning the front thereof, outwards, with fair Pillars of black Marble, and Statues of those Saxon Kings, which had been Founders, or Benefactors to the Church: beautified the inner part thereof, with figures of Angells; and all the wainscote work of the Quire, with excellent carving; *viz.* of Cherubins and other Imagery, richly gilded; adding costly suits of Hangings for the upper end thereof.[48]

Laud also refurbished his chapel at Lambeth Palace. Peter Heylyn recorded Laud's work there and in some other chapels:

> When he came first to Lambeth-house, where he found the chapel lye so nastily, (as his own words are) the Windows so defaced, and all things in it so disordered, that he was much ashamed to see it, and could not resort to it without disdain; the Images in the Windows

---

47 Gordon Higgott, 'The Fabric to 1670' in Derek Keene, Arthur Burns and Andrew Saint (eds), *St. Paul's: The Cathedral Church of London 604–2004* (New Haven, CT: Yale University Press 2004), pp. 171–89, p. 175.
48 William Dugdale, *The History of St. Pauls Cathedral in London* (London: Thomas Warren 1658), p. 160.

being broken in many places, and most deformedly patcht up with ordinary Glass, he caused to be repaired, and beautified according to their former Figure, his Glasiers Bill amounting to no less than 148li.7s.6d. With like care, but with far less Charges, he repaired the ruined Windows in the Chappel of his house in Croyden where he spent the greatest part of his Summers, and whither he retired at other times for his ease and privacy. And as for the Communion Table, which he found standing in the middle of the Chappel, a very sorry one in it self, he ordered it to be removed to some other Room, and caused a new one to be made, placed where the Altar sometimes stood, shadowed over-head with a very fair Frieze, and Fenced with a decent and costly Rail, the guilding of the one, and curious workmanship of the other, together with the Table it self, amounting to 33 pounds, and upwards; copes, Altar-cloaths, Plate, and other necessaries which belonged to the adorning of it he had been Master of before in his other Chappels, and therefore was at the less charge in compleating this. He put himself at some cost also in repairing and beautifying the Organs, which he found very much out of tune, and made great use of them in the celebrating of Divine service on Sundays and Holydays, when his leisure could permit him to be present at it; some Gentlemen of his Majesties Chappel assisting many times to make up the Consort when the solemnity required it. According unto which example of their Lord, and Chancellor, the principal Colledges in Oxon. beautified their Chappels, transposed their Tables, fenced them with rails, and furnished them with Hangings, Palls, Plate, and all other necessaries.[49]

These two accounts by contemporaries of Laud give a succinct picture of his concern for the beauty of holiness in worship.

WILLIAM HAYWOOD AT ST GILES
AND NICHOLAS FERRAR AT LITTLE GIDDING

William Haywood followed Roger Manwaring as Rector of St Giles in the Fields, London. Both were 'Laudian' supporters, Haywood having been one of Laud's chaplains. The divisive nature of the 'Laudian' quest for the beauty of holiness is evidenced in the opposing positions of petitioners in a complaint to Parliament in 1640, and both petitions gave

---

49 Peter Heylyn, *Cyprianus Anglicus, or the Life and Death of the Most Reverend and Renowned Prelate William by divine providence Lord Archbishop of Canterbury, etc.* (London: John Maycock 1671), p. 277.

information regarding the furnishings and ceremonial at St Giles. The 'puritan' faction complained that his church discipline was superstitious and idolatrous,

> manifested by strange antic gestures of cringings and bowings; by using and approving of many antiquated, obsolete, and popish cere-monies, both in the administration of the Holy Sacrament of the Lord's Supper, and in other holy duties, contrary to the laws estab-lished within this realm . . . In the exterior acts of administering the Sacrament, for the preparation to this duty, the said Doctor and the subdeacons do all go from the body of the said church unto the west end: being there clothed according to their order, some in scarlet, silk, and fine linen, they bend their course towards the east, every one at their first entrance saluting the church-door with low congies . . . The bread being set upon a plate, and some of the wine poured into a bowl, all are covered with a fine linen cloth, which cloth hath the corners laid in the figure of a cross . . . In these dumb devotions of his, the organs play in a doleful low tune . . . His altar stands decked continually, week-days and all, and mewed up within the screen and rails.[50]

Haywood's supporters countered this by claiming that the term sub-deacon was never used by Haywood, and that the screen was a gift of a 'religious lady' before Haywood's time. Furthermore:

> The ornaments of the Holy Table, the silk curtains, carpet, covering, books, and much plate, were all the pious gift of the same honourable lady which bestowed the screen: and being for the decency of God's service, and well accepted of by the parishioners, the Doctor had no reason to refuse them. As for the crucifix, organs, and church music mentioned in the petition, they were long before Dr. Haywood's coming. There is no desk upon the Lord's Table, only a little stay to hold up the plate, nor any such pictures on the books as the petition-ers speak of. For the ceremonies used in administering (the scornful description whereof, and his abusive wit that drew it, the Doctor much pities) they were none of them invented, nor new brought up,

---

50 *The Petition and Articles exhibited in Parliament against Doctor Heywood, Late Chaplen to the Bishop of Canterburie, by the Parishioners of S. Giles in the Fields* (1641) in Members of the Ecclesiological Late Cambridge Camden Society, *Hierurgia Anglicana, or Documents and extracts Illustrative of the Ritual of the Church in England* (London: Rivington 1848), pp. 250–1.

by Dr. Haywood. His pattern he had from his Majesty's Chapel not far from that place.[51]

Once more it is the Chapel Royal that is the standard for the ceremonial.

Another 'symptom' of 'Laudian' popery, according to Puritan-minded opponents, was the extended family community at Little Gidding, Huntingdonshire, under the leadership of Nicholas Ferrar. It brought forth a critical work entitled *The Arminian Nunnery: Or, A Briefe Description of the Late Erected Monasticall Place, called the Arminian Nunnery at Little Gidding in Huntington-Shire* (1641). Even allowing for the exaggeration of this hostile source, Trevor Cooper aptly commented: 'Although not a convent, the private devotional life of the Ferrar family – formal, intense, all-pervading – was indeed pushing the boundaries for the Church of England.'[52] Ferrar's widowed mother moved to Little Gidding in 1626 and was joined there by three of her children with their families, and so the household numbered between 30 and 40. Nicholas Ferrar had held office in the Virginia Company and, although unmarried and not the eldest son, nevertheless became head of the household which lived a life based around prayer and worship. He was extremely devout, and was ordained deacon by William Laud.

Ferrar himself made a distinction between the family's private prayers and their public worship that followed the Book of Common Prayer. The former were carefully regulated at certain times of the day, beginning at 4 a.m. in the summer, and 5 a.m. in the winter. These 'Hours' consisted of psalms, a reading from a harmony on the Gospels, and one of George Wither's hymns accompanied by a harmonium. The church at Little Gidding was in poor state, and in 1630 the Ferrars repaired and refurbished it; it was a parish church, not a private chapel. Though it underwent Victorian renovation, some things have survived. From a set of drawings of 1798, as well as material from the Ferrar papers, Trevor Cooper gives the following summary of the refurbishment:

As normal, there were a set of Commandments, Creed and Lord's Prayer in the Chancel, and they are still there, good London work, the chancel being distinguished visually from the nave by a step and a fine carpet. In the nave the Ferrars introduced identical twin pulpits

51 *An Answer to a lawless Pamphlet entitled 'The Petition and Articles exhibited in Parliament against Dr. Haywood'* (1641) in *Hierurgia Anglicana*, p. 251.
52 Trevor Cooper, '"Wise as serpents": The Form and Setting of Public Worship at Little Gidding in the 1630s' in Natalie Mears and Alec Ryrie (eds), *Worship in the Parish Church in Early Modern Britain* (Farnham: Ashgate 2013), pp. 197–219, p. 198.

(now disappeared): the one on the north was used by the minister to read the service, instead of the normal reading desk; and the other for Sunday sermons, and reading from the Book of Homilies on feast days when no minister was present. There was also a medieval eagle lectern, which may have come from Sawtry priory a few miles away, and, close to the pulpit, a font.[53]

The seating was collegiate style, though the altar was set tablewise and there is no evidence that there was a Communion rail. Since John Williams the bishop opposed the 'Laudian' altar, this may have been the reason. A rail was introduced in 1635 after the 'Laudian' provincial drive. Although it was far from the 'Laudian' ideal, the refurbishing and the private prayers at hours of the day were regarded by Puritan critics as being yet another example of a move back towards popish excesses.

THE PROPOSED PRAYER BOOK FOR SCOTLAND (1637)

It was the Durham House liturgical ideal derived from the English Chapels Royal that was taken up by Charles's Scottish bishops, and resulted in the ill-fated 1637 Book of Common Prayer for Scotland.[54] Though often referred to as 'Laud's liturgy', it was mainly the work of Bishops James Wedderburn and John Maxwell, but it was certainly a Durham House or 'Laudian' liturgical Prayer Book. Wedderburn had studied at St Andrews and then at Cambridge. He was ordained in England and was appointed to St Andrews; at the command of James VI, he used the English Book of Common Prayer in the college chapel. He returned to England and held English benefices and was a canon of Ely. He was appointed Dean of the Scottish Chapel Royal in 1635 and Bishop of Dunblane in 1636. He was indeed a friend of Laud, but no doubt shared both James VI's and Charles I's aims of greater uniformity between the English and Scottish Churches. Robert Baillie was to write of Wedderburn:

> though fugitive from our Church discipline for his Arminian lectures to his Schollers in Saint Andrewes was not onely kindly entertained and richly beneficed in England by the Arch-bishop but also sent

53 Cooper, '"Wise as serpents"', pp. 203–5.
54 G. Donaldson, *The Making of the Scottish Prayer Book of 1637* (Edinburgh: Edinburgh University Press 1954); see also Joong-Lak Kim, 'The Scottish-English-Romish Book: The Character of the Scottish Prayer Book of 1637' in Michael J. Braddock and David L. Smith (eds), *The Experience of Revolution in Stuart Britain and Ireland* (Cambridge: Cambridge University Press 2011), pp. 14–32.

backe by him Bishop of Dumblane, though hee had never beene a Minister amongst us, neither alone was hee returned a simple Bishop, but also Deane of that Royall Chappell, to the end that his gracious parts might be employed to instill the Canterburian Tenets, in the heads of the new Societie of the twenty foure Royall Chaplains lately instituted amongst us.[55]

Baillie saw the Scottish bishops as part of a huge plot by Laud to take over the Kirk. In fact, Laud had the full backing of Charles I, who was himself completing the wish of James VI to bring uniformity of worship and polity in the three kingdoms. The preface to the 1637 Prayer Book noted that though it is impossible for the whole Church of Christ to have uniformity in worship, 'at least in the churches that are under the protection of one sovereign prince the same ought to be endeavoured'. Charles, through Walter Balcanquhal, explained:

Our Father of blessed memorie immediately after his coming into England, comparing the decencie and uniformitie of Gods worship here, especially in the Liturgie of the Church, with that diversitie, nay deformitie which was used in Scotland . . . He did immediately, as became a Religious Prince, bethink himself seriously how His first reformation in that Kingdome might begin at the publike worship of God.[56]

But, of course, the liturgical experience of both James and Charles was mainly that of the Chapels Royal.

Charles I furthered his father's work in establishing daily sung services in the Scottish Chapels Royal, as well as furnishings in the English style. In 1630 Edward Kelly was appointed director of music of the Scottish Chapel Royal and travelled to London to see how services were conducted. At Charles's Scottish coronation in 1633, he brought with him musicians and singers from the English Chapel Royal. The service took place in the Abbey Church at Holyrood, and the Archbishop of St Andrews and the Bishops of Murray, Dunkeld, Ross, Dunblane and Brechin wore rochets and copes of blue silk. John Spalding remarked of the service:

---

55 Robert Baillie, *A Large Supplement of the Canterburian Self-Conviction* (1641), no pagination.
56 Charles I/Walter Balcanquhal, *A Large Declaration concerning the late Tumults in Scotland* (1639), pp. 15–16.

Now it is marked that there was a four-nooked tassil in manner of an altar, standing within the kirk, having standing thereupon two books, at least resembling clasped books, called *blind books*, with two chandlers and two wax candles, whilk were on light, and a bason wherein there was nothing; at the back of the altar (covered with tapestry) there was an rich tapestry wherein the crucifix was curiously wrought, and as thir bishops who were in service past by this crucifix, they were seen to bow their knee, and beck, which with their habit was noted, and bred great fear of inbringing of popery, for whilk they were all deposed, as is set down in thir papers. The archbishop of Glasgow, and remanent of the bishops there present, changed not their habit, being not in the service; but wore their black gowns without rochets, or white sleeves.[57]

On the following Sunday in St Giles', Edinburgh, Spalding wrote:

Sunday the 23d of June he came frae the Abbey by coach to St. Giles' kirk, and heard John bishop of Murray teach in his rochet, which is a white linen or lawn drawn on above his coat, above the whilk his black gown was put on, and his arms through the gown sleeves, and above the gown sleeves is also white linen or lawn drawn on, shapen like a sleeve. This is the weed of archbishops and bishops, and wears no surplice, but churchmen of inferior degree, in time of service, wears the samen, which is above their cloaths, a side linen cloth over body and arms like to a sack.

The people of Edinburgh, seeing the bishop teach in his rochet, which was never seen in St. Giles' kirk since the Reformation, and by him who was sometime one of their own puritan ministers, they were grieved and grudged hereat, thinking the samen smelled of popery, whilk helped to be the bishop's deposition, as after does appear.[58]

And on 25 June:

the king heard devotion in his own Chapel Royal. Doctor William Forbes, minister at Aberdeen, teached in his black gown, without either surplice or rochet; his text was at the 27th verse of the 14th chapter of John's Gospel; the English service was said both before

57 John Spalding, *The History of the Troubles and Memorable Transactions in Scotland 1624–1645*, Vol. 1 (Aberdeen: 1792), p. 23; see also Dougal Shaw, 'St. Giles' Church and Charles I's Coronation Visit to Scotland', *Historical Research* 77 (2004), pp. 481–502.
58 Spalding, *History of the Troubles*, p. 26.

and after sermon, as their use was, the chaplains and novices, having their white surplices on, the bishop of Dumblain, as chaplain of the Chapel Royal, had his rochet and white sleeves on, but none of our Scots bishops, except he, had the like, but only black gowns.[59]

In a letter sent to Bishop Bellenden in October 1633, Charles ordered that prayers twice a day in the Chapel Royal be according to the English Book of Common Prayer, that on Sundays and holy days the Bishop must wear his 'whites', that Communion be received kneeling, and that copes were to be worn when the sacrament was celebrated.[60] The Chapel Royal at Stirling Castle had been repainted by Valentine Jenkin in 1628 in anticipation of the coronation. Charles had a new ceiling decorated in the Chapel at Falkland Palace and he encouraged and enabled the refurbishing of cathedrals.[61] In establishing the See of Edinburgh in 1633, Charles commanded that

> Sanct Jeilles churche (designed by us to be the Cathedrall Churche of that bishoprik), be ordered as is decent and fitt for a church of that eminencie and according to first intentioun of the erectors and founders thairof which was to be keiped conforme to the lairgenes and conspecuitie of the fundatioun and fabrick, and not to be indirectlie parcelled and disjoynit by wallis and partitiounes as now it is.[62]

In 1636 the Dean of Edinburgh, James Hanney, was sent to visit Durham Cathedral to gain some idea of how St Giles' should be used after its extensive reordering that Charles had commanded. In May 1636 new Canons and Constitutions Ecclesiastical were published, which ordered that every church should have a baptismal font, a Communion table at the upper end of the chancel, that the sacrament should

---

59 Spalding, *History of the Troubles*, pp. 26–7.

60 Charles Rogers, *History of the Chapel Royal in Scotland* (Edinburgh: The Grampian Club), pp. clxxvi–clxxvii.

61 Andrew Spicer, '"Laudianism" in Scotland? St. Giles' Cathedral, Edinburgh, 1633–39: A Reappraisal', *Architectural History* 46 (2003), pp. 95–108; Simon Thurley, 'The Stuart Kings, Oliver Cromwell and the Chapel Royal 1618–1685', *Architectural History* 45 (2002), pp. 238–74. See also David Baldwin, *The Chapel Royal: Ancient and Modern* (London: Duckworth 1990), ch. 9; Anthony Milton, '"that sacred Oratory": Religion and the Chapel Royal during the Personal Rule of Charles I' in Andrew Ashbee (ed.), *William Lawes (1602–1645): Essays on His Life, Times and Work* (Aldershot: Ashgate 1998), pp. 69–96.

62 *Extracts from the Records of the Burgh of Edinburgh*, ed. J. D. Marwick, Scottish Burgh Records Society (Edinburgh: Oliver and Boyd 1936), Vol. 8, p. 134.

be received kneeling, and that all should stand to recite the creed.[63] As Joong-Lak Kim observed, this was part of the King's wish to bring the three Churches of his kingdoms into uniformity by introducing rites and ceremonies which he believed to be essential to decent, beautiful and orderly worship.[64]

Already by 1629 Bishop Maxwell had suggested that it would be best if a liturgy was drawn up by the Scottish clergy rather than have the English Book forced on them, whereas Charles and Laud were of the opinion that the English Book should be adopted. Renewed efforts at a liturgy were undertaken between 1634 and 1637, and the probable drafts, which include the Haddington Book, Egerton MS 2417 and the Christ Church Book, have been carefully discussed by Gordon Donaldson. The resulting 1637 Book represents a recycling of material from the 1549 Book, though with obvious concessions to a Scottish audience – the use of presbyter rather than priest, and Yule and Pascha instead of the English Christmas and Easter. A good many changes were made, indicating a move back towards the 1549 Book of Common Prayer, and these changes gave verbal support to the sacramental theology of the Durham House theology. In baptism, inserted into Luther's 'Flood Prayer' that Cranmer had used was a petition that asked: 'Sanctify this fountain of baptism, thou which art the sanctifier of all things', and in the prayer before the baptismal act the words were added of the water, 'which we here bless and dedicate in thy Name to this spiritual washing'. In the Communion service the compilers had glanced back to 1549 and perhaps to the usage of Lancelot Andrewes and John Overall. A rubric directed:

> The holy Table, having at the Communion time a carpet and a fair linen cloth upon it, with other decent furniture meet for the high mysteries there to be celebrated, shall stand at the uppermost part of the Chancel or Church, where the Presbyter, standing at the north side or end thereof, shall say the Lord's Prayer with this Collect for due preparation.

A rubric directed the preparation of bread and wine with these words: 'And the Presbyter shall then offer up and place the bread and wine prepared for the sacrament upon the Lord's Table, that it may be ready

---

63 Rogers, *History of the Chapel Royal of Scotland*, p. cxcv.
64 Joong-Lak Kim, 'Firing in Unison? The Scottish Canons of 1636 and the English Canons of 1640', *Records of the Scottish Church History Society* 28 (1998), pp. 55–77, p. 76.

for that service.' A reference to the departed was inserted in the Church Militant prayer. The *sursum corda* and preface were linked with the prayer with the words of institution, which was now called 'The Prayer of Consecration', into which was restored a petition for the word and Holy Spirit from the 1549 liturgy. The consecration prayer was followed immediately by the Prayer of Oblation, again suggested by the 1549 rite but also practised by Bishop John Overall. Then came the 'Collect of humble access', moved to being a pre-Communion preparation as it had been in 1549. The words of administration were those of 1549 without the additional words from 1552, thus stressing that the bread and wine were in some way the body and blood of Christ. Any consecrated elements were to be covered over and in the final rubric we find:

> And if any of the bread and wine remain which is consecrated, it shall be reverently eaten and drunk by such of the communicants only, as the Presbyter which celebrated shall take unto him; but it shall not be carried out of the church.

Though not Laud's composition, at his trial Laud was accused of inverting the order of prayers in the English Book. He replied to the accusation thus:

> though I shall not find fault with the order of the prayers, as they stand in the Communion-book of England, (for, God be thanked, 'tis well;) yet, if a comparison must be made, I do think the order of the prayers, as now they now stand in the Scottish Liturgy, to be the better, and more agreeable to use in the primitive Church . . . I think no man doubts, but that there is, and ought to be offered up to God at the consecration and reception of this Sacrament, *sacrificium laudis*, the sacrifice of praise: and that this ought to be expressed in the Liturgy, for the instruction of the people. And these words, 'We entirely desire Thy fatherly goodness, mercifully to accept this our sacrifice of praise, and thanksgiving, &c.' are both in the Book of England, and in that which was prepared for Scotland . . . In the meantime there is as little said in the Liturgy for Scotland, which may import an oblation of an unbloody sacrifice, as in the Book of England. As for 'the oblation of the elements,' that's fit and proper; and I am sorry, for my part, that it is not in the Book of England.[65]

---

65 William Laud, *The Works of the Most Reverend Father in God, William Laud, DD* (Oxford: John Henry Parker 1853), Vol. 3, pp. 344, 358–9.

The protests that followed the attempted introduction of the liturgy were carefully stage-managed and characterized in folklore in the story of Jenny Geddes hurling a stool in protest in St Giles', Edinburgh, shouting, 'Villain! Do you say mass at my lug.' Behind the folklore was the agenda of a Presbyterian party strongly opposed to episcopacy in any form, and the emergence of a radical party represented by such ministers as David Dickson and Samuel Rutherford, which was opposed to all set forms of public prayer. George Gillespie, who was one of the earliest to attack the new liturgy, sounded an apocalyptic alarm when he assessed the danger of the new Scottish liturgy:

> It is not this day feared but felt, that the rotten dregges of Poperie, which were never purged away from *England* and *Ireland*, and having once beene spewed out with detestation, are licked up againe in *Scotland*; prove to be the unhappy occasions of a woefull recidivation. Neither is there need of Lyncean eyes, for if we be not poreblind, it can not be hid from us, what dolefull and disasterous mutation (to be bewailed with teares of blood) hath happened to the Church and Spouse of Christ in these Dominions? Her comely countenance is miscoloured with the farding lustre of the mother of Harlotes. Her shamefaste forehead hath received the marke of the Beast. Her lovely-lockes are frizled with the crisping pins of Antichristian fashions. Her chaste Eares are made to listen to the friends of the great Whoore, who bring the bewitching Doctrine of enchaunting Traditions . . . Oh forlorne Princes Daughter! how art thou not ashamed to looke thy Lord in the face? Oh thou best beloved among Women what hast thou to doe with the inveagling appurtenances and abilement of *Babylon* the Whoore? – But among such things as have beene the accursed meanes of the Churches desolation, those which peradventure might seeme to some of you to have least harme or evill in them, are the Ceremonies of kneeling in the act of receiving the Lords Supper, Crosse in Baptisme, Bishopping, Holy-dayes, &c. which are pressed under the name of things indifferent.[66]

Joong-Lak Kim's conjecture that Charles intended to impose this Book on England as well, if it had not been rejected by the Scots, is intriguing but will remain merely a conjecture.[67] Events escalated with the 1638

---

66 George Gillespie, *A dispute against the English-popish ceremonies, obtruded upon the Church of Scotland* (Edinburgh: 1637), no pagination.
67 Kim, 'The Scottish-English-Romish Book', pp. 30–1.

National Covenant, ejection of episcopacy and the invasion of England, which in turn set off a series of events leading to the English Civil War and the prohibition of use of the Book of Common Prayer.

FROM THE CANONS OF 1640
TO A DIRECTORY OF PUBLIC WORSHIP

In addition to a proposed Prayer Book for Scotland, the bishops had proposed a new set of canons in 1636. As the Short Parliament in 1640 met to deal with the proposed threat from Scotland, Convocation met to draw up new canons for the Church of England. Canon VII was concerned with rites and ceremonies. It noted that although the place of the Communion table was an 'indifferent' matter, 'we judge it fit and convenient, that all Churches do conform themselves in this particular to the example of the cathedral or Mother Churches'.[68] It further noted that because of irreverent behaviour, such as people putting hats on Communion tables or even sitting on them, they were to be 'decently severed with Rails, to preserve them from such or worse profanation'.[69] Services were to be conducted 'with all possible decency and reverence', and 'obeysance' to the table and the 'mystical Elements' was enjoined.[70]

As matters between King and Parliament unravelled, the bishops found themselves the target of much of the unrest. David Cressy notes that early in October 1640, 'unruly people' committed 'a notorious misdemeanour' against a church near Reading, Berkshire, breaking in at night, smashing the organ and destroying the Communion rails; more Communion rails were destroyed in Suffolk, Essex and Buckinghamshire prior to the Long Parliament.[71] At Hingham, Norfolk, the minister prayed, 'Oh Lord, we have offended thee in wearing the surplice, in signing with the cross, and using the ring in marriage.'[72] Additionally, for some the Book of Common Prayer itself became a target of attack. More extreme 'godly' figures such as John Davenport renewed earlier attacks on set forms of prayer.[73] Petitions for and against the Book of

---

68 *Constitutions and Canons Ecclesiastical Treated upon by the Archbishops of Canterbury and York* (London: Robert Barker 1640), p. 20.
69 *Constitutions and Canons*, p. 20.
70 *Constitutions and Canons*, pp. 20–1.
71 David Cressy, *England on Edge: Crisis and Revolution 1640–1642* (Oxford: Oxford University Press 2006), p. 157, citing BL Ad. MS 110.45 vol. V f.125v; and PRO, SP 16/470/55.
72 Cressy, *England on Edge*, p. 195, citing CU Library, Ms.Mn,1.45 (Baker transcripts), 32.
73 John Davenport, *The triall of the English liturgie* (1638).

Common Prayer were submitted to Parliament.[74] As Parliament and the army took control, so the Church of England became a non-episcopal Church, operating on a compromise system between Presbyterianism and Independency. Eventually Ordinances from Parliament ordered the removal of superstitious images, altars and crucifixes, and forbad the use of organs.[75] William Dowsing was commissioned to carry out the removal and destruction of such items and he kept a diary recording his work. At St Peter's, Cambridge, 30 December 1643, he wrote that 'we brake downe ten popish pictures; we took 3 popish inscriptions for prayers to be made for their soules, and burnt the rayles, diged up the steps, and they are to be levelled on Wednesday.'[76] Local, less authorized destruction also took place. In Rutland, in September 1644, 'Cornet Sewal . . . tooke the surplice and common prayer book out of Ashwell church and tyed them to his horse tail . . . they were dragg'd in Derision and triumph thro the town.'[77]

In place of Convocation, Parliament appointed an assembly of divines, the Westminster Assembly. Although there were five Scottish representatives, this assembly was made up of some of the best theological minds of the Church of England. It produced the Westminster Confession and Catechisms. In an order of the House of Commons of 18 September 1643, which was finally passed as an Ordinance of both Houses on 12 October 1643, Parliament empowered the Westminster Assembly to debate and propound a Directory of Worship which would replace the Book of Common Prayer.[78] Though some of the Westminster Divines might have settled for the Genevan Form of Prayers of 1556, the appearance of Independents who shared the views of Davenport, that all set forms were against the word of God, meant that a Directory was all that could be agreed upon, giving the outline of the order of service with a summary of the themes and doctrines that might (or might not) be used by the minister. This liturgical guide would

74 Judith Maltby, 'Petitions for Episcopacy and the Book of Common Prayer on the Eve of the Civil War 1641–1642' in Stephen Taylor (ed.), *From Cranmer to Davidson: A Miscellany*, Church of England Record Society 7 (Woodbridge: Boydell and Brewer 1999), pp. 105–67.

75 C. H. Firth and R. S. Rait (eds), *Acts and Ordinances of the Interregnum 1642–1660*, 3 vols (London: His Majesty's Stationery Office 1911).

76 Trevor Cooper (ed.), *The Journal of William Dowsing: Iconoclasm in East Anglia during the English Civil War* (Woodbridge: Boydell 2001), p. 191.

77 Fiona McCall, *Baal's Priests: The Loyalist Clergy and the English Revolution* (Farnham: Ashgate 2013), p. 107, citing Bodley, J. Walker Manuscript, Bodleian Library, Oxford, C1. 220.

78 Firth and Rait (eds), *Acts and Ordinances*, pp. 755–7.

be used in the three kingdoms. The work of compiling this liturgy was given to a sub-committee under the chairmanship of Stephen Marshall, incumbent of Finchingfield, Essex. Members included Thomas Young, Herbert Palmer, Charles Herle, and one of the Independents, Thomas Goodwin. They were joined by four Scottish commissioners – Samuel Rutherford, George Gillespie, Robert Baillie and Alexander Henderson. Goodwin, on his own authority, co-opted a fellow Independent, Philip Nye. Of the Scottish Commissioners, Rutherford and Gillespie were against set forms of prayer, and since Herle usually sided with the Independents, half of the commission was opposed to set forms of public prayer. When reminded of something in the *Form of Prayers*, Rutherford replied, 'We will not owne this liturgy, Nor are we tyed unto it.'[79] With the exception of the Preface, the whole Directory was completed on 12 November 1644, though it was not until 17 April 1645 that the House of Commons enforced it and abolished the Book of Common Prayer.

In the Preface the compilers appealed to the word of God, both to justify the Directory and the laying aside of the Book of Common Prayer. The Directory gave only 'the general heads, the sense and scope of the Prayers'. The making of this liturgy was not an easy task, as the Minutes reveal.[80] The Sunday morning service began with a call to worship, prayer of approach with confession of sin and psalm reading. Readings from the Old and New Testament were followed by a sung psalm (metrical) and then a long prayer before the sermon. After the sermon came another lengthy prayer, the Lord's Prayer, sung psalm and a blessing. Something of the style may be illustrated from the first long prayer, or Prayer of Approach. The minister is to call on the Lord to this effect:

> To acknowledge our great sinfulnesse, First by reason of Originall Sin, Which (beside the guilt that makes us liable to everlasting Damnation) is the seed of all other sinnes, hath depraved and poisoned all the faculties and powers of Soule and Body, doth defile our best actions, and (were it not restrained, or our hearts renewed by Grace) would breake forth into innumerable transgressions, and greatest rebellions against the Lord, that ever were committed by the vilest of the sons of men.

---

79 Manuscript minutes of the Westminster Assembly, 1643–52, Dr Williams's Library, London, Vol. 2, p. 492.
80 Bryan D. Spinks, *Freedom or Order? The Eucharistic Liturgy in English Congregationalism 1645–1980* (Allison Park, PA: Pickwick Publications 1984).

The service itself allowed for some flexibility, not only in what could actually be said in the prayers, but also in the recommended sequence. For example, the thanksgiving and intercessions could come before or after the sermon. The flexibility is also further illustrated by the little-known *A Supply of Prayer for Ships*, where the Directory sequence was rearranged and the suggestions for themes were turned into actual prayers.[81] The Directory provided a comprehensive guide for sermon construction, being the work of the chairman, Stephen Marshall.[82] The provisions for the baptismal rite began by ruling out private baptism and lay administration of baptism. The initial exhortation, or 'Instruction', described baptism as a 'Seale of the Covenant of Grace, of our Ingrafting into Christ, and of our Union with him'. It is the seal of remission of sins, regeneration, adoption and life eternal. Appeal was made to the covenant of grace for infant baptism, because children are 'federally holy before Baptisme'. The Instruction also noted that the inward grace and virtue of baptism is not tied to the moment of baptism. In many ways, the 'Instruction' is a quasi-liturgical rehearsal of the section found in the *Westminster Confession*.

Once the 'teaching' was complete, the minister was to pray that God would bless and sanctify the ordinance, and join the outward to the inward. After the child was named, he or she was baptized with the triune formula. Afterwards the minister was to give thanks 'to this or the like purpose',

> Acknowledging with all thankfulnesse, that the Lord is true and faithfull in keeping Covenant and Mercy; That hee is good and gracious, not onely in that he numbreth us among his Saints, but is pleased also to bestow upon our children this singular token and badge of his love in Christ: That in his truth and speciall providence, hee daily bringeth some into the bosome of his Church, to be partakers of his inestimable benefits, purchased by the blood of his dear Son, for the continuance and increase of his Church.

Entirely omitted are the recitation of the Lord's Prayer and the Apostles' Creed. For the Lord's Supper the recommended order, following on from the usual Sunday service, was: exhortation on the benefit of the

---

81 See Appendix for the text.
82 Bryan D. Spinks, 'Brief and Perspicuous Text; Plain and Pertinent Doctrine: Behind "Of the Preaching of the Word" in the Westminster Directory' in Martin Dudley (ed.), *Like a Two-Edged Sword* (Norwich: Canterbury Press 1995), pp. 91–111.

sacrament, excommunication of the unworthy and encouragement to repentance; the recital of the words of institution; optional explanation of the words of institution; prayer of thanksgiving or blessing of the elements; fraction and delivery; exhortation; solemn thanksgiving. A rubric directed the minister 'to begin the action of sanctifying and blessing the elements of bread and wine', and in the prayer after the institution narrative to pray God 'to vouchsafe his gracious presence, and the effectual working of his Spirit in us; and so to sanctify these elements both of bread and wine, and to bless his own ordinance, that we may receive by faith the body and blood of Jesus Christ, crucified for us'. Communion could be at the table or around it. The Minutes show that the compilation was a contentious process, and the Independents continued to use separate blessings for the bread and wine.

Penalties were imposed for neglect of the Directory and for use of the Book of Common Prayer – £5 for the first offence, £10 for a second and a year in prison for a third offence. However, in spite of the fines, it would seem that the Book of Common Prayer was used more commonly than once thought. Fiona McCall notes that John Gregson claimed before the Wiltshire Committee to be the only minister in the county still using the Prayer Book, but from archival sources cites a number of examples from other parts of England of clandestine usage.[83] Furthermore, as McCall says, chopped up and memorized versions were another matter, and cites the example of Richard Newte who 'digested our incomparable Forms of Prayer into another Method'.[84] Robert Sanderson's *Liturgy in the Time of Rebellion* was such an adaptation and, for family use, Owen Felltham's *A Form of Prayer*.[85] Using less of the 'incomparable Forms' and more of Eastern and Roman liturgical sources, Jeremy Taylor compiled his *Collection of Offices* (1658). It has also been questioned as to whether the Directory was widely used. John Spurr estimated that only 25 per cent of parishes acquired a copy, though more recently Judith Maltby has pointed out that it went through 15 editions, was a relatively inexpensive book and was a ministerial

83 McCall, *Baal's Priests*, pp. 237–9.
84 McCall, *Baal's Priests*, p. 238.
85 For Sanderson, see William Jacobson (ed.), *Fragmentary Illustrations of the History of the Book of Common Prayer* (London: John Murray 1874). For Felltham, see Ted-Larry Pebworth, 'An Anglican Family Worship Service of the Interregnum: A Cancelled Early Text and a New Edition of Owen Felltham's "A Form of Prayer"', *English Literary Renaissance* 16 (1986), pp. 206–33. For Taylor, *The Works of the Right Rev. Jeremy Taylor*, Vol. 3 (London: Longman 1889).

rather than a parish book.[86] Attempts were made to replace Sternhold and Hopkins with the metrical psalms of Francis Rouse (1641) and William Barton (1644), but neither received support of both Houses of Parliament. The Directory had a continued life in Scotland but, with the events of 1660 heralding the Restoration, the Book of Common Prayer came out of hiding and was once more to be the liturgy of the Church of England.

---

86 Judith Maltby, '"Extravagencies and Impertinencies": Set Forms, Conceived and Extempore Prayer in Revolutionary England' in Natalie Mears and Alec Ryrie (eds), *Worship and the Parish Church in early Modern Britain* (Farnham: Ashgate 2013), pp. 221–43, p. 228.

Chapter 4

From the 1662 Book of Common Prayer to the 1789 American Prayer Book

THE 1662 BOOK

In his will (1727) John Hutchins, a London goldsmith, endowed an annual sermon on the excellence of the liturgy of the Church of England, to be preached each year on St Mark's Day. In the sermon preached on 25 April 1797, William van Mildert, later to be Bishop of Durham, claimed:

> Our Liturgy, indeed, in its present state, is a most valuable repository of Christian knowledge. It serves as a manual of faith and practice; nor can any person be thoroughly conversant in it, without finding his understanding enlightened, his thoughts spiritualized, and his heart improved . . . Upon the preservation, therefore, of our excellent Liturgy in its present improved state, must depend, in a great measure, the preservation of the Church of England.[1]

By van Mildert's time the 1662 Book of Common Prayer was firmly established and was regarded as the 'incomparable liturgy', though its framers probably had little idea that it would remain virtually unchallenged until the nineteenth century and officially unchanged in England until the twentieth century. The 1662 liturgy was certainly a revision of some of the language of the previous Book and had new material, both prayers and rubrics, but nevertheless was in the main the substance of the Cranmerian text as adopted in 1559.

---

1 William van Mildert, *The Excellency of the Liturgy, and the Advantage of being educated in the Doctrine and principles of the Church of England* (London: 1797), pp. 13, 15.

The death of Oliver Cromwell on 3 September 1658 led to the demise of the Commonwealth and protectorate, and eventually led to an invitation to Charles II to return as king. On 4 April 1660 Charles issued the Declaration of Breda, promising liberty to those of tender consciences, and since the 'Presbyterian party' had facilitated the return of the monarchy, some of the clergy presented Charles with an address requesting him not to reintroduce the Book of Common Prayer. On 25 October 1660 Charles issued *His majesty's Declaration to all his loving subjects of his kingdom of England and dominion of wales, concerning ecclesiastical affairs*, also known as the Worcester House Declaration, in which the King asserted:

> Though we do esteem the liturgy of the Church of England, contained in the *Book of Common Prayer* and by law established, to be the best we have seen (and we believe that we have seen all that are extant and used in this part of the world, and well know what reverence most of the reformed churches, or at least the most learned men in those churches, have for it), yet, since we find some exceptions made against several things therein, we will appoint an equal number of learned divines of both persuasions to review the same and to make such alterations as shall be thought most necessary, and some additional forms (in the scripture phrase, as near as may be) suited unto the nature of the several parts of worship; and that it be left to the minister's choice to use one or the other at his discretion.[2]

What was envisaged was a debate about certain things in the Book of Common Prayer and the authoring of alternative forms. A Royal Warrant was issued on 25 March 1661 establishing a commission to carry out this work. It met in April at the Master's Lodge of the Savoy in London and has become known as the Savoy Conference.[3] The Presbyterian party included Edward Reynolds, later to be Bishop of Norwich, and Richard Baxter, who would decline the see of Hereford. Among the episcopal party were Gilbert Sheldon, Bishop of London, and John Cosin, Robert Sanderson and William Sancroft. At the meeting the episcopal party announced that they found no fault with the Book of Common Prayer and invited the Presbyterian party to list their objections to it. This they did, setting out 19 general and 83 particular

---

2 Andrew Browning, *English Historical Documents, 1660–1714* (London and New York: Taylor and Francis 2006), pp. 360–1.

3 Colin Buchanan, *The Savoy Conference Revisited*, Alcuin/GROW Joint Liturgical Study 54 (Cambridge: Grove Books 2002).

'exceptions' (known as *The Exceptions*). In hindsight this was probably
a tactical error on the part of the Presbyterians, since many of the items
in this list, drawing on the objections made from Elizabethan times,
sounded petty and whining over nothing. Most were rejected by the
episcopal party. The Presbyterians turned their attention to the second
provision of the Worcester House Declaration and the task of writing
alternative forms was given to Richard Baxter, whose work is known
as the *Reformed Liturgy* or the *Savoy Liturgy*.[4] Baxter completed the
work in a fortnight, though he seems to have expanded his own use of
the Directory when minister at Kidderminster, used acceptable material from the Book of Common Prayer and drew heavily on scriptural
phraseology. Given that the Church of England morning service had
become Morning Prayer, Litany and Ante-Communion, it is possible
to see something of Baxter's idea of irenicism in the content of his alternative for morning worship on the Lord's day.[5] Baxter offered the following order:

Opening Prayer with shorter alternative
Apostles Creed, or Nicene Creed, and sometimes the Athanasian
    Creed
The Decalogue
Sentences of Scripture moving people to penitence
Confession of sin and prayer for pardon, and Lord's Prayer, with
    shorter alternatives
Some Scripture sentences for strengthening faith and raising the
    penitent ('comfortable words')
Psalm 95 or 10, or 84
Psalms of the day
Chapter of the Old Testament
A Psalm, sung, or Te Deum, said
Chapter of the New Testament
Prayer for the King and Magistrates
Psalm 67 or 98 or some other psalm, or Benedictus or Magnificat
Prayer for the Church, extemporized by the minister in the pulpit
Sermon

---

4 For the most thorough study, see Glen J. Segger, *Richard Baxter's Reformed Liturgy:
A Puritan Alternative to the Book of Common Prayer* (Farnham: Ashgate 2014).

5 Text in Segger, *Richard Baxter's Reformed Liturgy*, pp. 222–28, and Bard Thompson,
Liturgies of the Western Church (New York: World Publishing Company 1962), pp. 385–
93. See also Bryan D. Spinks, *Freedom or Order? The Eucharistic Liturgy in English
Congregationalism 1645–1980* (Allison Park, PA: Pickwick Publications 1984), pp. 53ff.

Prayer, including a blessing on the word of instruction and
   exhortation
Hymn (optional)
Blessing.

His rite of baptism reflected the covenant theology of the Reformed
divines, where infant baptism is based on the parents being in the covenant, on analogy with circumcision in the Old Testament. The opening exhortation mentioned the inherited sin of Adam, but that through
Christ 'God hath made and offered to the world a covenant of grace'.
The covenant is with the Trinity and results in washing away of original
sin, but faith and dedication on the part of parents is essential.

Baxter's eucharistic rite also had a Trinitarian base and was constructed
around the concepts of consecration, commemoration and communication. A prayer addressed to the Father, followed by the recitation of the
institution narrative and a declaration that the bread and wine were 'not
now Common Bread and Wine, but Sacramentally the Body and Blood
of Christ', was consecration. Commemoration was achieved by a prayer
to Christ asking for pardon through his sacrifice and a fraction of the
bread and outpouring of the wine, with the words 'The Body of Christ
was broken for us and offered once for all to sanctifie us; behold the sac-
rificed Lamb of God, that taketh away the sins of the World' and 'Wee
were redeemed with the precious Blood of Christ, as of a Lamb without
blemish, and without spot'. Communion was with a prayer addressed to
the Holy Spirit together with the reception of the elements.

Baxter's liturgy is interesting in that it represents what at least one of
the godly would have liked in place of the Book of Common Prayer.
However, just as *The Exceptions* were rejected so was Baxter's alternative
liturgy, and the meeting dispersed in July 1661. Segger writes:

> As notable as Baxter's liturgy may be, the *Reformed Liturgy* simply did
> not provide a viable liturgical alternative for the Restoration church.
> Baxter not only proposed forms that went well beyond the spirit of
> liturgical revision envisioned by the king, but the ecclesiology inher-
> ent in the *Reformed Liturgy* was completely incompatible with that of
> the diocesan episcopacy envisioned by the bishops. It is even debat-
> able whether the godly would have ultimately united around Baxter's
> *Reformed Liturgy*, for the puritans themselves practiced a diversity of
> worship styles and forms.[6]

---

6 Segger, *Richard Baxter's Reformed Liturgy*, p. 219.

Since the Savoy Conference ended with no agreement, the business of liturgical reform passed to the Convocations which met in November 1661. In the meantime, however, the Book of Common Prayer in its 1604/1625 format was being reintroduced ahead of any official liturgical settlement. Samuel Pepys recorded in his diary on 5 August 1660, 'After dinner to St. Margaret's [Westminster] where for the first time I ever heard Common Prayer in that Church.'[7] At his own parish church, St Olave's, Hart Street, on 4 November 1660, he recorded:

> In the morn to our own church, where Mr. Mills did begin to nibble at the Common Prayer, by saying 'Glory be to the father, &c', after he had read the two psalms; but the people had been so little used to it, that they could not tell what to answer. This declaration of the King's do give the Presbyterians some satisfaction, and a pretence to read the Common Prayer, which they would not do before because of their former preaching against it. After dinner to Westminster . . . where I went to the Abbey, where the first time that ever I heard the organs in a cathedral.[8]

The following Sunday, he wrote: 'This day also did Mr. Mills begin to read all the Common Prayer, which I was glad of.'[9] Shortly after the initial gathering of the Savoy Conference, on 23 April, Charles was crowned. Pepys also described some of the pageantry, which signalled that the traditional ceremonial associated with the Chapel Royal would be revived:

> And got to the abby, where I fallowed Sir J. Denham the surveyour with some company that he was leading in. And with much ado, by the favour of Mr. Cooper his man, did get up into a great scaffold across the north end of the abby – where with a great deal of patience I sat from past 4 till 11 before the King came in. And a pleasure it was to see the Abbey raised in the middle, all covered with red and throne (that is a chaire) and footstoole on the top of it. And all the officers of all kinds, so much as the very fidlers, in red vests.
>
> At last comes in the Deane and prebends of Westminster with the Bishops (many of them in cloth-of-gold Copes); and after them the nobility all in their parliament-robes, which was a most magnificent sight. Then the Duke and the King with a scepter

---

7 *The Diary of Samuel Pepys*, Vols 1–3 (1659–63), ed. Henry B. Wheatley (New York: G. Bell and Sons 1923), Vol. 1, p. 200.

8 *The Diary of Samuel Pepys*, Vol. 1, p. 255.

9 *The Diary of Samuel Pepys*, Vol. 1, p. 260.

(carried by my Lord of Sandwich) and Sword and mond before him, and the crowne too.

The King in his robes, bare-headed, which was very fine. And after all had placed themselfs – there was a sermon and the service. And then in the Quire at the high altar he passed all the ceremonies of the Coronacion – which, to my very great grief, I and most of the Abbey could not see. The crowne being put upon his head, a great shout begun. And he came forth to the Throne and there passed more ceremonies: as, taking the oath and having things read to him by the Bishopp, and his lords (who put on their capps as soon as the King put on his Crowne) and Bishopps came and kneeled before him.[10]

Even as the Savoy Conference was in session, Convocation met and drew up orders of service for 29 May, 5 November, and for 30 January for Charles the Martyr. They also wrote a baptismal service for those of riper years, though they did not proceed with attempting to authorize it, awaiting the outcome of the Savoy Conference.[11] Parliament held a Communion service on the first anniversary of the Restoration using the 1604/1625 Prayer Book, and in June the House of Commons introduced a Bill for the uniformity of worship, with the 1604/1625 Prayer Book annexed to it.[12] The Bill was sent to the House of Lords, but was never debated there. Matthew Wren, during his long years of imprisonment in the Tower of London, had drawn up the *Advices*, giving suggested revisions of the Prayer Book, and John Cosin, now Bishop of Durham, had made notes for revision in a 1619 edition of the Prayer Book, known as the Durham Book.[13] This latter incorporated material from 1549 and 1637. Cosin's secretary, William Sancroft, was given the task of copying some of this as well as some of *The Exceptions* into another Prayer Book, known as the Fair Copy. This was emended in Convocation, the results being known as the 'Convocation Book'. This in turn was copied and attached to a new Act of Uniformity, and is known as the 'Annexed Book'. The final version was known as the 'sealed' book, as it was certified under the Great Seal.

---

10 *Diary of Samuel Pepys*, Vol. 2, pp. 18–19.

11 Edward Cardwell, *Synodalia: A Collection of Articles of Religion, Canons, and Proceedings of Convocations in the Province of Canterbury. From the Year 1547 to the Year 1717* (Oxford: Oxford University Press 1842), Vol. II, pp. 641–2.

12 'House of Commons Journal Volume 8: 25 June 1661', British History Online, <www.british-history.ac.uk/commons-jrnl/vol8/pp279-280> (accessed 13 October 2016).

13 G. J. Cuming (ed.), *The Durham Book* (Oxford: Oxford University Press for the University of Durham 1961; London: Alcuin Club 1975).

Revision began in Convocation on 21 November 1661 and was completed in 22 days. In the Lower House of Convocation it was reported:

> Dr *Allen* of *Huntingdon-shire*, and Clerk in the Convocation, earnestly labored with the then Bishop of *London* [Gilbert Sheldon], afterwards Arch-Bishop, that they might so refine the Liturgy, that no sober Man might make Exception. He was wished to forbear, for what should be, was concluded on or resolved . . .
>
> [T]here were no debates to speak of; the greatest that I could hear of, was between the *Cambridg* Professor *Gunning* and the *Oxford* Professor Dr. *Creed*, about (a hard Point indeed) *the Age of Children to be Confirm'd.*[14]

The final Book (sealed) was to come into use by the Feast of St Bartholomew, 24 August 1662. Dean Honeywood of Lincoln expressed concern that copies had not reached him – in fact a copy arrived on 23 August. It was not read at Taunton until 25 August, and not until 30 May 1663 did Ralph Josselin of Earls Colne in Essex introduce the new Book.[15]

Compared with the previous Prayer Books of 1559 and 1604, this liturgy underwent much more revision. The language was updated, new services and new prayers were introduced, and rubrics were emended or added. With the Preface of the Directory of 1644 in mind, the new Preface of the 1662 Prayer Book, written most probably by Robert Sanderson, presented a reasonable and moderate liturgy that all reasonable and moderate people should be able to accept:

> It hath been the wisdom of the Church of England, ever since the compiling of her Publick Liturgy, to keep the mean between the two extremes, of too much stiffness in refusing, and of too much easiness in admitting any variation from it . . . Our general aim therefore in this undertaking was, not to gratify this or that party in any of their unreasonable demands; but to do that, which is to our best understanding we conceived might most tend to the preservation of Peace

---

14 E. Pearse, *The Conformists' Plea for the Nonconformists* (London: Jonathan Robinson 1681), pp. 28, 33.

15 Tanner MS.48, ff.17, cited by I. M Green, *The Re-Establishment of the Church of England 1660–1663* (Oxford: Oxford University Press 1978), p. 145; William Gibson, *Religion and the Enlightenment 1600–1800: Conflict and the Rise of Civic Humanism in Taunton* (Bern: Peter Lang 2007), p. 88; A. Macfarlane (ed.), *The Diary of Ralph Josselin 1616–1683* (Oxford: Oxford University Press for the British Academy 1976), p. 498.

and Unity in the Church; the procuring of reverence and exciting of Piety and Devotion in the publick Worship of God; and the cutting off occasion from them that seek occasion of cavil, or quarrel against the Liturgy of the Church.

Though not wanting to gratify any particular party, since Cosin, Wren and Sanderson were involved in much of the drafting of the revision it is no surprise that fewer concessions were made to the 'godly' than to those who had been aligned with the Durham House liturgical ideals. Yet Sancroft expressed what must have been disappointment for the Durham House survivors: 'My LL. Ye BB at Elie house Ordered all in ye old Method.'[16] When the liturgical ideals of this group were met, it was mostly through rubric rather than change in the prayer texts. For example, there was no restoration of the 1549/1637 petition for blessing and sanctifying the elements by the word and Holy Spirit. Instead, Cranmer's prayer that contained the words of institution was now titled (as the restored 1549 prayer in 1637 had been) 'The Prayer of Consecration', even though it contained no explicit request for consecration. Manual acts were now added during the recital of the words of institution, so that the fraction took place during the prayer. This was not what the 'godly' had asked for – it is clear from the versions of the *Form of Prayers*, the Directory and Baxter's *Reformed Liturgy* that they required a quite distinct faction and libation of the wine. The 'Black rubric' was restored, but had a significant verbal alteration. In 1552 the rubric repudiated belief in any 'reall and essential presence' in the elements of bread and wine. Now the rubric repudiated a 'corporal' (i.e. physical) presence, since by the seventeenth century many divines did believe in a 'reall and essential presence', or sacramental presence. Remaining consecrated elements were to be veiled and consumed. In the baptism of infants, an explicit blessing of the water was added to the prayer immediately before the baptismal act: 'sanctifie this Water to the mysticall washing away of sin'. The rite for baptism of those of riper years was added. The Ordinal now made clear that bishops constituted a separate ordering and were not merely priests 'consecrated' or appointed to that office. Cosin's version of 'Come Holy Ghost' from his *Devotions* replaced the rather poor hymn that Cranmer had provided at ordinations. New prayers were also added, including for Charles the Martyr, and, suggested by the Westminster Assembly's *A Supply of Prayer for Ships*, a service was now provided for those at sea.

---

16 Cuming, *The Durham Book*, p. 180.

The Directory itself supplied words for the new General Thanksgiving prayer. It was crafted by Edward Reynolds and was based on the thanksgiving over the bread and wine in the Directory service for the Lord's Supper.[17] Two new prayers were added at Morning Prayer.

The pattern of services established in Elizabeth's reign continued – Morning Prayer, Litany and Ante-Communion on Sunday morning and Evensong with catechism in the afternoon. To help re-establish the choral tradition which had been destroyed in the Interregnum, Edward Lowe published *A Short Direction for the Performance of Cathedral Service* in 1661, which offered advice for those who had forgotten the art of cathedral choral services. An expanded version was published in 1664. Lowe gave the music with a few directions for Morning Prayer, the Litany and the 'second service' or Ante-Communion. Of the latter, Lowe wrote:

> The second Service is begun by the Priest who reads the Lords Prayer in one grave tone, the deeper (if strong and audible) the better: Then the Collect before the Commandements, and the Commandements in a higher tone, the whole Quire (if no singing to an Organ) answering *Lord have mercy upon us &c.* after each Commandement in the same tone.
>
> Then the Priest reads the Prayers before the Epistle, the Quire answering *Amen.* When the Epistle is done and the Gospell named. The Quire sings, *Glory be to thee O Lord,* in either of the two formes here set downe; which will serve to the Key of any Service, as the Organist shall apply it.
>
> When the Gospell is ended, the Priest (or whole Quire) say (or sing) the *Nicene Creed.* And after that the Priest reads the Prayer for *Christ's Church Militant &c.* and so goes on to the end of the Morning Service.[18]

Commenting on a similar work by James Clifford, Christopher Dearnley noted:

> Agreeing with Lowe on the order of service, [Clifford] also indicated the place of anthems and organ voluntaries. One voluntary followed the psalms at Morning and Evening Prayer and another divided the composite morning service, being played after the Litany

---

17 G. J. Cuming, 'Two Fragments of a Lost Liturgy?', *Studies in Church History* 3 (London: E. J. Brill 1966), pp. 247–53.

18 Edward Lowe, *A Review of some short Directions for the performance of Cathedral Service* (London: 1664), p. 43.

(which concluded the 'First Service') and leading into the 'Second, or Communion Service'.

Two anthems are sung in the morning, the first after the third collect at Matins, the second after the sermon in the Communion service (following the Creed). This anthem concluded the choral service. At Evensong, in addition to an anthem in the usual place after the third collect, another was sung after the sermon.[19]

He also notes that the Restoration practice was to sing the Sanctus in place of an organ voluntary as a kind of introit to the Second service, and that the Gloria in excelsis often served as an anthem concluding the choral part; an anthem in this context was a musical setting of a sacred text from Scripture or the Book of Common Prayer.

New churches that were built were done so to showcase the 1662 rite. That is true of the new St Paul's Cathedral and other Wren churches, as well as those of Hawksmoor. Reflecting on his work of the 1670s and 1680s Wren wrote:

in our reformed religion, it should seem vain to make a parish church larger, than that all who are present can both hear and see. The Romanists, indeed, may build larger churches, it is enough if they hear the murmur of the mass, and see the elevation of the host, but ours are to be fitted for auditories. I can hardly think it practicable to make a single room so capacious, with pews and galleries, as to hold above 2000 persons, and all to hear the service, and both to hear distinctly, and see the preacher. I endeavored to effect this, in building the parish church of St. James's, Westminster, which, I presume, is the most capacious, with these qualifications, that hath yet been built; and yet at a solemn time, when the church was much crowded, I could not discern from a gallery that 2000 were present. In this church I mention, though very broad, and the middle nave arched up, yet as there are no walls of a second order, nor lanterns, nor buttresses, but the whole roof rests upon the pillars, as do also the galleries, I think it may be found beautiful and convenient, and, as such, the cheapest of any form I could invent.[20]

---

19 Christopher Dearnley, *English Church Music 1650–1750* (London: Barry and Jenkins 1970), p. 99.

20 Sir Christopher Wren, 'Letter of Recommendation to a Friend on the Commission for Building Fifty New Churches', reprinted in Pierre de la Ruffinière Du Prey, *Hawksmoor's London Churches: Architecture and Theology* (Chicago, IL: University of Chicago Press 2000), Appendix 2, pp. 135–6.

Yet any idea that the Act of Uniformity actually established uniformity is called into question by the report of the lawyer Dr Dennis Granville, who wrote in January 1683:

> I Confesse I am much offended and Disturbed, whensoever I hear any Minister Maime God's Publick Service, or add any New Matter of his own, or else Exalt his own Prudence, in Varying from the Forme or Order thereof, tho' hee should use no other Prayers, but what are Conteined in the Book . . . Wee have yet as many severall wayes of Worshipp, as wee have Ministers . . . One Cuts of[f] the Preparatory Exhortacion, Dearly Beloved Brethren etc., Another the Benedictus and Jubilate, and satisfyeth himself with a Psalme in Meeter in stead thereof, out of Sternald and Hopkins, which, all know, is no part of your Office, and a bad Translacion, considering the Language of our Age (tho' probably it was very tolerable when it was first Composed) and never approved of in a Convocacion. A Third brings in part of the Visitacion Office, Comanded to bee said in the Sick Man's presence, into the Publick Congregacion . . . A Fourth Adds very Formally a Preface of his own to the Recitall of the Creed . . . A Fifth Jumbles both first and Second Service together, Cutting of[f] not only the Concluding Prayer of St.Chrysostome, and the Grace of our Lord Jesus Christ, but allso our Lord's Prayer, in the Front of the Comunion Office . . . A Sixth more presumptuously not only Cuts of[f] the Lord's Prayer alone, but both the Lord's Prayer and Nicene Creed allsoe. A Seventh, who avoids those Irregularityes, yet Presumes after Sermon to Cut of the Prayer for the Church Militant, and the Final Benediction, The Peace of God, etc. hoping to satisfye his Congregacion, (but I am sure hee never Satisfied mee) with a Benediction of his own Choice, and Prayer of his own Composure.[21]

Much depended on the minister's personal liturgical style, as well as the architecture of the church in question, and local custom. Controversy continued over the placement of the minister in the second service. In 1683 a pamphlet entitled *Parish Churches Turn'd into Conventicles* argued that the canons and rubrics required the second service to be read at the north side of the Holy Table 'and that whosoever reads it at

---

21 Bodleian MS. Rawlinson D. 851, edited in J. Wickham Legg, *English Church Life from the Restoration to the Tractarian Movement* (London: Longmans, Green and Co. 1914), pp. 112–13.

any other place, breaks the Order of our Church'.[22] A reply of the same year, *Parish-Churches no Conventicles*, argued that the place was a matter of discretion.[23] Such matters were not confined to the performance of worship, but were also linked to the furnishings of the churches. The encouragement and then enforcement of a railed-in table altarwise in the 1630s was brought to an abrupt end in the 1640s, and the journal of William Dowsing is a testimony to the destruction carried out in East Anglia.[24] The years after 1660 witness the return of the railed altar almost immediately in the royal chapels and cathedrals; however, as Kenneth Fincham has shown, in parishes this did not happen overnight and in some places it did not happen at all.[25] At St Giles Cripplegate the parishioners in 1660 petitioned for a clergyman to replace the intruded Presbyterian Samuel Annesley. In 1662 Annesley was ejected, and under the incumbency of John Dolben, the chancel was reconstructed, with the ground raised and the table placed on a black marble step and railed in.[26] The subject was discussed in Parliament in March 1668 when Sir Thomas Littleton gave a speech 'to prove that in this government now in force there are many innovations, as the removing the Communion table from the body of the church to the place where it now stands altarwise, and bowing to the altar and many other ceremonies'.[27] This trend was encouraged by the rebuilding of 51 churches in London destroyed by the Great Fire. The 1670 act for the rebuilding of the city churches provided for the cost of the fabric to be paid for by the commissioners, but the furnishings by the parish. Fincham notes:

the detailed accounts approved by the commission indicate that the arrangements at the east end of each church followed a standardised

---

22 R[ichard] H[art], *Parish Churches Turn'd into Conventicles . . . in Particular, by Reading the Communion Service, or any Part Thereof at the Desk* (London: 1683), p. 5. The reply (note 23) suggested the work was really by T.A., a barrister at law.

23 O.U., *Parish-Churches no Conventicles* (London: 1683).

24 Trevor Cooper (ed.), *The Journal of William Dowsing: Iconoclasm in East Anglia during the English Civil War* (Woodbridge: Boydell Press 2001).

25 Kenneth Fincham, "According to Ancient Custom": The Return of Altars in the Restoration Church of England', *Transactions of the Royal Historical Society* 13 (2003), pp. 29–54. Kenneth Fincham and Nicholas Tyacke, *Altars Restored: The Changing Face of English Religious Worship, 1547–c.1700* (Oxford: Oxford University Press 2007). Regrettably this otherwise excellent study pays little attention to liturgical studies and only the final chapter deals with the post-1660 period.

26 Fincham, '"According to Ancient Custom"', p. 34.

27 Caroline Robbins (ed.), *The Diary of John Milward, Esq, Member of Parliament for Derbyshire September, 1666 to May, 1668* (Cambridge: Cambridge University Press 1938), p. 218.

format: the communion table was to stand on a black and white marble floor, resting on a black marble step, sometimes with a second plain step; the shallow depth of these ascents meant that the table could only be placed on them altarwise not tablewise. All were also railed, and most backed by an altarpiece, which usually contained the ten commandments, creed and Lord's prayer, and sometimes paintings of Moses and Aaron.[28]

There were legal wrestles over the position of the altar at Sandwich and St Mary's, Dover, in the 1670s and 1680s, with the railed altar finally triumphing; on the other hand, Bishop Thomas Barlow of Lincoln was firmly opposed to the altarwise position and as late as the 1690s some Lincolnshire churches had the table in the nave.[29] Clearly, 'uniformity' in worship was a negotiable term and the mode of furnishing was equally variable.

LITURGY AND THE CRISIS OF 1688/89

Charles II died without a legitimate heir and his Catholic brother James succeeded to the throne. James's wish for tolerance to Dissenters and Catholics caused alarm, and the arrest and trial of seven bishops over their protest against the Declaration of Indulgence fuelled Protestant fears of an imminent restoration of Catholicism. This resulted in talks between some prominent Presbyterians and the Established Church. As part of a response to the perceived creeping Catholicism, a proposed revision of the 1662 Prayer Book with a view to bringing back some of the Presbyterians was begun in 1688. Archbishop William Sancroft appointed a committee that included Simon Patrick, John Sharp, John Moore and Thomas Tenison. The results of these deliberations are found in a Folio Prayer Book (MS 886 in Lambeth Palace Library). With the arrival of William of Orange and the Dutch invasion, a new situation was created that would result in the Nonjuring crisis. A new commission began work on revision in October 1689, and its proposals are found in another Folio Prayer Book in Lambeth Palace Library (MS 2173), which has become known as the Liturgy of Comprehension.[30] Timothy Fawcett divided the committee into four parties or groups. The first he termed the 'pressure group', which included Simon Patrick,

---

28 Fincham, "'According to Ancient Custom'", p. 38, with reference to *The Wren Society* X (Oxford: 1933) and XIX (Oxford: 1942).

29 Fincham, "'According to Ancient Custom'", pp. 44, 46–8.

30 Timothy J. Fawcett, *The Liturgy of Comprehension 1689* (Southend-on-Sea: Mayhew-McCrimmon 1973).

Edward Stillingfleet and John Tillotson. A second group he labelled 'miscellaneous', and it included Henry Compton, Bishop of London. The 'High Church' group included Archbishop Thomas Lamplugh of York. A fourth group Fawcett called 'academics', two of whom never attended the meetings. Among the proposed revisions were the Beatitudes as an alternative to the Ten Commandments, and the term 'sacrifice' of Christ's body and blood added to the Prayer of Humble Access. As a concession to the Presbyterian tender conscience, the surplice, sign of the cross in baptism, the ring in marriage, kneeling for Communion and the phraseology of regeneration in baptism were to be made optional. In the rite of public baptism, a new rubric was proposed concerning sureties. Only communicants were to be sureties, but a longer proposed rubric noted that although the custom of godparents was ancient and would continue, the main responsibility for the child's Christian formation was with the parents. This may have been a pastoral observation, but is equally a reflection of covenant theology, where the right of infant baptism lies in the fact that the parents are Christian. In the Exhortation after the Gospel reading a reference was to be added concerning God's 'gracious Covenant', and the post-baptismal charge was addressed to the parents as well as the sureties.[31] A lower view of sacramental action is perhaps indicated in changes proposed to the first two prayers. The 1662 version of the 'Flood Prayer', derived from Luther, referred to the Christ who 'didst sanctify Water to the mystical washing away of sin'. This was to read, 'didst *appoint water to be used in this Sacrament for* the mystical washing away of sin', thus avoiding the idea of hallowing the element itself.[32] In the second prayer, 'may he receive remission of his sins by spiritual regeneration' was rendered 'may be regenerated & receive remission of sin', suggesting a more conditional regeneration.[33] Some 'modernizing' seems to be at work in the alteration of the renunciation to 'the pomps and *vanities of ye wicked world . . .* and *all ye sinfull Lusts*' in place of 'glory of the world' and 'carnal desires'.[34] Pouring and sprinkling were allowed modes of baptism alongside 'dip', and the signing of the cross became optional.[35]

The rite for 'The Ministration of Private Baptism of Children in Houses' was to be given a new title '. . . of Children in *Cases of*

---

31 Fawcett, *The Liturgy of Comprehension 1689*, pp. 116–17.
32 Fawcett, *The Liturgy of Comprehension 1689*, p. 117.
33 Fawcett, *The Liturgy of Comprehension 1689*, p. 117.
34 Fawcett, *The Liturgy of Comprehension 1689*, p. 118.
35 Fawcett, *The Liturgy of Comprehension 1689*, p. 119.

Necessitie.[36] This seems to represent a compromise between those who opposed all private baptisms (see Chapter 2 above) and those who would allow private baptism in cases of emergency. The changes in the text brought the private rite into harmony with the proposed changes for the public rite, as was the case with baptism of those of 'riper years'. In the Communion service a rubric notes that when there is no Communion, there should not be any Communion service, suggesting that the 'Second Service' would disappear from regular Sunday Morning worship.[37] However, the Ante-Communion is directed to be at the North side of the Table, seemingly a victory for those who argued that this was the correct place for the 'second service'.[38] In the Ante-Communion the most notable and creative change was to substitute the Beatitudes for the Ten Commandments, a suggestion made by Jeremy Taylor in his 1658 rite and in turn inspired by the Eastern Orthodox rite. The rubric 'Another Book of Homilies be added to ye former' indicated the need for a wider variety of set homilies, perhaps of a more contemporary nature.[39] A new prayer of preparation was inserted after the prayer for the Church Militant:

> O God who has ordained holy Mysteries for a comemoratio of or Saviour's wonderfull love in laying dow his life for us; & for ye comunicatio of ye benefits of his death & passion to Us; we beseech yee to dispose all Those who intend to be made partakers of them, to come to thy holy Table with such sincere repentance of all their sinns, & ufeigned Resolutios of better Obedience; wth such an humble Fayth & ardent love uto Thee & unto All men: That They may cofortably hope for thy gracious Pardon, & for ye powr of thy holy Spirit, to carry them, by patience in well doing, unto aetrnal life, through Jesus Christ our Lord. Amen.[40]

The final text was presented to Convocation on 4 December 1689, but with the flight of James II and the accession of William and Mary, any need for comprehension and Protestant solidarity evaporated, and with the dissolution of Convocation on 13 February the 1662 Book was left intact and unaltered. In Ireland the 1662 Book of Common Prayer was introduced by an Act of Uniformity in 1665. This 1665

---

36 Fawcett, *The Liturgy of Comprehension 1689*, p. 121.
37 Fawcett, *The Liturgy of Comprehension 1689*, p. 100.
38 Fawcett, *The Liturgy of Comprehension 1689*, p. 101.
39 Fawcett, *The Liturgy of Comprehension 1689*, p. 104.
40 Fawcett, *The Liturgy of Comprehension 1689*, pp. 106–7.

Irish Prayer Book was mainly the text of 1662 with the addition to the state prayers of a prayer for the Lord Lieutenant and a service for the Visitation of Prisoners; also bound with the Book was John Cosin's form of Consecration of a Church.

Something of how services were conducted was recorded by a Scottish minister, Robert Kirk, who visited London in 1689. Kirk noted:

> Every Church in London have not organs, but the most have – all the pulpits have a deep velvet cloth & cushion, Red, purple, checquerd & stript, or such other colours, with large fringes of the same colour intermixed with Gold, some are wholly gold or silver. They have their fonts within the entry of the Churches, & the minister or Reader (in orders) Christens the children after sermon, when the people are dismissed; Theye take the children in their own arms from the god-mother, sprinkles water on their faces, signs the cross with their fin-ger, then dryes the child's face with its own linens, & gives it back to the Godmother which named it, the Father & a Gossip standing by, but the Godfather & Godmother engaging to train up the Child in the true Religion.[41]

Covent Garden Church had no organ, 'but psalms once sung when the minister is a coming. Women sing little. The men sing divers grave tunes, but all the tunes have only 2 notes for easiness to the commons, a higher & a lower.'[42] On 8 March 1690 Kirk heard Henry Compton, Bishop of London, preach on John 14.15. Afterwards, Compton 'going to the communion table at the east end of the Church, he prayed & laid his hands on the heads of about 300 young men & gentlewomen to confirm them; having been examined the week before', which appar-ently he did in different London churches throughout the season of Lent.[43] Kirk observed that at Christmas all windows were beset with green laurel and holly berries. 'There is sermon in all the Churches before-noon; most of the people communicate that day, & then feast sumptuously for that & some days after.'[44] The seats in churches were also adorned with green branches. On the twelfth day, Epiphany, Kirk recorded a strange custom. The shops were all shut for this holy day, and at night cakes were made throughout the city,

---

41 Robert Kirk, *Sermons, Conferences . . . with a Description of London. Ann 1689*, University of Edinburgh Department of Manuscripts, La.III.545, folio 157.
42 Kirk, *Sermons, Conferences*, folio 22.
43 Kirk, *Sermons, Conferences*, folios 85–6.
44 Kirk, *Sermons, Conferences*, folio 123.

very fair & delicious, and then cut in square pieces, with shreds of paper put in each piece, having a name of King, Knave, Wiseman, apeface, & such, in them, with so much money of value on each paper written to be spent in the Company, and payed by him that draws that fragment out of the hat as it chances.

The season of Christmas was observed until Candlemas and then the greenery was removed.[45]

In a letter to Archbishop Tenison, Edward Bowerman who became incumbent of Caddington, Bedfordshire, in 1691 explained the state of worship when he arrived, and what he had done to improve the situation.[46] Many fell asleep in the service,

> out of which they were awakened by ye singing of ye Clark alone, for not one of ye whole Congregation bore a part with him: when I began to pray in ye Pulpit some of them got upon their legs, & yawned & stretched themselves; & after I had named my text many of them put on their hatts, thou it was in ye most schorching time of July.[47]

They rarely observed a holy day, had no knowledge of the liturgical calendar, and had baptisms and churching of women in their homes.

The first reform was 'to get off their hats'. Next,

> care was taken, to have ye upper part of ye Chancell raised, & ye Communion Table railed in; in ye times of confusion ye Railes were pulled down, & ever since converted to a Profane use in ye Parish: at my first coming here ye Chancell lay in a disorderly & neglected manner, & ye Communion table loose from ye frame, & ye frame disjoynted & in pieces.[48]

In 1691 only 24 parishioners attended the Christmas Communion. But at Easter 1692, 100 attended and the parishioners

> begun now to put on a new face, & much decency & order was seen in ye Church; their irreverence & drouziness was changed into

---

45 Kirk, *Sermons, Conferences*, folio 116.
46 Lambeth Palace Library MS 933.9, Edward Bowerman to Thomas Tennison, p. 2.
47 Bowerman, p. 4
48 Bowerman, p. 6.

Devotion & serious attention; & those that could read bore their parts in the service, & many now joyned in ye responses & singing, wch before were confined to the Clark alone. & all stood up when the Psalms were sung.[49]

He also attempted to complete the morning service as per the rubrics, and introduced the Church Militant prayer after the sermon, the 'clark singing ye 134 psalm, that ye People might be imployed while I descended from ye Pulpit, put on ye Surplice, & breathed a little' and 'I proceeded to those Prayers that had for a long time been disused'.[50]

There were continued efforts to improve the standard of music in Church of England parish churches. In his sermon preached on the occasion of the new organ at St Andrew Undershaft, London on 31 May 1696, Gabriel Towerson proclaimed:

> The organ, in particular, both by the *loudness* and the *harmoniousness* thereof doth, with a kind of grateful violence, carry the voices of men along with it, and not only prevents any such indecent discords as might otherwise arise, but makes their voices indeed and in truth to answer that melody, which is here exhorted to, and is, it may be, the only instrument that can with any certainty procure it.[51]

However, few churches were able to afford an organ and providing a financial base for competent liturgical music was not an easy matter. Nicholas Temperley notes that a shift in culture resulted in psalm singing being identified with Puritanism, and by extension, with the common people. The result was that

> the idea was fast taking root that an English gentleman should have nothing to do with music of any kind . . . Rarely did a noblemen or a wealthy squire or merchant see fit to present his parish church with an organ, or endow a parish clerkship, or even accept the dedication of a collection of psalm tunes.[52]

---

49 Bowerman, p. 13.
50 Bowerman, p. 15.
51 Gabriel Towerson, *A Sermon concerning vocal and instrumental musick in the church, as it was delivered in the parish church of St. Andrew, Undershaft, May 31st, 1696* (London: 1696), p. 26.
52 Nicholas Temperley, *The Music of the English Parish Church*, Vol. 1 (Cambridge: Cambridge University Press 1979), p. 87.

Nevertheless, John Playford's *A brief introduction to the skill of music* (1658) had seen five editions between 1660 and 1670, and a revised version also went through several editions. Abraham Barbar published *A book of psalme tunes in four parts* (York, 1687), and Thomas Matthews, *The whole booke of psalmes, as they are now sung in the churches* (1688). The text of the metrical psalter remained that of Sternhold and Hopkins of 1562. In 1679 John Patrick had published *A Century of Select Psalms, and Portions of the Psalms of David, Especially those of praise. Turned into Meter, and fitted to the usual Tunes in Parish Churches, For use of the Charter-House, London*, as an attempt to improve the language of Sternhold and Hopkins. Psalm 6, sung to the Old Hundredth, had eight stanzas, the first of which read:

> Lord, I can suffer thy rebuke,
> When thou dost kindly me chastise;
> But thy fierce wrath I cannot bear,
> O let not that against me rise.[53]

It appears that this collection became popular with dissenting congregations, but was not widely used in the Church of England. However, 1696 saw the publication of the metrical psalter by Nahum Tate and Nicholas Brady, which became known as the 'New Version'. Tate was the poet laureate and a librettist, and Brady, a prebendary of Cork, was incumbent of St Katherine Cree, London. The pair attempted to improve on the linguistic style of the sixteenth-century psalter. J. R. Watson noted that in 1664 the Royal Society had set up a committee for improving the English language, and its members made a constant resolution 'to reject all the amplifications, digressions, and swellings of style: to return back to the primitive purity, and shortness, when men deliver'd so many things, almost in an equal number of words'.[54] According to Watson, Tate and Brady's version 'caught the moment', exchanging the active mood for the passive mood, providing clear subjects and verbs, and using the two halves of the Common Metre stanza to balance simile and statement.[55] The contrast with the 'Old Version' of Sternhold and Hopkins is illustrated in Psalm 4:

---

53 John Patrick, *A Century of Select Psalms, and Portions of the Psalms of David, Especially those of praise. Turned into Meter, and fitted to the usual Tunes in Parish Churches, For use of the Charter-House, London* (London: 1679), p. 5.

54 Thomas Spratt, *History of the Royal Society* (London: 1667), p. 113; J. R. Watson, *The English Hymn: A Critical and Historical Study* (Oxford: Clarendon Press 1997), p. 98.

55 Watson, *The English Hymn*, pp. 98–9.

Sternhold and Hopkins	*Tate and Brady*
O God, thou art my righteousness,	O Lord, thou art my righteous Judge,
Lord, hear me when I call:	To my complaint give ear:
Thou hast set me at liberty,	Thou still redeem'st me from distress;
when I was bound in thrall:	have mercy, Lord, and hear.

Whereas the Sternhold and Hopkins version had nine stanzas, the 'New version' of Tate and Brady had eight. However, although endorsed by influential clergy and dedicated to King William, this 'New Version' did not successfully compete with the 'Old Version' of Sternhold and Hopkins until the mid-eighteenth century.[56] Tate and Brady provided no music, but their version was designed to be sung to the customary tunes used for Sternhold and Hopkins. In most parish churches, the singing was still led by the parish clerk, and the people joined in, all *a capella*. Though exaggerated, there was unfortunately some truth in the rhyme of Elias Hall:

> Then out the people yawl an hundred Parts,
> Some roar, some whine, some creak like Wheels of Carts:
> Such Notes the Gam-ut yet did never know,
> Nor num'rous Keys of Harps'cals on a row.
> Their Heights or Depths cou'd ever comprehend,
> Now below double A re some descend:
> 'Bove E la squealing now ten notes some fly;
> Straight then as if they knew they were too high
> With headlong haste down Stairs they again tumble,
> Discords and Concords, O how thick they jumble;
> Like untam'd horses, tearing with their Throats
> One wretched Stave into an hundred Notes.[57]

HIGH CHURCH AND NONJURING LITURGIES

The Dutch invasion and the subsequent events of 1689 caused both a constitutional crisis and a crisis of conscience, particularly for High

---

56 See the chart of editions in Temperley, *The Music*, Vol. 1, p. 122.
57 Elias Hall, *The psalm-singer's compleat companion* (London: 1706), Introduction, p. 2.

Churchmen for whom the Divine Right of Kings and loyalty to the Established Church were crucial. Archbishop William Sancroft, together with Bishops Turner of Ely, Lake of Chichester, Thomas of Worcester, White of Peterborough, Ken of Bath and Wells, Lloyd of Norwich and Frampton of Gloucester were unable in conscience to take new oaths of allegiance to William and Mary and were deprived. Some 400 priests were also deprived, and from this was born the Nonjurors. Some who felt able to take the oath or for some reason had not been required to do so, remained in the Church, but had close friendships and sympathies with many of those who had left. Although not all Jacobites (those who politically and militarily supported James and his male heir) were Nonjurors, and not all Nonjurors were Jacobites, nevertheless the three great waves of Jacobite activity (1689–96, 1714–23 and 1745–53) were all marked by High Church and Nonjuring liturgical enterprises.

High Church liturgies appeared from the pens of Edward Stephens and Dr Johannes Grabe. Stephens was a lawyer and member of the Middle Temple, and had initially welcomed William's accession. Later he became disillusioned with both the monarch and the Church of England and declared himself out of communion with all but a handful of High Churchmen and Nonjurors. He had little sympathy with the Book of Common Prayer; his theological objections were expressed in a tract entitled *The Cranmerian Liturgy, Or, The Subtilty of the Serpent in Corrupting the True English Liturgy by Cranmer and a Faction of Calvinists* (1696). He particularly complained of the omission of commemoration of the saints, prayer for the dead and petition for sanctification of the elements and oblation of the unbloody sacrifice. Stephens had his own oratory and authored a liturgy which he used there, *The Liturgy of the Ancients Represented, As near as well may be, In English Forms* (1696).[58] The Preface claimed that it had been in use in some 'Publick Churches' in London since January 1694. The service was divided into two, corresponding to word and sacrament. The first part, clearly based on 1662, incorporated also the Te Deum, and other pieces from Morning Prayer. The Second part included the initiatory anthem from 1549, 'Christ our Paschal Lamb is offered for us once for all', the 1662 invitation, confession, absolution (preceded by a short prayer for forgiveness) and, in capitals, 'THE OFFERTORY'. A Preface was compiled from the Prayer of General Thanksgiving, Sanctus and 'Worthy is the Lamb' from Revelation. The Church Militant prayer followed, in its 1549

---

58 W. Jardine Grisbrooke, *Anglican Liturgies of the Seventeenth and Eighteenth Centuries* (London: SPCK 1958), pp. 60–70.

format, and then the Prayer of Consecration followed by the Prayer of Oblation, both from 1637, though the latter prayer was expanded with petitions from the Litany. The Lord's Prayer and Prayer of Humble Access preceded the Communion.

The second part of this service was enlarged and published separately in 1700. In this version the Eucharistic Prayer was inspired by *Apostolic Constitutions* VIII, but also material from St Basil and St James.

A close associate of Stephens was Johannes Grabe. Grabe was a Lutheran, but because of his ecumenical spirit was regarded by the stricter confessional Lutherans as a syncretist. He was ordered by the Consistory of Samland to submit any doubts he had concerning Lutheran theology and was imprisoned for a while. Grabe considered becoming a Moravian, but was persuaded by the Moravian bishop and Reformed Court Chaplain Daniel Jablonski to turn to the Church of England. He was ordained, and settled at Worcester College, Oxford, where he was a distinguished patristic scholar. He eventually concluded that the 1662 Prayer Book was deficient and attended Stephens' oratory in London. He wrote two eucharistic liturgies, one in English and one in Greek, closely modelled on that of Stephens.[59] His method of working was by expansion of the 1662 or older Prayer Book texts, and by borrowing from Eastern liturgical material. For example, whereas Stephens reproduced the 1549 petition, 'that they may be unto us the Body and Blood of thy most dearly beloved Son', Grabe strengthened the petition with 'that they may now *become* unto us the Body and Blood'. His Greek liturgy emended the 1662 Prayer of Consecration by rendering 'Satisfaction' with 'suitable ranson', and by adding an epiclesis before the narrative of institution: 'Hear us, o merciful Father, we humbly beseech thee, and send down thy Spirit on us and on these gifts here laid before, and make this bread the precious Body of thy Christ, and that which is in the cup the precious Blood of thy Christ.'

Both Stephens and Grabe were concerned to express the concept of sacrifice in the Eucharist and consecration by Word and Holy Spirit. The theological underpinning of both of these was set forth by John Johnson of Cranbrook in his 1710 *The Propitiatory Oblation in the Holy Eucharist* and the two-volume (1714 and 1718) *The Unbloody Sacrifice and the Altar, Unvail'ed and Supported*. Concerning the idea of the Eucharist as a sacrifice, Johnson wrote:

---

59 Günther Thomann, *John Ernest Grabe's Liturgies: Two Unknown Anglican Liturgies of the Seventeenth Century*, privately printed (Nürnberg: 1989); 'Studies in English Church History', privately printed (Stoke-on-Trent 1995).

[T]he bread and Wine, or, which is the same thing, the Sacramental Body and Blood, were by the Ancients esteemed, not only the Representation of a Sacrifice, but a real Sacrifice; and that the sacred Symbols were thus offer'd to God, the Liturgies are a Demonstration; in every one of which a solemn Tender of the Symbols is made to God, after the Words of Institution have first been pronounced over them.[60]

Johnson rejected the Roman doctrine of transubstantiation and argued instead for a change in power and effect through the Holy Spirit:

We may from hence learn, for what Reason the Ancients call'd the Eucharistical Bread, the spiritual Body of Christ, *viz.* because it was what it was by the peculiar Energy of the Holy Ghost: And what they meant by spiritual eating and drinking, *viz.* doing those outward Actions in the Eucharist, with a sincere Faith in the Passion of Christ, and receiving the Symbols, not as bare Bread and Wine, but as Divine powerful Representations of the Original Body and Blood.[61]

The liturgical experiments of Stephens and Grabe, and the eucharistic theology of Johnson represent catalysts and precursors for the liturgies of the Nonjurors.

The original Nonjurors of 1689 seem to have regarded the separation as personal and temporary, but after the deaths of three of their bishops, and then with the death of Archbishop Sancroft, leadership fell to Bishop Lloyd, and the decision was taken to keep a line of succession. In 1693/94 George Hickes and Thomas Wagstaffe, with permission of the exiled James II, were consecrated. All the original bishops had died by 1711, and when Wagstaffe died in 1712, Hickes arranged with the Scottish Bishops Archibald Campbell and James Gadderar to continue the English Nonjuring succession. The Scottish bishops and the episcopal clergy of the Church of Scotland had been ejected by the Presbyterians in 1689. The Scottish Episcopal Church was also a Nonjuring Church, refusing to take the oath to King William. Thus in 1713 Jeremy Collier, Nathaniel Spinckes and Samuel Hawes were consecrated. On Hickes's death in 1715,

---

60 John Johnson, *The Unbloody sacrifice and Altar, unvail'd and Supported*, Part I (London: 1714), p. 44.
61 Johnson, *The Unbloody sacrifice*, p. 209.

two further bishops were consecrated, Dr Thomas Brett and Henry Gandy. However, in 1716 a dispute began among them over what has become known as the Usages controversy.[62] The Usagers, led by Collier and Brett, argued that the liturgical witnesses of the first five centuries demonstrated that water should be added to the wine in the chalice, that there should be prayer for the departed, an explicit offering of the bread and wine, and an explicit epiclesis of the Holy Spirit, and that these were lacking in the 1662 Prayer Book. They appealed especially to the Clementine Liturgy of *Apostolic Constitutions* VIII.[63] The Non-Usagers, led by Spinckes, argued that these were adiaphora, and that the Nonjurors should be loyal to the 1662 Prayer Book. A tract warfare ensued and the Nonjurors split into two factions.[64]

At a meeting of the Usagers on 19 December 1717, an injunction signed by Collier and Brett directed that celebrants were to leave out the Ten Commandments and substitute the Summary of the Law; they were to openly mix the chalice with water; they were to omit the words 'militant here on earth' from the prayer of intercession, and were to add to it a prayer for the departed; and, after the words of institution, they were to pray the Prayer of Oblation and Invocation from the Clementine liturgy.[65] On 11 March 1718 the text of a eucharistic liturgy was issued which gave full expression to the theology of John Johnson and the 1717 Injunctions, with a rationale being set out at great length in Thomas Brett's *A Collection of the Principal Liturgies, Used by the Christian Church in the Celebration of the Holy Eucharist: particularly the Ancient* (1720), which also gave the texts of the liturgies from *Apostolic Constitutions* VIII, St James and St Basil.[66] Of note is the offertory prayer, which spoke of offering 'this reasonable and unbloody Sacrifice for our Sins, and the Sins of the people'.[67] The post-Sanctus was inspired by the anaphora of St Basil and St James, and the anamnesis by *Apostolic Constitutions* VIII, with a distinct epiclesis after the

---

62 See James David Smith, *The Eucharistic Doctrine of the Later Nonjurors*, Alcuin Club/GROW Joint Liturgical Study 46 (Cambridge: Grove Books 2000).

63 Leonel L. Mitchell, 'The Influence of the Rediscovery of the Liturgy of *Apostolic Constitutions* on the Nonjurors', *Ecclesia Orans* 13 (1996), pp. 207–21.

64 See Smith, *Eucharistic Doctrine*, and Bryan D. Spinks, *Liturgy in the Age of Reason: Worship and Sacraments in England and Scotland 1662–c.1800* (Farnham: Ashgate 2008), ch. 5.

65 Henry Broxap, *The Later Non-Jurors* (Cambridge: Cambridge University Press 1924), p. 62.

66 For detailed commentary, see Grisbrooke, *Anglican Liturgies*, pp. 95ff.

67 Thomas Brett, *A Collection of the Principal Liturgies, Used by the Christian Church in the Celebration of the Holy Eucharist* (London: Richard King, 1720), p. 139.

institution narrative, 'and send down thine Holy Spirit, the witness of the passion of our Lord Jesus, upon this sacrifice, that he may make this Bread the Body of thy Christ, and this Cup the Blood of thy Christ'.[68]

A compromise between the two parties was reached in 1732, between Bishops Brett, Smith and Gandy, in which the mixed chalice would be done privately, the words 'Militant here on earth' would be omitted, and the words in the 1662 Prayer of Consecration, 'Hear us etc', were to be counted as an epiclesis, and the 1718 rite was to be laid aside. This group became known as the Unionists. Sadly, some Usagers felt too much had been conceded, and some Non-Usagers felt similarly, and the result was that there were then three Nonjuring factions. A Scottish bishop, Robert Forbes, recorded the worship of the 'Unionist' Nonjuror Bishop Robert Gordon when visiting London in 1763. On St Luke's day, 18 October, he recorded:

> I read matins for Bishop Gordoun [when he informed me, upon ask-ing, that there was none of the same character, but himself only, in England], he performing the second service, the reading of the Law, &c., at the Altar. And here it is proper to observe that all the time I was in London I never heard any (Nonjuring) clergyman use the words *Militant here in Earth*, and I heard both Bishop Gordoun and Mr Conachar read prayers. Yea, remarkable is it that the former made considerable alterations in reading the prayers, particularly in the Litany he used *direct* for *keep*, and made this great addition – 'All sick *and distressed Persons, particularly such as may be suffering in the cause of Truth and Righteousness, and those that either need or desire the Charity of our Prayers,*' or words to that purpose; and then added *Exiles* to 'Prisoners and Captives'. Then, in performing the altar service, he not only omitted *Militant here in Earth*, but likewise he made a long pause in that same prayer after these words – '*Departed this Life in thy Faith and Fear,*' during which he and his people, with hands and eyes lifted up unto heaven, were commemorating mentally such of the faithful departed as they should judge most proper at the time; and in the prayer of Consecration he also made a long pause after these words – *Hear us, O Merciful Father, we most humbly beseech Thee,* in order to introduce mentally the Invocation of the Holy Spirit of God upon the elements of Bread and Wine. Immediately after the Prayer of Consecration he used the Oblatory Prayer.[69]

---

68 Grisbrooke, *Anglican Liturgies*, p. 289.
69 J. B. Craven (ed.), *Journals of the Episcopal Visitations of the Right Rev. Robert Forbes, MA* (London: Skeffington and Son Ltd 1923), pp. 37–8.

Among the Usagers, Bishop Thomas Deacon of Manchester became one of the leading liturgical revisers.[70] Deacon became a Nonjuror in 1716 and was made bishop in 1733, and made his living as a physician. In 1734 he published *A Compleat Collection of Devotions*, which in fact was a complete set of liturgical services, including a second part containing daily private prayers for morning and evening, and for nine, twelve and three o'clock. The opening preface noted that the best liturgical method for the Church to follow was that of the ancient, universal Church to the end of the fourth century, and that the *Apostolic Constitutions* is the most ancient of liturgies. Morning Prayer had opening versicles, the Gloria in excelsis, the proper prefaces from the 1662 Communion rite, a selected psalm, and then the psalmody of the day, a lesson, Te Deum or Benedicite, second lesson, Benedictus or Psalm 8, creed, homily, dismissals of the catechumens, kyrie, Lord's Prayer, preces and collects, Litany, prayers and dismissal in peace. It included a service using suggestions from *Apostolic Constitutions*, such as prayers for the catechumens and a penitential rite. The eucharistic liturgy followed the structure of the Prayer Book, but with liberal use of material from *Apostolic Constitutions* in the eucharistic prayer, including an explicit oblation and epiclesis.[71] The baptismal rites included the use of oil, and a form for blessing oil for the sick was included. Yet as interesting as the 1718 and 1734 liturgies are to Anglican liturgical scholars, the number of people who experienced them is greatly disproportionate to the scholarly attention that they receive. Bishop Forbes noted the poor attendance at Bishop Gordon's London church, and it is estimated that Deacon's congregation in Manchester was somewhere between 20 and 100, 'the greater part of them women'.[72] These liturgies, like those of Stephens and Grabe, were exotic compilations, but were used by only a small minority of people in a movement that atrophied to extinction.

THE NEWTONIAN AND LOCKEAN CHURCHMEN AND LITURGICAL REVISION

The long eighteenth century was also the Age of Reason, and two early eighteenth-century intellectual giants of the period were Isaac Newton (1642–1727) and John Locke (1632–1704). Newton was a mathematician and experimental physicist who also had a keen interest

---

70 Henry Broxap, *A Biography of Thomas Deacon* (Manchester: Manchester University Press 1911).

71 For full commentary, see Grisbrooke, *Anglican Liturgies*, pp. 113–35.

72 Broxap, *A Biography of Thomas Deacon*, pp. 99–100.

in biblical prophecy and alchemy, making him what Michael White has called 'the last sorcerer'.[73] As a Cambridge fellow and Lucasian Professor of Mathematics, Newton was expected to be in holy orders. He had studied theology with that end in mind, but he managed to avoid the requirement since it is clear from his unpublished writings that he did not believe in the Trinity.[74] Locke's great *Essay Concerning Human Understanding* (1690) and *The Reasonableness of Christianity* (1695) were based on a 'rational' reading of Scripture without dogma, and raised questions about Christology and Trinitarian doctrine. His posthumously published paraphrases of the Pauline Epistles play down the divinity of Christ and in consequence, give a 'low' concept of sacraments.[75] Philip Dixon observed that, given the Trinitarian controversies of the 1690s, Locke's silence is 'stunningly eloquent', and his shift of definition from 'person-as-substance' to 'person-as-consciousness' left no room for three persons as one.[76] Newton and Locke were close acquaintances and their published works were cutting-edge learning in the universities.

Two close associates and pupils of Newton were William Whiston and Samuel Clarke. Both were ordained, both questioned the received doctrine of the Trinity and both suggested liturgical revision in the light of their understanding of the Trinity.

William Whiston

Whiston was born in Leicestershire in 1667. His father had been a Presbyterian who had reluctantly conformed after the Restoration and had become Rector of Norton juxta Twycross. He attended Tamworth School, entered Cambridge University in 1686 and excelled at mathematics. He graduated BA in 1690 and was elected a fellow of Clare Hall. In 1693 he became MA, and was also ordained that year by Bishop William Lloyd of Coventry and Litchfield. Whiston was to become Vicar of Lowestoft and Kessingland in Suffolk in 1698, and he proved to be a zealous pastor; however, his ability in mathematics had already gained him the attention and friendship of Sir Isaac

---

73 Michael White, *Isaac Newton: The Last Sorcerer* (London: Fourth Estate 1997).

74 See James E. Force and Richard Popkin, *Essays on the Context, Nature and Influence of Isaac Newton's Theology* (Dordrecht: Kluwer Academic 1990); Spinks, *Liturgy in the Age of Reason*, ch. 6.

75 Arthur W. Wainwright (ed.), *John Locke: A Paraphrase and Notes on the Epistles of St. Paul to the Galatians, 1 and 2 Corinthians, Romans, Ephesians*, 2 vols (Oxford: Clarendon Press 1987).

76 Philip Dixon, *Nice and Hot Disputes: The Doctrine of the Trinity in the Seventeenth Century* (London: T & T Clark 2003), pp. 139, 142.

Newton, and in 1701 Newton asked him to be his substitute. Whiston was to succeed Newton to the Lucasian Chair in 1701. He was a polymath and published books on mathematics, astronomy and the chronology of the Bible. He also had a particular interest in prophecy and millenarianism. Whiston presents an interesting figure in whom Enlightenment and rationalist learning were combined with a strong conviction of the supernatural. However, his undoubted competence in several fields also led to a certain overconfidence in his own scholarship and reasoning ability.

It is difficult to know exactly at what point Whiston came to have doubts about the doctrine of the Trinity, but his teacher Sir Isaac Newton had abandoned Trinitarian belief, and Newton's two great pupils, Whiston and Dr Samuel Clarke, had sided with their teacher.[77] Whiston's training led him to a particular method of examining evidence, and he was also concerned with the purity of inspired scripture. The Athanasian (though more accurately, Constantinopolitan) Christology and Trinitarian theology he found to be lacking in the earlier and purer sources of the New Testament, and it would seem that already by 1705 Whiston had become 'inclin'd to what has been late called Arianism'.[78] He gave the Boyle Lectures in 1707 and then turned to pursue his new discovery in further depth. His study of the *Apostolic Constitutions* in 1708 confirmed his Arian hypothesis, and it was at that point that he wrote to both Archbishops. In August 1708 Whiston applied to the Vice-Chancellor of the university for a licence to print the results of his discovery, under the title *Essay on the Apostolical Constitutions*. Permission was refused because the work was deemed unorthodox. Whiston went ahead and published some of his findings in *Sermons and Essays Upon several Subjects* (1709). In short, Whiston concluded that 'I have studied these Points to the Bottom, and am thoroughly satisfied the Christian Church has been long and grossly cheated in them; and, by God's Blessing, if it be in my Power, it shall be cheated no longer.'[79] In 1710 Whiston was charged with breaking a university statute by teaching heresy, found guilty and deprived of his Chair. Undeterred and unrepentant, in 1711 he published his *Primitive*

---

77 James E. Force, *William Whiston: Honest Newtonian* (Cambridge: Cambridge University Press 1985).

78 William Whiston, *Historical Sketches of the Life of Dr. Samuel Clarke* (London: 1730), p. 13. He asserted that in a sermon of 1704, he still held the traditional doctrine as set forth in the Athanasian Creed.

79 William Whiston, *Memoirs of the Life and Writings of Mr. William Whiston* (London: 1749), Vol. 1, p. 151.

Christianity Reviv'd, with a full-scale defence of *Apostolic Constitutions* as an apostolic document and of the Arian doctrine.

What did Whiston believe about the *Apostolic Constitutions*? Whereas others found its apostolic claim to be suspect, Whiston believed it to be 'an authentic account of the worship, discipline and institutions of the gospel of Christ, and of the whole Christian economy, both for faith and practice, as they were left by the apostles, and their companions, in the latter end of the first, and former part of the second century'.[80] Since Whiston already viewed Arian doctrine as more primitive, he regarded this Arian or semi-Arian work as primitive. Thus he wrote:

> For now it appears by Church History, that since these *Old Constitutions* would not patronize the Athanasian Corruptions in Faith and Practice, *New ones* were fram'd that did; and since the *Old* Original *Liturgy*, did not appoint the Worship of Christians agreeably to the novel Notions, *New Liturgies* were fram'd, or rather the old one transform'd, modell'd and interpolated till it did.[81]

Again, in chapter 2.VIII:

> The *Liturgies*, and Forms of publick Devotions, and Administration of Baptism and the Eucharist here Extant, for their Piety, Simplicity, Zeal, fulness of Matter, and close Adherence to the Scripture Methods and Language, are exceeding admirable: Nay, far beyond the Composures of all the latter Ages; and highly worthy of the Apostles themselves.[82]

As might be expected, Whiston was particularly interested in the doxologies which supported his own anti-Trinitarian stance. Yet to be fair to Whiston, it was not just the anti-Trinitarian material that he took seriously. Chapter VI drew the inferences of his survey. Since in Whiston's mind *Apostolic Constitutions* was an apostolic document, it provided an exact order for worship, and there were also important liturgical implications:

> XVII. Hence we learn that the Eucharist is properly an *Oblation*, or *unbloody Sacrifice of Commemoration*; as those Antiently were *bloody*

---

80 Whiston, *Memoirs* (1753 edn), p. 210.
81 William Whiston, *Primitive Christianity Reviv'd*, Vol. 3, ch. 1.XXIII, p. 157.
82 Whiston, *Primitive Christianity*, Vol. 3, p. 183.

Sacrifices of Prefiguration; but both owing their proper Influence to the *one Sacrifice of Christ on the Cross*; and that this *Commemorative Sacrifice* is to be offer'd for the Faithful, both quick and dead, in the Christian Church.

XVIII. Hence we learn that Prayers *for* the Faithful departed, especially at the Eucharist, and in the Commemorations of them, is an Original Institution of the Gospel; as Prayers *to* them was afterward an Institution of Antichrist.

XIX. Hence we learn that Baptism is to be celebrated not by a *single sprinkling*, but by a *trine Immersion*; that the Person to be baptiz'd, is to be anointed with consecrated Oil before; and sealed with consecrated Ointment after it; in order to its Completion; and the later as the *Confirmation* of the baptized Persons also.

XX. Hence we learn that the Eucharist is to be celebrated with *Bread*, and a Mixture of *Wine* and *Water*, according to our Saviour's own Example and Appointment; and to be consecrated by the Invocation of the Father for the Descent of the Holy Spirit upon the Oblations, to make them the Body and Blood of Christ to the Communicants.[83]

In 1713 Whiston attempted to put some of this into practice within an Anglican framework, in *The Liturgy of the Church of England reduc'd nearer to the primitive Standard. Humbly propos'd to Publick Consideration.* The Preface to the Reader complained that the Prayer Book had been too influenced by Calvin (for which, of course, there is no evidence whatsoever) and had departed from the Primitive Forms. In his proposals, the Anglican liturgy is brought into some conformity with *Apostolic Constitutions*.

However, if Whiston used the semi-Arian doctrine of *Apostolic Constitutions*, he also used the document to enrich the Anglican rite. The 'Prayer of Consecration' of the 1662 rite was remodelled according to the 1549 rite, with its petition for Holy Spirit and Word to bless and sanctify the elements, and also in the anamnesis, an offering of the gifts. He inserted the *Hagia Hagiois* from *Apostolic Constitutions* VIII.XIII as an invitation to Communion. He also provided an alternative prayer of consecration, being that part of the eucharistic prayer of *Apostolic Constitutions* VIII from the institution narrative as far as the epiclesis, and the words of administration from the same source. A second edition was published in 1750, by which time Whiston had become a Baptist,

---

83 Whiston, *Primitive Christianity*, Vol. 3, p. 223.

and so whether the new edition was for academic or practical reasons, or at Whiston's whim, is difficult to know for certain.

Samuel Clarke

Samuel Clarke was born in 1675 in the city of Norwich. He attended the local free Grammar School where he was taught by Samuel Hoadly, father of Benjamin, and went up to Cambridge in 1690.[84] He took his BA in 1695 and was ordained in 1698; he became a Fellow of Gonville and Caius and succeeded Whiston as chaplain to the Bishop of Norwich. At Cambridge he acquainted himself with both the work and person of Sir Isaac Newton. Newton engaged him to translate his *Opticks* (1704) into Latin, and he defended Newton against Cartesianism in correspondence with Leibniz. Clarke was regarded as one of the most brilliant minds of the Church of England, and in 1704 and in 1705 gave the Boyle lectures. It is said that after his examination for the DD, the Regius Professor of Divinity Dr Henry James emended the usual 'I will now finish, as I have tested you enough' to 'You have taxed me enough'.[85] In 1709 he was appointed Rector of St James, Westminster, which was frequently a stepping stone to a bishopric. Clarke's preferment came to an end in 1712 with the publication of *Scripture-Doctrine of the Trinity*, which many of his contemporaries regarded as heterodox.[86] This work was divided into three parts. In the first Clarke collected passages of Scripture relating to God the Father, the Son of God and the Holy Spirit of God, paying attention to the subordination of the Son and Spirit to the Father. In Part II he expounded the doctrine which he found in the passages, concluding there is only one supreme cause and original, namely the Father. In Part III Clarke set out the reforms necessary to the Book of Common Prayer to bring it in line with the Scripture doctrine that Clarke had expounded. At a later date, and privately, he outlined further what form this would take. The British Library has an interleaved Book of Common Prayer printed in 1724, which has Clarke's hand-written emendations. For example, in place of the Gloria Patri, Clarke suggested either 'Glory be to God, by Jesus Christ, through the heavenly assistance by the Holy Ghost', or 'Unto God be glory in the Church, by Christ Jesus'. The Te Deum was

---

84 See J. P. Ferguson, *Dr. Samuel Clarke: An Eighteenth Century Heretic* (Kineton: The Roundwood Press 1976) for fuller biographical details.

85 Ferguson, *Dr. Samuel Clarke*, pp. 40–1.

86 For the view that he was simply arguing for a modern expression of the Trinity, see Thomas C. Pfizenmaier, *The Trinitarian Theology of Dr. Samuel Clarke (1675–1729): Context, Sources, and Controversy* (Leiden: E. J. Brill 1997).

altered, as was the punctuation of the Apostles' Creed; the Athanasian Creed was crossed out in its entirety. It appears that Clarke used the emended texts in his services at St James Church, Westminster. In his posthumously published lectures on the Catechism, Clarke argued that the sacraments had no physical efficacy, but only a moral qualification, and when received worthily, conferred an inward blessing.[87] A similar 'Newtonian-Lockean' approach to sacraments was represented by Bishop Benjamin Hoadly, a close friend of Clarke and a former friend of Whiston. In his *A Plain Account of the Nature and End of the Sacrament of the Lord's Supper* (1735), Hoadly argued that the Eucharist was a federal rite, a covenant, a seal and a remembrance of a covenant, but primarily a moral duty. Hoadly seems to have been quite content with the 1662 Prayer Book and never published ideas of revision, and Clarke himself never published a revised liturgy. Others, however, took up some of Clarke's suggestions. John Jones, Vicar of Alconbury, published *Free and candid Disquisitions relating to the Church of England* in 1749, arguing for shortened services, and removing the Athanasian Creed. His plea for publication of experimental revisions resulted in such works as *The Liturgy of the Church of England in its ordinary Service, reduced nearer to the Standard of Scripture* (1763) by William Hopkins, Vicar of Bolney. More importantly, in 1774 Theophilus Lindsey published *The Book of common Prayer reformed according to the Plan of the Late Dr. Samuel Clarke*. This seems to have been based on the ideas that Clarke published in *Scripture-Doctrine of the Trinity*, and is rather different from Clarke's own emendations as found in the interleaved Prayer Book of 1724. Lindsey's reforms included only the 1552 words of administration at the Communion, giving an explicit memorialist interpretation. Lindsey's congregation became Unitarian, and his 1774 liturgy inspired a host of non-subscribing Presbyterian and Unitarian liturgies.[88]

EIGHTEENTH-CENTURY PRAYER BOOK WORSHIP

A German visitor in the 1780s, Gebhard Friedrich Augustus Wendeborn, gave this assessment of Church of England worship:

> Whoever has not been brought up in the English church, will not think himself much edified, when he attends in it for the first time divine service. The Common-Prayer book contains some very

---

87 Samuel Clarke, *An Exposition of the Church-Catechism* (Dublin: 1730), pp. 155–6.
88 See A. Elliott Peaston, *The Prayer Book Reform Movement in the XVIIIth Century* (Oxford: Blackwell 1940).

excellent prayers; but as they are read all the year round, and frequently without much devotion in a hasty manner, with a voice not always sufficiently loud and intelligible, it is no wonder, that the congregation should appear rather tired, and without many signs of fervent devotion. The alternate reading verses of the Psalms, by the clergyman and the congregation, the loud repeating of the Litany, the Creed, and other parts of the service by the latter, makes it rather resemble a Jewish synagogue. The frequent repetition of the reading of the prayers, and the psalms, is the cause, that many of those who constantly attend the church, know both by heart; and therefore their thoughts seem to be much absent, when they recite this part of the service . . . [T]he singing is generally not very harmonious; that recitation of some parts of the service, which, as I have observed before, is divided between the clergyman and the congregation, is done in a manner that betrays rather carelessness than attention; the perpetual motion of kneeling and rising again, that monotony which prevails, and that inanimated manner in which sermons are commonly delivered, have, in my opinion, nothing of solemnity in them, and can hardly promote edification and devotion.[89]

The Revd James Newton, Rector of Nuneham Courtenay, attended morning service on his way back from Bath in June 1761, and commented: 'The Parson's reading of the Prayers was very poorly indeed & without any Piety & Devotion, a fault I hope I shall never fall into.'[90] The diarist farmer James Warne commented on his incumbent at Wool in Dorset in 1758: 'Mr. Fisher is a comical Man to Preach and as Odd Way of Reading Prayers as ever I heard. He reads so fast.'[91] Viscount Torrington was reasonably impressed with the service he attended at Middleham in 1792:

There was a decent, well-dressed, well-behaved congregation; with a singing-loft, from which there was too much singing from, about, a dozen voices, male, and female; and two bassoons, of better accompanyment than an organ: one of their attempts was too powerful for them, 'And the Trumpet shall sound', the bassoons imitating the

89 F. A. Wendeborn, *A View of England Towards the close of the Eighteenth Century by Fred. Aug. Wendeborn, LL.D*, 2 vols (Dublin 1791), Vol. 2, pp. 207–8.

90 Gavin Hannah (ed.), *The Deserted Village: The Diary of an Oxfordshire Rector, James Newton of Nuneham Courtenay, 1736–86* (Dover: Alan Sutton 1992), p. 109.

91 J. F. James and J. H. Bettey (eds), *Farming in Dorset: Diary of James Warne, 1758, Letters of George Boswell, 1787–1805* (Dorchester: Dorset Record Society 1993), p. 50.

trumpet. The service lasted long, but our service is much too long; The Curate, *the deputy* of *Mr Dean*, had a good voice, and perform'd tolerably.[92]

He was far less impressed by the cleric who officiated at Folkham in Lincolnshire:

> Here were a numerous, and decent congregation, with a singing loft crouded; and amongst them one lady in a blue silk bonnet, who sang *notably*; but the bassoons, and hautboys, were too loud and shrieking: as for the clergyman, he went off in a loud, unintelligible key, like a lawyer reading deeds, and was truly intolerable. Had I been in the company of those I knew, I could not have refrain'd from laughter. – Much singing before the service; likewise the Magnificat, and two psalms: during the sermon mine host slept, and I slumber'd.[93]

In 1790 at Knutsford Church, which was neat and 'well-pew'd' and 'was well fill'd with well-dress'd company', he observed: 'The service open'd with a psalm, accompany'd by an organ, and the Te Deum, and were chaunted; so these with two other psalms, gave me singing enough: as for the sermon, it had the merit of being short.'[94] Parson Woodforde recorded that when in the parish of Babcary, unless away from his cure, every Sunday he 'read Prayers and preached', with quarterly celebrations of the sacrament. Some Sundays he also baptized, churched women and performed the marriage service.[95] The parish clerk also had a crucial role: he not only led responses, but also was sometimes the only singer.[96] Woodforde noted that he and his clerk were up drinking late and as a result the clerk did not get up in time for the services the next day; Woodforde admonished him.[97] He complained of his new parish in 1775 that it had 'the worst singing I ever heard in a Church, only the Clerk and one man, and both intolerably bad'.[98] Woodforde also

---

92 C. Bruyn Andrews (ed.), *The Torrington Diaries: Containing the Tours Through England and Wales of the Hon. John Byng (Later Fifth Viscount Torrington) Between the Years 1781 and 1794*, 4 vols (New York: Henry Holt and Company 1936), Vol. 3, p. 58.
93 Andrews, *The Torrington Diaries*, Vol. 2 (1935), p. 338.
94 Andrews, *The Torrington Diaries*, Vol. 2, p. 175.
95 John Beresford (ed.), *The Diary of a Country Parson*, 3 vols (Oxford: Oxford University Press 1924–27), Vol. 2, p. 207; Vol. 3, pp. 57, 170.
96 James and Bettey, *Farming in Dorset*, p. 109.
97 Beresford, *The Diary of a Country Parson*, Vol. 1, p. 46.
98 Beresford, *The Diary of a Country Parson*, Vol. 1, p. 152.

recorded a struggle he had in November 1769 with the parish singers at Castle Cary, who sang from the West Gallery:

> I read Prayers and preached this morning at C. Cary Church. I was disturbed this morning at Cary Church by the Singers. I sent my Clerk some time back to the Cary Singers, to desire that they would not sing the Responses in the Communion Service [i.e. Antecommunion], which they complied with for several Sundays, but this morning after the first Commandment they had the Impudence to sing the Response, and therefore I spoke to them out of my desk, to say and not sing the Responses which they did after, and at other places they sang as usual. The Singers in the Gallery were, John Coleman, the Baker, Jonathan Croker, Willm Pew Junr., Thos Penny, Willm Ashford, Hooper the Singing Master, James Lucas, Peter, Mr. Francis's man, Mr. Melliar's man James, Farmer Hix's son, Robert Sweete and the two young Durnfords.[99]

The singers were absent from church on 26 November, 'they being highly affronted with me at what I lately had done'.[100] On 17 December Woodforde noted: 'The Singers at Cary did not please me this afternoon by singing the 12th Psalm, New Version, reflecting upon some People', which began, 'Help me, Lord, for there is not one godly man left.' On 24 December he gave them a lecture on their recent behaviour, and 'on promise of amendment have 0.2.0'.[101] The struggle between singers wanting to sing what they wanted over against clergymen's wishes was probably not uncommon. But Woodforde here gives us a very human picture of parish worship as it was often performed.

The singers at Cary seem to have been an example of the popular 'rustic' West Gallery music that came into vogue in parish worship in the eighteenth century. Nicholas Temperley observed of the popular composers and the local musicians, 'if they sang, they wanted to sing with unabashed feeling, exuberance, and ostentation – and most of the time, loudly'.[102] The first generation of these musicians – John and James Green, Matthew Wilkins and Israel Holdroyd – began by copying the professionals, but moved further and further away over time, drawing on the style of ballads, folk songs and dances. Vic Gammon observes

---

99 Beresford, *The Diary of a Country Parson*, Vol. 1, p. 92.
100 Beresford, *The Diary of a Country Parson*, Vol. 1, p. 93.
101 Beresford, *The Diary of a Country Parson*, Vol. 1, p. 95.
102 Nicholas Temperley, 'Present at the Birth' in Christopher Turner (ed.), *Georgian Psalmody 1: The West Gallery Tradition* (Corby Glen: SG Publishing 1997), pp. 1–7, p. 4.

that many West Gallery pieces used repetition as a musical device, which was known as 'fuguing', and it was common to repeat the last two lines of each stanza.[103] Gammon notes of the music manuscripts:

> The mixing of the religious and the secular in a number of manu-script books from the period leads one to think that the separation was not always seen as too important; sometimes dance tunes were at one end of the book and psalms at the other. But in other cases the two were intermixed. Much evidence suggests that the connection between church bands and social dance was strong and widespread. Looked at another way it could be said that playing in church was just one of a number of musical activities that rural musicians might undertake.[104]

When visiting Oxford in 1773, Woodforde recorded that he had read the Epistle 'at the Altar', and in 1784 he preached at Norwich Cathedral:

> I was full dressed and being Preacher sat next to the Sub-Dean Dr. Hammond. Whilst the Anthem was singing I was conducted by the Virger to the Pulpit and there Preached a Sermon from these Words 'Let your light so shine before Men that they may see your good Works and glorify your Father wch. is in Heaven.' After Sermon was over I walked back to the vestry, had my Hood taken of, and then a Person came to me and gave me for Preaching 1.1.0.[105]

English cathedral worship seems to have varied in quality. In his tours through England in the 1720s, Daniel Defoe recorded of Exeter Cathedral:

> The Solemnity, Decency, and affecting Harmony, with which the Service, and Music, vocal and instrumental, is generally performed, by the Choral Vicars, Organists, and Choristers; and (which is well-worthy of Imitation) the numerous Congregation, which, Winter and Summer, attend the daily Prayers at Six in the Morning; and their grave and pious Behaviour there; I say, all this together, renders

---

103 Vic Gammon, 'The Performance Style of West Gallery Music' in Turner, *Georgian Psalmody 1*, pp. 43–51, p. 44. For examples of the written scores, see Dave Townsend, 'Processes of Transmission in the Country Psalmody Tradition' in Turner (ed.), *Georgian Psalmody 1*, pp. 31, 33.
104 Turner (ed.), *Georgian Psalmody 1*, p. 46.
105 Beresford, *The Diary of a Country Parson*, Vol. 2, p. 118.

this Cathedral a Glory to the Diocese, the Envy of other Choirs, and the Admiration of Strangers.[106]

Defoe noted that it was not unusual for there to be 500 people present on a morning six o'clock service – five times as many as St Paul's Cathedral – and the Reader did not omit parts of the service as was a custom in other places.[107] The future succentor of York, William Richardson, wrote of his visit to York in October 1769:

> The evening service was then performed by candlelight. I had never before been in the Minster but in the middle of a summer's day. The gloom of the evening, the rows of candles fixed upon the pillars in the Nave and Transept, the lighting of the Chancel, the two distant candles glimmering like stars at a distance upon the Altar, the sound of the Organ, the voices of the Choir raised up with the pealing Organ, in the chaunts, services, and anthem, had an amazing effect upon my spirits as I walked to and fro in the Nave. The varied tones, sometimes low, sometimes swelling into a great volume of harmonious sound, seemed to anticipate the songs of the blessed, and the chorus of praise round the Throne of God and the Lamb.[108]

A number of talented musicians contributed music in the long eighteenth century. Jeremiah Clark composed some excellent anthems as well as two morning services in C minor and G minor but his career was cut short by suicide. His successor at the Chapel Royal, William Croft, together with Maurice Greene, William Boyce, William Hayes and Samuel Arnold, all added to the growing repertoire of English choral music. Cathedral organists also printed chant books, such as John Alcock's *Divine Harmony* (Birmingham, 1752) and Thomas S. Dupuis's *Sixteen Single and Double Chants* (London, 1775). The widely read work of John Chetham of Skipton and Thomas Bisse, Chancellor of Hereford, urged parishes to follow their mother churches, the cathedrals, and some did try to emulate them.[109] However, cathedral usage

106 Daniel Defoe, *A Tour Thro' the whole Island of Great Britain*, Vol. 1 (London: 1762, 6th edn), p. 352.

107 Defoe, *A Tour*, p. 352.

108 E. Gray, *Papers and Diaries of a York Family 1764–1839* (London: Sheldon Press 1927), p. 13.

109 John Chetham, *A Book of Psalmody* (London: 1718); Thomas Bisse, *Decency and Order in Public Worship Recommended in Three Discourses, Preached in the Cathedral Church of Hereford* (London: 1723).

differed considerably. Thomas Sharp, in *The Rubrick in the Book of Common Prayer* (1753), observed:

> It is said of the *Venite Exultemus*, the Hymns for Easter-day, *Gloria in Excelsis*, the *whole Psalter*, and *Gloria Patri*; that they shall be said or sung. But it is not said whether this shall be done by the Priest or the People; or if by both, whether jointly, or *alternatim*. Custom therefore is our only authority for those various ways, in which we perform these parts of the Office in Choirs and Parish Churches.[110]

THE SCOTTISH EPISCOPAL CHURCH

As a result of the Glorious Revolution, the Scottish bishops were unable to take the oath to William and Mary, and episcopacy was ousted from the Church of Scotland. The Church of Scotland became Presbyterian in polity, and those remaining loyal to the ousted bishops became a Scottish Nonjuring Church. For a number of years the worship in these two Scottish Churches was almost identical, as evidenced by the accounts of the Lord's Supper recorded by James Gordon in 1694.[111] This was to change partly as a result of the Act of Union (1707). In 1709 James Greenfield, who had taken the oath to Queen Anne, opened a meeting house opposite St Giles', Edinburgh, and used the Book of Common Prayer. Greenfield was arrested and imprisoned but appealed to the House of Lords, who found in his favour and awarded costs against the Edinburgh magistrates. By an Act of 1712, toleration was allowed to 'Dissenters' and chapels for English expatriates began to appear. Meanwhile the Scottish Episcopal Nonjurors began to use material from the English Book of Common Prayer and the proposed 1637 Book of Common Prayer for Scotland. From 1722 onwards, to save printing costs, only the Communion office from the latter was printed; these began at the offertory and omitted two exhortations as well as some rubrics and collects. Thus there came about a Scottish Communion office. Like their English counterparts, some of the Scottish bishops experimented with Eastern forms of liturgy, and Bishop Thomas Rattray's *The Ancient Liturgy of the Church of Jerusalem* was published posthumously in 1744, which offered reconstructions of the rite as Rattray imagined it in earlier centuries. *An Office for the Sacrifice of the*

---

110 Thomas Sharp, *The Rubrick in the Book of Common Prayer* (London: 1753), p. 77.
111 G. D. Henderson and H. H. Porter (eds), *James Gordon's Diary 1692–1710* (Aberdeen: Spalding Club 1949), pp. 48–9.

Holy Eucharist, being the Ancient Liturgy of the Church of Jerusalem, to which Proper Rubricks are added for Direction was published in 1748. It is clear that this liturgy was intended for use. Stuart Hall has described the leather-bound manuscript book he found in the safe of St John's Church in Pittenweem, now deposited in St Andrews University Library. It seems to be Rattray's compilation and, in Hall's words, 'is plainly intended as a manual of public worship'.[112] It included directions for psalms for introits, lessons for Morning and Evening Prayer, orders for Morning and Evening Prayer, the Litany and penitential rites, as well as 'An Order for the Sacrifice of the Holy Eucharist'. Though it draws on the 1637 Book of Common Prayer, Rattray's use of his liturgical reconstructions had played a major role in the manuscript services. With the death of Charles Edward Stuart in 1788, the Scottish bishops agreed to submit to the government of King George II, and they ceased to be a Nonjuring Church. The Scottish Episcopal Church became an Anglican Church using its own Communion office based on that of 1637.

OTHER REVISIONS: WESLEY, THE COUNTESS OF HUNTINGDON AND THE ANGLICAN CHURCH IN AMERICA

Among a good many movements that were born in the eighteenth century, the Evangelical Revival remains one of outstanding importance. In the Church of England it included those who may be styled 'Parish Evangelicals', such as Samuel Walker of Truro, William Grimshaw of Haworth and John Fletcher. Others operated on the boundaries of the parochial system, such as the Evangelical Calvinists like George Whitefield and the Countess of Huntingdon, and the Evangelical Arminians, led by John and Charles Wesley. Although some of those in the first group may have had reservations about certain parts of the Book of Common Prayer, they seem to have used it without alteration. However, both the Countess of Huntingdon and John Wesley made alterations to the liturgy.

Selina, Countess of Huntingdon, was the patroness of Whitefield and other preachers, and claimed the right as a peer of the realm to have private chaplains and chapels. The chaplains were Church of England and the liturgy was the 1662 Book of Common Prayer. However, in 1779 she purchased Spa Fields. The incumbent of the parish took legal action against her using it as a private Church of England chapel. He won his

---

112 Stuart G. Hall, 'Patristics and Reform: Thomas Rattray and *The Ancient Liturgy of the Church of Jerusalem*' in R. N. Swanson (ed.), *Continuity and Change in Christian Worship* (Woodbridge: Boydell and Brewer 1999), pp. 240–60, p. 257.

case and, in order to save her other chapels, Lady Huntingdon seceded from the Church of England and trained her own Protestant clergy. The Book of Common Prayer was provided for use in the chapels, but in modified form. Her own recommendations for alterations to the morning service survive in the Cheshunt Foundation archives and perhaps give some idea of the ad hoc emendations that were used in her Chapels:

Sentences
The exhortation beginning 'Dearly beloved Brethren' – to be
    omitted –
The General Confession to be read – & followed by the Lords
    prayer & the following sentences –
The absolution being omitted –
Any of the occasional Psalms, O Come let us sing unto the Lord
    &c &c are to be said or Sung, & then the Psalm for the day – the
    lessons to be chose by the minister –
If the occasional Psalms are not chaunted a Hymn to be sung
    between the lessons instead of the Psalm.
Then the apostles creed
The Litany – omitting the petition for the Bishops, Priests, Deacons
    &c &c & inserting in its place a Petition for all faithful ministers
    & servants [of] God of every denomination over the world who
    preach Jesus Christ & him Crucified & Salvation alone in His
    name.
The Lords prayer after the Litany to be omitted
The Prayer immediately following it to be read
Then the General Thanksgiving & the Concluding Collect –
    almighty God who hast given – & Grace of our Lord Jesus Christ
A Second Hymn
In the Communion service the Lords prayer & Commandments to
    be ommitted (sic)
To begin with the Collect 'almighty God unto whom all hearts be
    open' –
Then this Sentence – God spake these words & said I am the Lord
    Thy God Thou shall have none other Gods but me
Then the Epistle & Gospel
Then follow the two last collects in the Communion service before
    the Peace of God – viz Assist us mercifully O Lord – & almighty
    Lord & Everlasting God vouchsafe &c &c
The Peace of God
Conclude with a Hymn

The minister to pray for the King & Royal Family in his Prayer in
    the Pulpit – Then a Verse or two sung before Sermon –
N.B:
When the Litany is omitted the Prayer for All mankind to be read
    in its place –
In reading the Lessons the Minister to be at liberty to make any
    occasional observations to the People – [113]

What is significant here is the place of hymns. This was to be the
great contribution of the Parish Evangelicals, as well as the Countess
of Huntingdon and the Wesleys. Although often intended originally
for worship at meetings rather than at public services, the evangelical
hymns began to migrate into public worship, paving the way for the
Church of England hymn revolution of the nineteenth century.

Both Wesleys were staunch Prayer Book men, though not uncritical
of some of its features. Yet already in 1766, at an annual conference of
Wesley's Methodist Societies, it was recorded:

> But some may say 'Our own service is public worship.' *Yes, in a sense*:
> but not such as supercedes the Church Service. We never designed
> it should . . . It presupposes public prayer, like the sermons at the
> university. Therefore I have over and over advised, use no *long prayer*,
> either before or after sermon. Therefore I myself frequently use only
> a collect, and never enlarge in prayer, unless at intercession, or on a
> Watch night, or on some extraordinary occasion.
>
> If it were designed to be instead of Church Service, it would be
> essentially defective. For it seldom has the four grand parts of public
> prayer: deprecation, petition, intercession and thanksgiving. Neither
> is it, even on the Lord's day, concluded with the Lord's Supper.[114]

John was well aware of the contemporary debates, and was acquainted
with the Savoy *Exceptions* (1661) as well as with John Jones's *Free
and Candid Disquisitions* (1749). He also knew the liturgical work of
Thomas Deacon, and may have met Deacon during visits to Manchester
in the 1730s.[115] These influences, together with his experience in

---

113 Cheshunt Foundation Archives at Westminster College, Cambridge, A4/5, 25.
114 *Minutes of the Methodist Conference*, Vol. 1 (London: The Conference Office 1812),
p. 58.
115 Henry Broxap, *A Biography of Thomas Deacon* (Manchester: Manchester University
Press 1911), pp. 75–6; Karen B. Westerfield Tucker, 'John Wesley's Prayer Book Revision:
The Text in Context' in *Proceedings of the Charles Wesley Society* 1 (1994), pp. 119–35.

Georgia, were brought to bear on an abridgement of the Book of Common Prayer for the Societies in America, *The Sunday Service of the Methodists in North America* (1784), and a version for British Methodists was published in 1786. The note in the 1784 book explained:

> I BELIEVE there is no LITURGY in the world, either in ancient or modern language, which breathes more of a solid, scriptural, rational Piety, than the COMMON PRAYER of the CHURCH OF ENGLAND. And though the main of it was compiled considerably more than two hundred years ago, yet is the language of it, not only pure, but strong and elegant in the highest degree.
>
> Little alteration is made in the following edition of it, (which I recommend to our SOCIETIES in AMERICA) except in the following instances:
>
> 1 Most of the holy-days (so called) are omitted, as at present answering no valuable end.
> 2 The service of the LORD'S DAY, the length of which has been often complained of, is considerably shortened.
> 3 Some sentences in the offices of Baptism, and for the Burial of the Dead, are omitted. – And,
> 4 Many Psalms left out, and many parts of the others, as being highly improper for the mouths of a Christian Congregation.[116]

Concern about the 'improper' psalms, and the need to shorten the service of Morning Prayer, Litany and Ante-Communion were commonplace in the eighteenth century. Wesley's third point places him alongside most of the other Evangelicals. Wesley was certain that regeneration was part of baptism, but may not coincide with the rite's administration. He thus retained references to regeneration prior to the act of baptism, but removed the references which came after the baptism.[117] The Lord's Supper was little altered and provision was made for extempore prayer after Communion. To avoid paying duty, the abridgement was shipped unbound and was bound in America. One puzzle is that

---

116 See James F. White (ed.), *John Wesley's Prayer Book: The Sunday Service of the Methodists in North America* (Akron, OH: OSL Publications 1991), p. 2.
117 This is discussed in more detail in Bryan D. Spinks, *Reformation and Modern Rituals and Theologies of Baptism: From Luther to Contemporary Practices* (Aldershot: Ashgate 2006), pp. 107–11. See also Bernard G. Holland, *Baptism in Early Methodism* (London: Epworth Press 1970); Gayle Carlton Felton, *This Gift of Water: The Practice and Theology of Baptism among Methodists in America* (Nashville, TN: Abingdon Press 1992).

certain copies have the prayer of consecration without the manual acts, and omit the sign of the cross in baptism. It would seem that Dr Coke, who Wesley ordained as Superintendent for America, may have been responsible for the substitution, which was later rectified. However, the sign of the cross disappeared in the 1786 edition. The book was used out of loyalty to John Wesley and after his death it was laid aside.

Wesley was not the only person considering the need for a revised Book of Common Prayer for America. The War of Independence placed the Church of England in the newly independent colonies in a difficult position. It was a Church that was sworn to uphold the lawful monarch, but was ministering in colonies seeking independence, who were at war with the armies of the lawful monarch, and then independence was seized through victory. The answer was an independent Anglican Church in the new United States. Samuel Seabury, a priest from Connecticut, was elected as bishop and was duly sent to England to be consecrated. There was no legal machinery for making anyone bishop without the Royal Mandate, and then only for England, Wales and Ireland. Thus it was that Seabury turned to the Nonjuring Scottish bishops. They had no such legal problems, and he was consecrated on 15 November 1784. He also allegedly signed a concordat – itself based on an earlier unsuccessful attempt by the Nonjurors to enter communion with the Greek Orthodox – in which he agreed to take a serious view of the Communion service of Scotland. Seabury wrote home to say that the Scottish bishops hoped that the Connecticut clergy would use the English book except with regard to the Communion service.

The New England clergy were, however, airing their own ideas of liturgical revision, based on mild Lockean and Newtonian ideas.[118] The Connecticut clergy welcomed Seabury back, made their proposals for revision known to him, and sought his opinion at meetings at Middletown and later at New Haven. At this stage there seems no mention of the Scottish Communion service.

Meanwhile, the Southern States were planning a Convention at Philadelphia, which duly met in 1785. At the Convention they discussed suggestions that had already been made for revision of the liturgy. They set about appointing a committee to undertake such a revision and were encouraged by Seabury in letters. Leading names in this committee were Samuel Provoost, William White and William Smith. At

---

118 The material in this section is derived from Marion J. Hatchett, *The Making of the First American Book of Common Prayer* (New York: Seabury Press 1982), and Paul Victor Marshall, *One, Catholic and Apostolic: Samuel Seabury and the Early Episcopal Church* (New York: Church Publishing 2004).

this Convention a letter was sent to the Archbishop of Canterbury requesting bishops. But the task of revising the liturgy was seriously undertaken. The Committee took into consideration the attempt at comprehension of the Presbyterians in 1689, the publication of John Jones of Alconbury on *Free and Candid Disquisitions*, as well as discussions in Connecticut and elsewhere. There were alterations of saints' days; psalms and hymns were left to the choice of the minister.

In Morning and Evening Prayer the words 'absolution' and 'priest' were removed. In the marriage rite everything after the blessing was deleted; a service for the Visitation of Prisoners from the 1711 version of the Irish Prayer Book was included. Reactions to the proposals varied considerably from place to place. The proposals went through an editorial committee and a final printed book appeared in 1786 for consideration. The Preface listed 12 particular matters under review, and included the length of the Sunday Public Service, a need to eliminate repetition, a choice of psalms, and selections which remove unchristian material, and the Athanasian Creed to be omitted or left optional. The Preface announced: 'It is far from the intention of this Church to depart from the Church of England, any further than local circumstances requires, or to deviate in any thing essential to the true meaning of the 39 articles.'

This book, in addition to changes proposed by the Committee, removed references to priest and replaced it by minister or pastor. Baptismal regeneration was toned down in the baptismal rite, and hymns were included by Phillip Doddridge and Samuel Wesley.

Reaction was mixed. William Smith wrote that the hymns were well received, but older persons disliked any change. Some felt it was Presbyterian and thought that baptismal regeneration was being denied. The Church Convention in the state of Maryland in April 1786 adopted the book with one alteration in the Communion service – the inclusion of a petition for consecration before the words of institution. The New Jersey Convention was hostile to the book; Pennsylvania proposed alterations; Virginia ratified it; South Carolina proposed emendations, but adopted it; and New York deferred a decision. Bishop Samuel Seabury generously wrote that he never thought there was any heterodoxy in the book, but 'I do think the true doctrine is left too unguarded, & that the Offices are, some of them, lowered to such a degree, that they will, in a great measure, loose their influence'.[119] More honest were Thomas Bradbury Chandler, who noted that on the subject of liturgy,

---

119 Samuel Seabury to Samuel Parker, 13 February 1788, in Francis L. Hawkes and William Stevens Perry, *Documentary History of the Protestant Episcopal Church in the United States of America: Connecticut*, 2 vols (New York: J. Pott 1863–64), Vol. 2, p. 321.

the *Free and Candid Disquisitions* was the oracle they consulted, and Samuel Peter, who felt it offended no one except Christians, and that the authors had much improved on Lindsey's and on Arius's system.[120] In June 1786 a bill was passed in the English Parliament making it possible for the English bishops to consecrate bishops for America. Three clergy were elected as bishop – Griffeth for Virginia, Provoost for New York, and William White for Pennsylvania. The English bishops let it be known that they were unhappy about the fact that the proposed book dropped the Nicene Creed from the Communion and had left out the Athanasian Creed. While the Southern States were concerned with procuring bishops and giving trial use of the 1786 liturgy, the Church in Connecticut was also proceeding with liturgical change. Seabury was concerned that liturgical revision should be informed by antiquity, and go back to a time before the Church was corrupted by popery. The book of 1786 he rightly perceived to be latitudinarian and informed by passing fashion. He was now prepared to advocate the Scottish Communion consecration prayer, though not the whole liturgy. In his version which he wrote, he in fact changed some phrases back to 1662. He insisted that the chalice should be mixed, and the words 'that we and all others who shall be partakers of this holy communion' replace 'that whosoever shall be partakers of this holy communion'. Seabury tried to impose his Communion office by Episcopal Supremacy, and seems to have failed. However, trial liturgies were for the moment the order of the day.

In July 1789 deputies from the seven Southern States met at Christ Church, Philadelphia, to ratify the 1786 liturgy. They then postponed action in the hope that New England would participate. On 4 August Massachusetts and New Hampshire each elected a deputy, and Connecticut too was to be represented. In the meantime, William Smith now wrote to all the deputies urging them to adopt a more primitive type of liturgy, drawing on antiquity. The bishops were to be part of the process, but would not be able to impose. Seabury brought with him a notebook which contained various new prayers, a form for consecrating churches by Thomas Wilson, Bishop of Sodor and Man, and a Deed of Consecration for a new church. He also advocated the Scottish Communion prayer of consecration.

The Convention reconvened on 29 September. The bishops tried hard to get the Athanasian Creed readmitted, but the Deputies would not allow it. Seabury was still wedded to the Scottish Communion prayer of consecration. In the end, his proposal was accepted. The

120 Marshall, *One, Catholic and Apostolic*, p. 172.

deputies were persuaded by the chairman, Dr William Smith, himself a Scot. It is said that as soon as there seemed to be dissension, Smith told them to listen, and he read the whole prayer of consecration, in his Scots brogue, and all thought it beautiful and accepted it. Here accent rather than theological debate won the day. The final form agreed upon at this convention was to be used in the Church from 1 October 1790. It was a less liberal book than that of 1786. The psalter was restored, but provision was made for selections. The word 'priest' was restored in some places, but not all. The rubrics about ornaments and chancels were omitted. In Morning and Evening Prayer there were two new opening sentences, a small change in the exhortation. The words 'absolution' and again 'priest' were restored. The words in the Lord's Prayer 'on earth' replaced 'in earth', as in Wesley's Abridgement. At Evening Prayer both Magnificat and Nunc Dimittis were omitted. Marion Hatchett wrote:

> It has been fashionable to minimize the influence of the Proposed Book (1786) upon the Prayer Book of 1789. The 1789 book restored the whole psalter, the teaching of baptismal regeneration, and the use of the word priest. It incorporated a Eucharistic Prayer from the Eastern . . . Non-Juror Scottish tradition. But the basis for the Preface, Lectionary, Occasional Prayers and Thanksgivings, and hymns, and the revision of almost every one of the Offices was the version of the Proposed Book. Other sources included not only the 1662 book but also *Free and Candid Disquisitions*, *A New Liturgy* (1749), Jeremy Taylor's *The Rule and Exercise of Holy Dying*, Bishop Gibson's *Family Devotion*, Bishop Seabury's notebook, and the proposals of various state conventions.[121]

Thus, alongside the 1662 Book of Common Prayer, there now existed two other Anglican forms – one in Scotland based directly on the Communion service of 1637, and an American revision, though neither departing too greatly from the Cranmerian and Restoration texts. In the Hutchins sermon of 1752, Samuel Shuckford noted the biblical nature of the Prayer Book, in its provision for confession of sin and the recitation of the psalms. One of its 'excellencies' was 'in that its Service is performed in short Prayers; and that these are so composed as to fill our Minds continually with a right Sense of almighty God, and of our blessed Saviour'.[122] Though it was not absolutely perfect, nevertheless,

---

121 Hatchett, *The Making of the First American Book of Common Prayer*, p. 129.
122 Samuel Shuckford, *The Use of a Liturgy, and the Excellency of the Liturgy of the Church of England Considered, in a Sermon . . .* (London: 1752), p. 18.

'its Worship is so framed, as to answer well all the Ends of a reasonable Service of God, truly to set forth his Honour and Glory, by leading his People, to believe and to do *as becometh the Gospel of Christ*'.[123] In the sermon for 1760, Henry Stebbing argued that a public liturgy seems essential for maintaining public devotion, and there was no more need to change the Church of England liturgy than there was for changing the government. In conclusion he stated:

> The liturgy of the Church of England is a treasure of Christian devotion, both publick and private. And those who are true christians and soberly devout have always esteemed and used it as such. As to those who, by making alterations in it, would lead the way to an entire abolition of it; and to others who, under the pretence of a more convenient liturgy, have a secret wish for the removal of what a Christian Church cannot part with, and an Established Church ought not; they are Both out of the question; because they are no friends to the Church of England, or not sound friends to Christianity.[124]

Many in the eighteenth century would agree with East Apthorp that the liturgy of the Church of England – and its Scottish and American variants – was indeed 'so rational, so touching, so eloquent, so pious, devout and scriptural'.[125]

---

123 Shuckford, *The Use of a Liturgy*, p. 22.

124 Henry Stebbing, *A Sermon Preached at the Parish Church of St. Mary-le-Bow, on St. Mark's Day, 1760* (London: 1760), p. 19.

125 East Apthorp, *The Excellence of the Liturgy of the Church of England: A Sermon at the Church of St. Mary le Bow* (London: 1778), p. 21.

Chapter 5

The nineteenth century: undermining the sure foundation

The Book of Common Prayer moved into the early nineteenth century unscathed from the demands of High Churchmen, Newtonians and Evangelicals for any reform. In a sermon on the excellency of the liturgy of the Church of England in 1804, the Revd S. Crowther told the assembled congregation: 'That the compilers of our Liturgy have established their doctrine upon *"the foundations of the apostles and prophets"*, is evident from the spirit and tendency of the whole of the Common Prayer', and he added that it was a book inferior only to the Bible itself.[1] The Victorian era, however, saw new and irreversible assaults on the liturgical adequacy of the Book of Common Prayer as well as on the manner in which the services were performed. The Report of the Royal Commission on Ecclesiastical Discipline (1906) would indeed note that there was:

> no justification for any doubt that in the large majority of parishes the work of the Church is being quietly and diligently performed by clergy who are entirely loyal to the principles of the English Reformation as expressed in the Book of Common Prayer.[2]

But more tellingly, the Commission noted:

---

1 *A Sermon Preached at St. Mary-Le-Bow, by the Rev. S. Crowther, A.M. Vicar of Christ Church in the City of London on St. Mark's Day, April 25 1804* (London: J. Adlard 1804), pp. 23, 18.
2 <www.anglicanhistory.org/pwra/rced11.html> (accessed 20 January 2012).

the law of public worship in the Church of England is too narrow for the religious life of the present generation. It needlessly condemns much which a great section of Church people, including many of her most devoted members, value; and modern thought and feeling are characterised by a care for ceremonial, a sense of dignity in worship, and an appreciation of the continuity of the Church, which were not similarly felt at the time when the law took its present shape.[3]

The consequences of that particular observation, which would end the hegemony of the Book of Common Prayer, were to unfold in the twentieth century.

THE 'EXCELLENT LITURGY'

The esteem with which Crowther and others held the Prayer Book was echoed by many writers throughout the nineteenth century. During 1802 in Wakefield Parish Church, Thomas Rogers gave a series of lectures on the service of Morning Prayer which were published in 1816. In the Introduction, Rogers eschewed any originality for the substance of his lectures and explained that they were intended to impress upon the minds of the recipients 'a due sense of the excellency and utility of the Liturgy of our Church'.[4] He exhorted his readership:

> These excellent compositions of the Common Prayer, have a strong claim to your serious attention, not only for the plainness and simplicity of their style, and the admirable order in which they are arranged, but for their direct tendency to produce and establish in you that humility and spirituality of mind which every real Christian would wish to possess, when approaching the throne of Grace . . . Suffer me to exhort you, as members of the Established Church, to hold fast the form of sound words.[5]

Similarly, Charles Simeon, the noted Cambridge Evangelical, preached four sermons on the Book of Common Prayer, which were published in 1812 under the title *The Excellency of the Liturgy in Four Discourses*. Presumably having in mind Evangelical scruples over regeneration in the baptismal rite and the words 'sure and certain hope of the resurrection'

---

3 <www.anglicanhistory.org/pwra/rced11.html> (accessed 20 January 2012).
4 Thomas Rogers, *Lectures Delivered in the Parish Church of Wakefield in the Year 1802 on that part of the Liturgy of the Church of England contained in the Morning Prayer* (London: 1816), p. xi.
5 Rogers, *Lectures*, pp. iv–v.

in the Burial rite, Simeon admitted that the liturgy was not absolutely perfect. He nevertheless considered:

> as one of the highest excellencies of our Liturgy, that it is calculated to make us wise, intelligent, and sober Christians; it marks a golden mean; it affects and inspires a meek, humble, modest, sober piety, equally remote from the coldness of a formalist, the self-importance of a systematic dogmatist, and the unhallowed fervour of a wild enthusiast. A *tender seriousness, a meek devotion* and an *humble joy*, are the qualities which it was intended, and is calculated, to produce in all her members.[6]

As his title reinforced, Simeon defended what he termed the 'unrivalled excellence' of the Book of Common Prayer.[7] John Skinner, the incumbent of Camerton, Somerset, claimed that 'even those who could not read might easily join in the excellent Liturgy of the Church'.[8] In a sermon preached in 1822, he contrasted the educated clergy of the Church of England with many uneducated local Methodist preachers and rhetorically asked, 'Is it the same thing to attend the crude, undigested effusion of a cobbler or a collier, under the name of prayer, as the beautiful service of our Liturgy?'[9] Joseph Leech, the Bristol newspaper publisher, on his rides to services in the villages around Bristol in 1845, encountered a cleric en route to preach at Iron Acton, who in conversation purportedly asserted:

> One page of our beautiful liturgy, uttered in the spirit that God requires, and the Church directs, 'with a lowly, penitent, and obedient heart', would fall like refreshing dews on the soul, and leave us in a holier, happier frame of mind than a hundred discourses. The best and most elaborately prepared sermon is to my mind a poor, bald, and meagre composition, compared with the touching beauty and true piety of a single sentence of the Litany.[10]

---

6 Charles Simeon, *The Excellency of the Liturgy, in Four Discourses. Preached Before the University of Cambridge, in November 1811* (Cambridge: 1812), p. 54. See also Andrew Atherstone, *Charles Simeon on The Excellency of the Liturgy*, Alcuin Club/GROW Joint Liturgical Study 72 (Norwich: Hymns Ancient and Modern 2011).

7 Simeon, *The Excellency of the Liturgy*, p. 23.

8 John Skinner, *Journal of a Somerset Rector 1803–1834*, ed. Howard and Peter Coombs (Oxford: Oxford University Press 1984), p. 269 (entry for 1824).

9 Skinner, *Journal of a Somerset Rector*, p. 213.

10 Joseph Leech, *Rural Rides of the Bristol Churchgoer*, ed. Alan Sutton (Stroud: Nonsuch Publishing Ltd 2004), pp. 171–2. Journalistic licence is no doubt at work here, giving voice to Leech's own views.

Leech himself told the account of a particular individual who had been brought up in the Dissenting tradition, but at the age of 18 first encountered 'our inimitable Liturgy',

> which came upon him with its piety breathing and comprehensive petitions, the simple and beautiful majesty of its addresses to the Almighty, the contrite humility which pervades its penitential confessions, and the fervour with which it enables faith to express itself – all these, presented to him for the first time in the full force of freshness and novelty, made such an impression on him that from that day forward he was a churchman, declaring that he could never again bear to listen to the bald and erratic extemporisings of Dissent.[11]

In his 1848 sermons on the Prayer Book, Frederick Denison Maurice stated that 'I hope you will never hear from me any such phrases as our "excellent or incomparable" Liturgy' because it was not there to be praised but used.[12] Although he rejected the term 'excellent', Maurice held that the Prayer Book was at the heart of English national identity and morality; along with many other nineteenth-century churchmen and churchwomen, he regarded the liturgy as essential to the English Church.[13]

THE BOOK AS USED

John Skinner of Camerton recorded in his journal for Sunday 6 January 1828, 'I read the prayers as usual'.[14] But what was 'usual'? Contemporary journals and diaries such as Skinner's and the newspaper articles of Joseph Leech allow us to flesh out the Prayer Book services as performed during the first part of the nineteenth century.

The rubrics of the 1662 Book of Common Prayer insisted that Morning Prayer, the Litany and Ante-Communion were to be celebrated

---

11 Leech, *Rural Rides*, p. 195.

12 Frederick Denison Maurice, *The Prayer-Book considered especially in Reference to the Roman System. Nineteen Sermons preached in the Chapel of Lincoln's Inn 1848* (London: Macmillan and Co. 1893), p. 6.

13 See further, Andrew Braddock, *The Role of the Book of Common Prayer in the Formation of Modern Anglican Church Identity: A Study of English Parochial Worship, 1750–1850* (Lewiston, NY: Edwin Mellen Press 2010). For a contemporary argument that the Prayer Book was 'implicated in establishment, development, and consolidation of the national identity of early modern England', see Timothy Rosendale, *Liturgy and Literature in the Making of Protestant England* (Cambridge: Cambridge University Press 2007).

14 Skinner, *Journal of a Somerset Rector*, p. 309.

every Sunday, and the three rites were celebrated consecutively. Communion itself was in most churches only quarterly. When Communion was administered, only those wishing to receive stayed for that part of the service. The surplice was worn for all services but, although not sanctioned by rubric, it had become the custom for the priest to remove the surplice and put on a black gown for preaching the sermon. At the evening service the catechism was expounded; because it was a shorter service, it may account for the higher attendance. William Holland, incumbent of Over Stowey, Somerset, noted in 1800 that 'In Country Parishes there are always more in the afternoon than in the morning', which was also the experience of the Revd Francis Witts in the 1820s at Upper Slaughter in the Cotswolds, and of Joseph Leech around Bristol in 1845.[15] The 'occasional' services were often celebrated on Sundays too. William Holland recorded on 1 April 1804, Easter Day:

> Not many at Church but a good many at the Sacrament, two or three and twenty. The Church at Asholt very full indeed. I received three children into the Church first and then I read the Baptism over again for another child, the elder of the first three was ten years old. The Duty of this day almost fatigued me, I had prayers twice, a Sacrament, two Sermons, two Christenings, and a Churching and so I went into Mr Blake's and they gave me a glass of mead and I drank tea there.[16]

Francis Witts had a christening and churching after the morning service on Sunday 12 April 1807 at Erchfont, and the following Sunday a burial after the evening service.[17] On Sunday 20 September 1820 John Skinner recorded that after Evening Prayer he buried a child who had died from the measles.[18] Morning and evening services usually needed the assistance of the church clerk who led the congregational responses and sometimes led the singing where there was no parish band or singers. Most parishes had a clerk, and a good many also had the singers and a band.

---

15 Jack Ayres (ed.), *Paupers and Pig Killers: The Diary of William Holland, a Somerset Parson, 1799–1818* (Gloucester: Alan Sutton Publishing 1984), p. 33; Francis E. Witts, *The Complete Diary of a Cotswold Parson. Vol. 2: The Curate and Rector* (Chalfont: Amberley Publishing 2008); Joseph Leech, *Rural Rides, passim*.

16 Ayres (ed.), *Paupers and Pig Killers*, pp. 95–6. Though Holland wrote 'Asholt', the name today seems to be Aisholt.

17 Witts, *The Complete Diary*, Vol. 2, pp. 109, 111.

18 Skinner, *Journal of a Somerset Rector*, p. 138.

At St George's, Somerset, Joseph Leech stated that the Vicar was 'an admirable reader, impressive without ostentation', and at Slimbridge, where two curates occupied the reading desk and divided the duty, the service combined 'the utmost solemnity and simplicity'.[19] Leech also described the dignity of a service at St John's, Torquay, at which three priests and Bishop Henry Phillpotts officiated. Of Phillpotts, Leech observed:

> At the rehearsal of the Commandments he advanced to the steps of the altar, and facing the congregation, read, while the three clergymen knelt towards the East. His delivery of the Decalogue was beautifully judicious: without any appearance of acting, no acting could yet be employed to produce more effect: conscious of his want of strength, there was an earnest and emphatic effort to make up for his physical debility, as was evinced by the impressive shake of the head and the upraised hand at the close of almost every period.[20]

Not all clergy and churches, though, were meticulous about dignity, decency and good order. Henry Moule, Vicar of Fordington in Wiltshire, told Francis Kilvert something of the state of things when he had first arrived in that parish in the late 1820s:

> No man had ever been known to receive the Holy Communion except the parson, the clerk and the sexton. There were 16 women communicants and most of them went away when he refused to pay them for coming. They had been accustomed there at some place in the neighbourhood to pass the cup to each other with a nod of the head. At one church there were two male communicants. When the cup was given to the first he touched his forelock and said, 'Here's your good health, Sir'. The other said, 'Here's the good health of the Lord Jesus Christ'.
> One day there was christening and no water in the Font. 'Water, Sir!' said the clerk in astonishment. 'The last parson never used no water. He spit into his hand.'[21]

19 Leech, *Rural Rides*, pp. 221, 232.
20 Joseph Leech, *The Church-Goer's Rural Rides* (Bristol: 1851, 3rd edn), pp. 245–50, p. 247.
21 William Plomer (ed.), *Kilvert's Diary 1870–1879. Selections from the Diary of the Rev. Francis Kilvert* (New York: The Macmillan Company 1947), pp. 279–80.

In his 1845 visit to Bleadon church, Joseph Leech recorded:

> The Rev. David Williams was in the reading-desk when I entered,
> going through the service, just as you would suppose the service to
> be gone through in such a church as I have described. He seemed
> to be suffering from flatulency, for at every other verse he was
> obliged to pause, afterwards wiping his mouth with an old brown
> handkerchief, and occasionally varying the act by using the sleeve of
> his surplice (which was far from clean) for the purpose. There was no
> singing or musical service whatever, the Rev. Gentleman objecting
> to it, as I have heard, on the grounds that it affects his head, but he
> has never complained of it affecting his heart . . . he has occasionally
> paused in the midst of the Psalms, to correct the clerk for reading too
> fast or too loud, but by way of reprisals the clerk has sometimes had
> to correct the parson for reading the wrong psalm, an incident of this
> kind having occurred, I think, on Whitsunday last.[22]

At Yatton church, Leech complained of the speed with which the parson read the service. He commented:

> There is an old joke of an Oxford spark saying he would give any
> man the Creed and beat him before he came to the end of the Litany.
> I really believe from the rate at which he read, the incumbent of
> Yatton might do this with ease: I attempted to keep up with him,
> but finding the pace impossible I closed my book, and listened with
> resignation . . . I cannot bear to hear the beautiful prayers of the
> church, which so abound in fervent appeals, in deep devotional and
> penitential expressions, and awful epithets, being skipped through by
> clergyman and congregation, as if they were performing a mere daily
> task, the primary object of which was expedition.[23]

Perhaps with such incumbents in mind, Richard Cull, a tutor in elo-
cution, had in 1840 published *Garrick's Mode of Reading the Liturgy of
the Church of England*. David Garrick, the famous eighteenth-century
actor, had instructed some clergy in the art of speech delivery; the
manuscript notes of one cleric were published in 1797, and now repub-
lished by Cull. Cull noted:

---

22 Leech, *Rural Rides*, pp. 297–8.
23 Leech, *Rural Rides*, p. 180.

It is a subject of deep regret that this prominent duty (publicly reading service) is commonly so ill performed, even by Clergymen of
high mental endowments and of great acquirements, and the object
of the present work is to supply the Clergy with some principles to
guide them in their public reading.[24]

Thus with the opening three words of the exhortation to confession
at Morning Prayer, 'Dearly beloved brethren', the advice Garrick had
given was:

> Here, make a pause much longer than the comma, or, indeed, than
> the time which is thought to be necessary after a semicolon. – Then
> proceed with a *solemn dignity* of tone, and with a *tenor* of *smooth,*
> *regular* delivery.
> *the scripture moveth us in sundry places to acknowledge –*
> Not ac*know*ledge (the second syllable very long,) as it is pro-
> nounced by many.[25]

For the Communion (second service) he suggested a low but strong
and audible tone for the Lord's Prayer, and for the Collect of Purity, 'Be
very *awful,* and *reverentially impressive* in commencements of this kind',
and 'Conclude it with a *round* voice, very *articulately,* and with much
deliberation'.[26]
In the original Preface that was reprinted by Cull, the intention was
to redress 'the slovenly and irreverent manner in which the Common
Prayer was read by the generality of Divines'.[27]
But parish clerks also had a crucial role too. Joseph Leech, on his
1844 visit to Redcliff Church, opined:

> I don't know whether or not parish clerks may be out of my prov-
> ince: if it were not taking a liberty, however, I would meekly beg that
> the rev. the vicar might devote a spare hour to teaching the clerk to
> deport himself with more reverend humility in his business: he lolled
> upon the left hand with an air of the utmost complacency, and cast-
> ing a side-long glance towards the ceiling said, 'We beseech thee to

24 Richard Cull, *Garrick's Mode of Reading the Liturgy of the Church of England*
(London: John Parker 1840), p. vii.
25 Cull, *Garrick's Mode,* pp. 67–8.
26 Cull, *Garrick's Mode,* pp. 131–2.
27 Cull, *Garrick's Mode,* p. 63.

hear us, good Lord,' as if it did not greatly concern him whether his prayers were complied with or not.[28]

Writing in 1803, William Jones, incumbent of Broxbourne, Hertfordshire, complained that the deputy parish clerk, a tailor called Mr Rogers, kept losing his place in the book and fumbling over words:

> Upon the whole, he made a sad, bungling piece of work of it, & if he acquits himself no better in his tailoring capacity than he does in supplying a Church-clerk's place, he must be what is called a miserable hand, a mere *botcher*. The whimsically wretched mistakes he made, & which I have heard too many fixed in that high office make, in reading the psalms, etc, are incredible . . . In some parishes, one might suppose that miserable reading was considered as a first-rate qualification in a parish-clerk. They *jabber*, as fast as they can pelt out the words, right or wrong.[29]

The parish musicians and singers, using the metrical psalms of the old version of Sternhold and Hopkins or the new version of Tate and Brady, often preferring the folk music style of 'fuguing', could make or mar the service.[30] The pipe organ and barrel organ were becoming more common in the early nineteenth century, though most churches used a medley of instruments. Although hymns were not unknown, they were regarded by many bishops as expressions of Methodism, and discouraged.[31] At Abbott's Leigh in 1845 Leech noted that in the West Gallery there were a big fiddle, a flute and a bassoon, 'together with sundry persons who perform on these musical implements, severally and respectively – I wish I could add respectably'.[32] William Holland recorded on Sunday 15 April 1804 that at Asholt Church (Somerset),

> A disagreeable fellow was playing his fiddle in the Church when I came in, without tune or harmony, intending I presume to accompany

---

28 Leech, *Rural Rides*, pp. 41–2.

29 O. F. Christie (ed.), *The Diary of the Revd. William Jones 1777–1821. Curate and Vicar of Broxbourne and the Hamlet of Hoddesdon 1781–1821* (London: Brentano's 1929), pp. 149–50.

30 See Christopher Turner (ed.), *Georgian Psalmody 1: The West Gallery Tradition* (Corby Glen: SG Publishing in association with Anglia Polytechnic University 1997).

31 See Thomas K. McCart, *The Matter and Manner of Praise: The Controversial Evolution of Hymnody in the Church of England 1760–1820* (Lanham, MD: Scarecrow Press 1998).

32 Leech, *Rural Rides*, p. 243.

the Psalm Singers. I however ordered him to stop his noise which he would hardly do and then he began trying his discordant hautboy.[33]

John Skinner had to ban his singers when they arrived intoxicated, and who, 'being offended because I would not suffer them to chaunt the service after the First Lesson, put on their hats and left the Church'.[34] Joseph Leech, noting that in some 'primitive' parishes the custom was to write the psalms to be sung on a slate which was hung over the gallery, recalled one occasion at Isle Brewers:

> the clerk, when he had partly given out the psalms, discovered that the usual telegraph had not been lowered; his announcement, therefore, when interrupted, ran thus: 'Let us sing to the praise and . . ., I say (looking up to the gallery), why don't thee hang out the slate there?' I mention this incident only to illustrate that parish orchestras look for the most part upon themselves in the light of mere parish musicians, and have little or no sense of the solemnity of their situation or of that portion of the service which appertains to them.[35]

But there were success stories too. Holland spoke well of the singers and two flautists in 1805, and in December they had new instruments from London.[36] Leech's visit to Thornbury, Christmas 1844, reveals that this church had an organ and organist, as well as a gallery choir. The voluntary was 'dashing', and followed by the Gloria sung by the gallery singers, though perhaps this was because it was Christmas and because the Mayor and Corporation were in attendance.[37] Furthermore, at least some cathedrals maintained a reasonable choral tradition.[38] Help for improvement of lay devotion was also not neglected. In 1808 a new corrected edition of *Directions for a Devout and Decent Behaviour in the Public Worship of God; more particularly in the Use of the Common Prayer appointed by the Church of England* was published, the tract itself already being in its sixteenth edition in 1761; and further editions appeared in 1821 and 1823, suggesting that this was a very popular work. However, even while Leech was making his 1845 visits, the liturgical practices of

---

33 Ayres (ed.), *Paupers and Pig Killers*, p. 96.
34 Skinner, *Journal of a Somerset Rector*, p. 200; cf. p. 162.
35 Joseph Leech, *The Bristol Church Goer: His Visits to Bitton, &c.* (Bristol: John Riddler 1849), p. 16.
36 Leech, *The Bristol Church Goer*, pp. 120, 125.
37 Leech, *Rural Rides*, pp. 207ff.
38 William J. Gatens, *Victorian Cathedral Music in Theory and Practice* (Cambridge: Cambridge University Press 1986).

parish churches across the country were beginning to undergo considerable change. Isaac Williams, in his prefatory thoughts to his poems published in 1842, wrote:

> The Church, 'tis thought, is wakening through the land
> And seeking vent for the o'erloaded hearts
> Which she has kindled, – pours her forth anew, –
> Breathes life in ancient worship, –from their graves
> Summons the slumbering Arts to wait on her,
> Music and Architecture, varied forms
> Of Painting, Sculpture, and of Poetry.[39]

Williams alluded rather obliquely here to what was, in fact, the double tsunami of Tractarianism and the Ecclesiologists, the aftershocks of which would completely alter the inherited pattern and forms of Church of England worship.[40]

THE PRAYER BOOK ASSAILED: TRACTARIANISM

It is doubtful whether those who gathered at Hadleigh Rectory and planned the *Tracts for the Times* could have foreseen the liturgical revolution that would ensue. Calls for shortening the Prayer Book services had already begun in the latter decades of the seventeenth century and periodically throughout the eighteenth century. Such calls were renewed at the beginning of the nineteenth century by those viewed as representing a more liberal voice – Connop Thirlwall, Charles Wodehouse and Edward Berens. They argued for an abridgement of the morning services, the omission of the Athanasian Creed and rubrics such as mentioning the dipping of children in baptism.[41] The Tractarians initially called for no changes at all, only the enforcement of the rubrics regardless of whether or not they had long fallen into abeyance. In Tract 3 Newman argued that only rationalists and Evangelicals wanted alteration to erode the Church, and he returned to this theme in Tracts 38

---

39 Isaac Williams, *The Baptistery, or, The Way of Eternal Life* (Oxford: John Henry Parker 1842), p. x.

40 Nigel Yates, *Anglican Ritualism in Victorian Britain 1830–1910* (Oxford: Oxford University Press 1999); *The Anglican Revival in Victorian Portsmouth* (Portsmouth: Grosvenor Press for Portsmouth City Council 1983); Dominic Janes, *Victorian Reformation: The Fight over Idolatry in the Church of England 1840–1860* (New York: Oxford University Press 2009); Teresa Berger, *Liturgie- Spiegel der Kirche: Eine systematische-theologische Analyse des liturgischen Gedankenguts im Traktarianismus*, Forschungen zur Systematischen und ökumenischen Theologie 52 (Göttingen: Vandenhoeck and Ruprecht 1986).

41 R. C. D. Jasper, *Prayer Book Revision in England 1800–1900* (London: SPCK 1954).

and 41. In Tract 9 Hurrel Froude turned his attention to the plea for shortening services. He retorted that they had already been shortened at the Reformation. Furthermore, they were intended for daily use, but now had become weekly. The logical trend would be that they would become monthly and then disappear altogether. The Tractarian ploy was to observe the rubrics diligently so that bishops in turn would enforce them. However, when High Church bishops such as C. J. Blomfield of London in 1842 and Henry Phillpotts of Exeter in 1845 – neither of whom were Tractarians – attempted simply to enforce the wearing of the surplice for preaching, they met with protest, and resistence.[42] The Ornaments Rubric, which had lain dormant since 1559, was to become a storm centre and was appealed to for support of practices from lighted candles on the altar to full eucharistic vestments and incense. The Tracts also made appeal to the pre-Reformation medieval services, and later Tractarians would begin to interpret the Prayer Book through the lenses of the medieval liturgies, and even replace Prayer Book formularies with those of the medieval rites or the contemporary Catholic rites. Newman had begun using the Roman Breviary in 1837, a practice that Pusey adopted in 1839.[43] Pusey defended baptismal regeneration in Tracts 67–69, and in Tract 81 defended the concepts of real presence and sacrifice in the Eucharist, which many regarded as smuggling popery into the Church of England.

If the Oxford Tracts were one assault, the Cambridge Ecclesiologists were another. The evangelical Francis Close astutely observed:

> as Romanism is taught *Analytically* at Oxford, it is taught *Artistically* at Cambridge – that it is inculcated theoretically, in tracts at one University, and it is *sculptured, painted* and *graven* at the other . . . in a word, that the 'Ecclesiologist' of Cambridge is identical in doctrine with the Oxford *Tracts for the Times*.[44]

---

42 L. E. Ellsworth, *Charles Lowder and the Ritualist Movement* (London: Darton, Longman and Todd 1982), p. 8, citing their Diocesan Charges. The Revd Dr John Allen Giles recorded in March 1855, 'A letter from Mr. Adams told me that Mr. Newman the new curate at Bampton now preached in his surplice, which was thought a novelty and was much talked about.' Leech had remarked that the Revd Williams at Bleadon had kept his surplice on for the sermon, simply because, like many others, it saved the necessity of changing. Elsewhere it became a liturgical controversy. David Bromwich (ed.), *The Diary & Memoires of John Allen Giles* (Taunton: Somerset Record Office 2000), p. 319; Leech, *Rural Rides*, p. 298.

43 Ellsworth, *Charles Lowder and the Ritualist Movement*, p. 10.

44 F. Close, *The Restoration of Churches is the Restoration of Popery: A Sermon* (London: Hatchard 1844), p. 4.

In May 1839 John Mason Neale and Benjamin Webb had founded the Cambridge Camden Society, later to become the Ecclesiological Society. While by no means the first to promote neo-Gothic architecture,[45] the Society's publications promoted this style as the only true Christian style, and their principles would be embraced by William Butterfield and Richard Carpenter. Christopher Webster observes:

> Within a generation, Anglican churches and the worship within them, were indeed undergoing a far-reaching process of transformation and *The Ecclesiologist* could claim with a good deal of justifiable pride in its last edition in 1868 'we have the satisfaction of retiring from the field as victors'.[46]

Both Neale and Webb were concerned with the interiors as well as exteriors, and strengthened the growing criticism of box pews and rented pews.[47] But they were also interested in ceremonial. Neale and Webb published the translation of Durandus of Mende's *The Symbolism of Churches and Church Ornaments* in 1843 and Camden Society members edited *Hierurgia Anglicana* between 1843 and 1848, recording the survival of pre-Reformation ornaments and rituals in the Church of England. These works coalesced with the convictions of Tractarians, such as J. R. Bloxam, who has been described as 'the real originator of the ceremonial revival in the Church of England'.[48] Geoffrey Brandwood notes that although Webb never adopted vestments or incense, Neale, after he started the sisterhood of St Margaret's, East Grinstead, did, and also introduced exposition of the sacrament.[49] Recently, George

---

45 For varied styles, including Gothic revival, see M. H. Port, *Six Hundred New Churches: The Church Building Commission 1818–1856* (Reading: Spire Books 2006); Nigel Yates, *Buildings, Faith, and Worship: The Liturgical Arrangement of Anglican Churches 1600–1900* (Oxford: Oxford University Press 1991).

46 Christopher Webster, "'Absolutely Wretched"': Camdenian Attitudes to the Late Georgian Church' in Christopher Webster and John Elliott (eds), *'A Church as it Should Be': The Cambridge Camden Society and Its Influence* (Donington: Shaun Tyas 2000), pp. 1–21, p. 2. Cf. *The Ecclesiologist* 29 (1868), pp. 315–16.

47 See Trevor Cooper and Sarah Brown (eds), *Pews, Benches and Chairs: Church Seating in English Churches from the Fourteenth Century to the Present* (Donington: Ecclesiological Society/Shaun Tyas 2011).

48 A. Symondson, 'Theology, Worship and the Late Victorian Church' in C. Brooks and A. Saint (eds), *The Victorian Church: Architecture and Society* (Manchester: Manchester University Press 1995), p. 195.

49 Geoffrey K. Brandwood, "'Mumeries of a Popish Character'" – the Camdenians and Early Victorian Worship' in Webster and Elliott (eds), *'A Church as it Should Be'*, pp. 62–97, pp. 76–7.

Herring has questioned whether the later ritual developments were a true development of Tractarianism or a diversion from its main theological and pastoral purposes.[50] He notes how in the wake of Orby Shipley's essays on Ritualism, the Evangelical *Record* observed that the doctrines of the Ritualists were now 'asserted with a boldness at which most High Churchmen would have stood aghast twenty years ago'.[51] The point, though, seems academic, since the second-generation Tractarians did indeed morph into Ritualism.

Few churches adopted such extreme Catholic ceremonial in the 1850s, but the wide ripple effects should not be underestimated. For example, the *Essex Standard* newspaper of 21 February 1845 carried an article under the title 'Rubrical Changes at Witham', which began:

> The changes in the performance of Divine service introduced in this county immediately after, and some of them in accordance with the suggestions and directions of the Bishop of the Diocese, were carried out more extensively at Witham than in other places; and on the chancel of the church being repaired, a cross and other matters, novel in Protestant churches, were introduced. These changes occasioned the most uncomfortable sentiments in the minds of the parishioners; but, as in the generality of instances, the objections to these unwelcome changes were suppressed, partly from respect to the minister, and partly from the commendable wish to avoid disputes. Recently, however, it has been respectfully intimated to the Vicar, the Rev. John Bramston, that a return to the old form of service was desirable: and it was suggested that a private meeting of the Vicar and his leading parishioners should be held on the subject. This was done, and in the evening of the 10 instant between 20 and 30 of the principal inhabitants met Mr. Bramston at the house of one of the churchwardens, when the various points were discussed in a friendly spirit. Upwards of twenty objections were presented to the reverend gentleman, including the preaching in the surplice, the offertory, the cross erected at the altar, the credence or side table for the elements of the holy communion, the placing of the alms basin on the altar at All Saints Church, the manner of singing in the morning service, the minister turning from the people during prayer, the performance of baptism in the congregation, the

---

50 George Herring, *The Oxford Movement in Practice: The Tractarian Parochial World from the 1830s to the 1870s* (Oxford: Oxford University Press 2016).

51 Herring, *The Oxford Movement in Practice*, p. 195.

application of the alms for other purposes than those of the poor of the parish, and other points.[52]

Bramston, later to be Dean of Winchester, was no extreme ritualist.[53] He inherited from his predecessor the scheme to build a new church in the town centre, since the old parish church of St Nicolas was some distance away. The building committee rejected George Gilbert Scott in favour of the Norwich architect John Brown, a decision that cost them dearly.[54] However, when the new All Saints Church was opened, Bramston seems to have taken the opportunity to introduce, both there and at St Nicolas, some of the newer, more moderate fashions in worship.

Others did similarly. In 1850 Lady Charlotte Guest complained of the Revd Walter Ponsonby, 'Ist., the intoning of the service, 2ndly., the print of a crucifix and dead Christ on the Altar of the Mortuary Chapel, 3rdly., the total disuse of the gown which, however unimportant of itself, I looked upon as a badge of party. I remonstrated on the Popish tendency of his formalities.'[55] Ponsonby 'referred to his obligation to follow the rubric, and seemed greatly shocked and hurt at being suspected of anything like a Romanising tendency'.[56]

Benjamin Armstrong, Vicar of Dereham 1850–88, noted the changes made in 1855 at St Ethelburga's, Bishopsgate:

Mr. Rodwell has Holy Communion every Sunday; a surpliced choir; intones the service; has nothing but Gregorian tones; rings the Sanctus bell in service; preaches in his surplice; kneels east and, in short, has adopted the whole feature of Catholicity of which our system is capable.[57]

---

52 'Rubrical Changes at Witham', *Essex Standard*, 21 February 1845, no pagination, but sheet 2. The paper also printed the sermon that Bramston preached the following Sunday defending the changes. He took his text from 1 Cor. 14.1, 20, 26, 33, 40. Sheets 3 and 4.

53 Witham Church did not regularly use eucharistic vestments until 1968 when they were introduced by Canon Leslie John Derrett. During my curacy at St Nicolas, Witham (1975–78), I borrowed High Mass vestments for festivals, though the ceremonial was hardly a High Mass by Knott's *Ritual Notes* standard. William van Mildert had been curate of Witham. The Revd John Suddards was Team Rector of Witham for ten years and in 2011 left for Thornbury, one of the churches visited by Leech. Sadly, John Suddards was murdered at Thornbury in February 2012.

54 Janet Gyford, *A History of Witham* (Witham: Janet Gyford 2005), pp. 73–5.

55 The Earl of Bessborough (ed.), *Lady Charlotte Guest: Extracts from her Journal 1833–1852* (London: John Murray 1950), p. 238.

56 Earl of Bessborough (ed.), *Lady Charlotte Guest*, p. 239.

57 Herbert B. J. Armstrong (ed.), *Armstrong's Norfolk Diary: Further Passages from the Diary of the Reverend Benjamin John Armstrong* (London: Hodder and Stoughton 1963), p. 54.

Surpliced choirs and good music, and even the wearing of the surplice for sermons in one or two places, predate the Tractarian movement, such as at Leeds, where the Revd Richard Fawcett formed a surplice choir in 1818, and Richard Waldo Sibthorp did so at St James's Church, Ryde, in 1838.[58] But fear of Romanism also led to disruptions and protests. The hymn writer and cleric Sabine Baring-Gould noted of an Evensong in St George's in the East, in East London during 1859 or 1860:

> At Evensong a pair of candles lighted, a surplice choir in the stalls, and the surplice worn in the pulpit.
> Directly the doors were opened, the mob surged into the church, scrambling into the pews, some over their backs, and into the galleries. Police were stationed down the middle passage, but had been given orders to do nothing unless personal violence were offered. There ensued talking, laughing, and cracking of vulgar jokes before the service began.
> When choir and clergy entered there burst forth booing and hooting, and during the service unseemly mimicry of the intoning, and indecent parodies chanted as responses. When the choir turned East at the Creed, the mob turned bodily west.[59]

However, there is little doubt that the movement gave such practices further impetus and they also became a part of worship even in churches that most certainly disowned Tractarianism.

In 1869 Benjamin Armstrong visited the rector of Whissonsett, and noted:

> He showed us his banners, eucharistic vestments and scarlet cassock and laced cotta for the thurifer! Who could ever suppose that such things would be used again and in the heart of Norfolk! The object of the Ritualists is to make our services as glorious and beautiful as any in the world.[60]

---

58 Bernarr Rainbow, *The Choral Revival in the Anglican Church (1839–1872)* (New York: Oxford University Press 1970), p. 3; see also Michael Trott, *The Life of Richard Waldo Sibthorp* (Brighton: Sussex Academic Press 2005).

59 Sabine Baring-Gould, *The Church Revival: Thoughts Theron and Reminiscences* (London: Methuen 1914), p. 232. Baring-Gould was himself a hymn writer, most famous for 'Onward Christian Soldiers'. See J. E. Thomas, *Sabine Baring-Gould: The Life and Work of a Victorian* (Stroud: Fonthill Media 2015).

60 Herbert B. J. Armstrong (ed.), *A Norfolk Diary: Passages from the Diary of the Rev. Benjamin John Armstrong* (London: George Harrap and Company Ltd 1949), p. 119.

Armstrong made changes at a slower pace at Dereham. In 1861 he introduced a surpliced choir at all services, but didn't preach in his surplice until 17 May 1868, though he still wore his black gown when preaching in Norwich Cathedral in 1871.[61] On 7 December 1873 he celebrated choral Communion, and thought that it was probably the first time in Dereham since the Reformation.[62] In October 1870 he had recorded with pride and satisfaction:

> To-day I have completed twenty years in this parish. Preached on retrospection, drawing a comparison between the state of things now and twenty years ago. Nothing could be worse than the state of the Church in 1850. Then, the altar was a miserable mahogany table with a covering fifty years old; there was a vile yellow carpet; a Grecian reredos with daubs of Moses and Aaron; no painted glass, and the rail for the communicants intersecting the sedilia. Look at it now – an altar and super-altar of full dimensions, with flower-vases always replenished with flowers; candlesticks and candles (now introduced); three altar-cloths changed at the seasons; the windows painted; a stone reredos highly painted and with a central Cross; a rich carpet; credence table; Bishop's chair, etc, etc.[63]

On the other hand, St Barnabas, Jericho, Oxford, had been built in 1869 to showcase Tractarian ceremonial from the start. Francis Kilvert described a service that he attended in 1876:

> The large Church was almost full, the great congregation singing like one man. The clergy and choir entered with a procession, incense bearers and a great gilt cross, the thurifers and acolytes being in short white surplices over scarlet cassocks and the last priest in the procession wearing a biretta and a chasuble stiff with gold . . . The poor humble Roman Church hard by is quite plain, simple and Low Church in its ritual compared with St. Barnabas in its festal dress on high days and holidays.[64]

---

61 Herbert B. J. Armstrong, *A Norfolk Diary: Passages from the Diary of the Rev. Benjamin John Armstrong* (London: George Harrap and Company Ltd 1949), pp. 82, 135, 163.

62 Armstrong, *A Norfolk Diary*, p. 177.

63 Armstrong, *A Norfolk Diary*, p. 156.

64 Kilvert, *Diary*, p. 365. St Barnabas was funded by Thomas Combe, Printer to the University and a Tractarian supporter, who was connected with Magdalen College, where Bloxham was a Fellow. See Roy Judge, 'May Morning and Magdalen College, Oxford' in *Folklore* 97 (1986), pp. 15–40, for the intersection of Bloxham, Combe and Holman Hunt.

Some 14 years later, the young Ursula Bethell wrote:

> We went together to the afternoon service at St. Barnabas . . . What wd.you have said to it! The Altar with a gorgeous canopy over it &seven red lamps always burning before it – & many candles & crucifixes. The clergyman decked out to a degree – he was robed & unrobed several times during the service by two little acolytes who always stood by him – & he looked like the pictures of Roman Catholic Priests. While singing a hymn they marched round the church – many men clothed in red holding banners & crucifixes – & then a boy with incense which filled the church![65]

Bishops attempted to stem the tide, and outlaw those who in their eyes were the more extreme exponents. In 1847 J. M. Neale was inhibited by Bishop Gilbert of Chichester because of his High Church ceremonial and furnishings in Sackville College Chapel and the inhibition lasted until 1863. In 1873 John Bacchus Dykes, Vicar of St Oswald's, Durham, was refused a curate by the Bishop of Durham unless Dykes and the curate agreed that the latter be not required to:

1st That he wear coloured stoles.
2nd That he take part in, or be present at the burning of Incense.
3rd That he turn his back to the congregation during the celebration of the Holy Communion, except when 'ordering the bread'.[66]

The new good taste in church architecture and furnishing meant that whereas at the Reformation the question had been, 'How could Gothic interiors be adapted for the celebration of Prayer Book liturgies?', now the question was, 'How could Prayer Book liturgies be adapted for Gothic and neo-Gothic interiors and furnishings?' A committee of the Lower House of the Canterbury Convocation rightly noted in 1866, 'some advance in Ritual is the natural sequel to the restoration and adornment of Churches which has so remarkably prevailed during the last twenty-five years'.[67]

---

65 Peter Whiteford (ed.), *Vibrant Words: The Letters of Ursula Bethell* (Wellington, New Zealand: Victoria University Press 2005), p. 5. Letter dated 1890/91.

66 Letter to Dykes, 4 July 1873 in J. T. Fowler (ed.), *Life and letters of the Rev. John Bacchus Dykes* (London: John Murray 1897), p. 304. See also G. Roe and A. Hutchings, *J.B. Dykes (1823–1875): Priest and Musician* (Durham: St Oswald's Parochial Church Council 1976).

67 Cited in Ellsworth, *Charles Lowder and the Ritualist Movement*, p. 84.

Dale Adelmann has documented the other important contribution of the Ecclesiologists – the revival of quality choral worship.[68] Both Webb and Neale subscribed to the Musical Antiquarian Society, from which evolved the Motet Society with its concern for sacred music. This together with the work of Revd Thomas Helmore at the recently opened St Mark's Training College, Chelsea, saw the encouragement of plainsong. John Hullah, a member of the Camden Society from 1843, gave classes on sight-singing at Exeter Hall from 1841. Other pioneers included Robert Druitt, Frederick Helmore and Gore Ouseley, the latter founding a college and new church at Tenbury.[69] The aim, though, was congregational singing:

> and by *choral service* is meant the mode of celebrating the public service by both priests and people, in which they sing all portions allotted to each respectively, so as to make it one continued psalm of praise, confession, and intercession, from beginning to end.[70]

The publication of the *Hymnal Noted* (1860) drew heavily on the hymns of the Sarum use. Neale translated many pre-Reformation hymns, and would be a main contributor to the hugely successful *Hymns Ancient and Modern* (1861). This hymnal, conceived on a journey on the Great Western Railway, bore a Tractarian stamp, though the collection drew on a variety of traditions and centuries.[71] Richard Watson has drawn attention to the collection's provision for the liturgical year and that after the section on 'Morning' came three hymns for the third, sixth and ninth hours: 'The link with western monasticism is clear.'[72] However, music was able to cross boundaries in ways that Tractarian theology and

---

68 Dale Adelmann, *The Contribution of Cambridge Ecclesiologists to the Revival of Anglican Choral Worship 1839–62* (Aldershot: Ashgate 1997). See also Trevor Beeson, *In Tuneful Accord: The Church Musicians* (London: SCM Press 2009). For the founding of choir schools at this period, see Alan Mould, *The English Chorister: A History* (London: Continuum Press 2007), p. 194.

69 See Rainbow, *Choral Revival.*

70 *The Parish Choir* 1 (1846), p. 26. This was a monthly journal that promoted parochial choirs.

71 See Susan Drain, *The Anglican Church in Nineteenth Century Britain: Hymns Ancient and Modern (1860–1875)* (Lewiston, NY: Edwin Mellen Press 1989), pp. 101–2, p. 105; Trevor Beeson, *The Church's Folk Songs from Hymns Ancient and Modern to Common Praise 1861–2011* (Norwich: Canterbury Press 2011).

72 Richard Watson, 'Texts and contexts: the first edition of *Hymns Ancient & Modern*' in Janet Butler et al. (eds), *Hymns Ancient & Modern and Henry Williams Baker* (Leominster: The Leominster History Study Group 2013), pp. 27–40, p. 39. This collection also contains useful essays by John Harper and Jeremy Dibble.

Ecclesiologist ceremonial could not, and *Hymns Ancient and Modern* was used in many churches that would never have regarded themselves as remotely connected with Tractarianism. Charles Box, a noted musician, described services at various London churches he visited in 1882. At Holy Trinity, Gray's Inn Road, morning service on 12 March:

> First portion of prayers read; second intoned. Venite and Psalms chanted. Te Deum (Hopkins' Service in G); Anthem, 'Turn Thy face from my sin' (Atwood); Versicles and Litany (after Tallis). No Communion service. Hymn before sermon, and hymn during the offertory. A surpliced choir of twenty-four voices. 'Church Hymns' used. Singing congregational, very hearty and well attuned. Out voluntary, 'Let their celestial concerts all unite'.[73]

Holy Trinity, Minories, used *Hymns Ancient and Modern,* and St Alban, Wood Street, with St Olave, used *Hymnal Companion.*[74] At St Bartholomew, Moor Lane, Cripplegate, on 11 June 1882, Box recorded the following:

> Prayers intoned. A surpliced choir of sixteen voices. Venite, Te Deum, and Jubilate chanted. Psalms chanted in choral unison, but the Glorias according to score. Hymn at the end of the third Collect. No Litany. Musical responses to the Decalogue. Nicene Creed, (Goss). Musical accompaniments to the celebration of the Eucharist. Hymn at the close. 'Church Hymnal' used.[75]

On 26 March 1882 he wrote of St Ethelburga's:

> Prayers intoned. Surpliced choir of fifteen voices. Here the singing and order of the service was so dissimilar to any other, that it would be difficult for a stranger without a guide-book to give a fair account of the proceedings. They neither belonged exclusively to the Church of England nor the Church of Rome, but were perplexingly compounded of both, with other ingredients added. When the summoning bell ceased tolling at eleven o'clock, the congregation was composed of seven persons, but during the morning, this number

---

73 Charles Box, *Church Music in the Metropolis* (London: William Reeves 1884), p. 129.

74 Box, *Church Music in the Metropolis*, pp. 128, 129.

75 Box, *Church Music in the Metropolis*, p. 133.

was nearly trebled. The Communion service was a somewhat elaborate affair, but three only of the congregation 'drew near' to partake of the sacred emblems. Two hymns from the 'Ancient and Modern' book effected a slight relief to the overpowering weight of other music, far more chromatic than pleasing. The building wore a dim, dingy and damp aspect, and the two tall lighted candles placed on the altar presented a sickly appearance when an occasional streak of sunlight pierced the windows.[76]

Of course this was London, but such musical changes would be replicated in many other urban churches and not a few rural churches by 1882. The story of the choral revival that stemmed from Tractarianism and the Ecclesiologists has been recounted by Bernarr Rainbow.[77] Nicholas Temperley points out that at the beginning of the nineteenth century there was a rush to provide organs, either pipe or barrel, and this trend continued throughout the century.[78] No longer clerk and gallery singers with flute, but organ with surpliced choir became the Anglican norm.

CATHEDRALS AND MUSIC

In 1843 John Jebb published his survey of the liturgical system of the cathedrals and collegiate churches, and found many wanting in sense and decency in singing and provision for Communion.[79] Of London's St Paul's Cathedral he complained:

> But surely the Chapter of St. Paul's must at length perceive how sacrilegious a mockery they have long sanctioned: suffering a pretence to be made of weekly Communion, the Holy Table being arranged for the Feast, so as thereby to invite communicants, the Clergy being in numerous attendance; and then when the time arrives for its celebration, the Clergy are dispersed, the Altar is forsaken, and the expectant worshippers dismissed by the notice of a Verger, without even a diaconal benediction![80]

---

76 Box, *Church Music in the Metropolis*, p. 141. The population of the parish was 315.
77 Rainbow, *Choral Revival*.
78 Nicholas Temperley, *The Music of the English Parish Church*, Vol. 1 (Cambridge: Cambridge University Press 1979), pp. 234–8, 310–14.
79 John Jebb, *The Choral Service of the United Church of England and Ireland: Being an Enquiry into the Liturgical System of the Cathedral and Collegiate Foundations of the Anglican Communion* (London: John Parker 1843).
80 Jebb, *Choral Service*, p. 521.

Among other things, Jebb noted that except for the coronation, the wearing of copes in cathedrals had fallen into abeyance.[81] Yet just as worship in the parish churches improved, so too choral music, decency and ceremonial changed in the cathedrals. At St Paul's an improvement came with Henry Hart Milman's appointment as dean in 1849 and, in addition to the statutory services, special services of national significance were revived, and a series of popular evening services were introduced under Milman's successor, Dean Mansel, who also introduced decorations on the altar at Christmas and had choral services for Holy Week. By 1872 the pattern of services on Sundays was 8 a.m. Communion; 11.30 a.m. Morning Prayer with choral celebration and sermon; 3.15 p.m. the Litany with anthem, sermon and hymn; and 7 p.m. Evening Prayer with hymn and sermon.[82] At Queen Victoria's Jubilee service (1897), not only were copes worn, but skull caps of cardinal-red velvet were also worn by the clergy.[83] In his study of the English cathedrals in the nineteenth century, Philip Barrett notes that in the early decades of the nineteenth century nearly all cathedrals had two choral services on Sundays, and Holy Communion was celebrated weekly in twelve cathedrals, and monthly in seventeen.[84] Barrett noted that it was the celebration of Holy Communion that had changed more than any other during the nineteenth century. Weekly celebrations became the norm, and celebrations on saints' days were also introduced in a number of cathedrals. As the influence of the Oxford Movement developed, an increasing emphasis was placed on early morning celebrations.[85] Throughout the nineteenth century, organists and composers continued to add significant settings to the ever-growing choral repertoire, such as Samuel Wesley and Thomas Attwood in the first decades, and Thomas Attwood Walmisley, S. S. Wesley, John Goss, Frederick Arthur Gore Ouseley, John Stainer and John Bacchus Dykes in the latter part. These and many other Victorian composers greatly enriched the choral celebration of the Prayer Book services.[86]

---

81 Jebb, *Choral Service*, pp. 216–17.

82 Philip Barrett, *Barchester: English Cathedral Life in the Nineteenth Century* (London: SPCK 1993), p. 116.

83 Donald Gray, 'Liturgy, 1714–2004' in Derek Keene, Arthur Burns and Andrew Saint (eds), *St. Paul's: The Cathedral Church of London 604–2004* (New Haven, CT: Yale University Press 2004), pp. 352–62, pp. 355–7 and illustration pp. 305, 359.

84 Barrett, *Barchester*, p. 115.

85 Barrett, *Barchester*, p. 138.

86 John S. Bumpus, *A History of English Cathedral Music 1549–1889* (Westmead: Gregg International Reprint 1972); William Gatens, *Victorian Cathedral Music in Theory and Practice* (Cambridge: Cambridge University Press 1986).

REACTIONS IN CHURCH AND STATE

J. M. Neale, in his *Essays on Liturgiology and Church History*, published in 1863, had argued that the Prayer Book was too narrow, lacked beauty and needed supplementing from ancient liturgies. As second-generation Tractarianism developed into Anglo-Catholicism, the Prayer Book rites were found inadequate and were supplemented or even replaced with liturgy from Catholic sources. Notable among these were Peter Medd's *The Priest to the Altar* (1861), Frederick George Lee's *The Altar Book* (1867), Orby Shipley's *The Ritual of the Altar* (1870) and A. H. Stanton's *Catholic Prayers for Church of England People* (1880).[87] Bishops could and did make life difficult for the Ritualist clergy. Both Evangelicals and Broad Churchmen responded. As early as 1842 Thomas Spencer had published *The Reformed Prayer Book*, which removed from the Prayer Book those things to which the Tractarians appealed and the things that Evangelicals found objectionable. In 1859 Lord Ebury founded an association for reforming the Prayer Book, later to become the Prayer Book Revision Society. In 1873 Ebury and his associates published *The Book of Common Prayer Revised*, carried out in such a manner as to exclude any Tractarian or Anglo-Catholic interpretations.[88] Evangelical clergy who seceded from the Church of England and formed what later became the Free Church of England adopted a reformed Prayer Book on the lines of Ebury's.[89] Another move was to purchase advowsons to insure a continued Low Church succession or to reverse a Ritualist tradition.[90]

At an official level, 1854 saw the appointment of a committee to take stock and action in the light of the 1851 census. An official change occurred in the Prayer Book – the removal of the commemoration of the death of Charles I on 30 January, the birth and restoration of Charles II on 29 May, and the Gunpowder Plot on 5 November. They had been added to the 1662 Book of Common Prayer on the authority of Convocation and the Crown, and were continued by Royal mandate.

87 Mark Dalby, *Anglican Missals and their Canons: 1549, Interim Rite and Roman*, Alcuin/GROW Joint Liturgical Study 41 (Cambridge: Grove Books 1998).

88 A. Elliott Peaston, *The Prayer Book Revisions of the Victorian Evangelicals* (Dublin: APCK 1963).

89 See further below. Also, A. E. Peaston, *The Prayer Book Tradition in the Free Churches* (London: James Clarke 1964), pp. 70–87; John Fenwick, *The Free Church of England* (London: T & T Clark 2004), pp. 225–43.

90 An example of the latter is St Michael's Church, Braintree, Essex. It was still an Anglo-Catholic church under J. W. Kenworthy in the early twentieth century. The vestments were destroyed under Peter James in the late 1950s and the remaining candlesticks 'disappeared'.

They were removed by royal warrant on 17 January 1857. Technically they were never part of the liturgy as authorized by Parliament, but arguably the commemorations had marked the extremes between which the 1662 liturgy was intended to be the mean. Though certainly not the intention, their removal was symbolic of the fact that the 1662 mean was no longer an acceptable mean. Notable ritualist court cases were Westerton v. Liddell (1855–57), Martin v. Mackonochie (1867–68), Sumner v. Wix (1870) and Hebbert v. Puchas (1870–71), with inconsistent conclusions. Gary Graber lists 11 proposed but failed attempts at Parliamentary ritual legislation between 1860 and 1873, such was the concern to bring order out of increasing chaos.[91] After much debate in Parliament, 1867 saw the appointment of the Royal Commission on Ritual. It resulted in four reports. The first dealt with vesture; the second with candles and incense; the third considered Prayer Book revision and recommended the shortening of lessons and the provision of proper lessons and alternative lessons. The fourth report dealt with services, and among its recommendations suggested that Morning Prayer, Litany and Holy Communion might be used together (as was the custom) or as separate services at the discretion of the minister. The Act of Uniformity Amendment was passed in 1872, which, in addition to allowing the shortening of Morning and Evening Prayer on weekdays, and the three Sunday Morning services to be used separately, sanctioned a 'third service' on Sundays as a supplement to the statutory services of Morning and Evening Prayer provided in the Prayer Book.[92] The materials of the latter were to come from the Prayer Book, but Evangelicals had already established mission-type services which used hymns and extempore prayer and saw this as sanctioning their own extra-liturgical practice. The Royal Commission also gave birth to the 1874 Public Worship Regulation Act that resulted in the Ridsdale case and the imprisonment of some Anglo-Catholic clergy, notably Arthur Tooth of St James, Hatcham, R. W. Enraght of Birmingham and S. H. Green of St John's, Miles Platting, Manchester. This in turn brought the Act into disrepute, and bishops refused to use it.[93] The fourth

91 Gary Graber, *Ritual Legislation in the Victorian Church of England: Antecedents and Passage of the Public Worship Regulation Act, 1874* (Lewiston, NY: Edwin Mellen Press 1993), p. 42.

92 Bryan D. Spinks, 'Not so Common Prayer: The Third Service' in Michael Perham (ed.), *The Renewal of Common Prayer: Unity and Diversity in Church of England Worship* (London: SPCK 1993), pp. 55–67.

93 Graber, *Ritual Legislation*, pp. 123–30; James Bentley, *Ritualism and Politics in Victorian Britain* (Oxford: Oxford University Press 1978).

report also resulted in discussion of a revised Prayer Book, known as the *Convocation Prayer Book* (1880). Among recommended changes were modification of the ornaments rubric, permission to sing an Introit to the Holy Communion service, the reduction of sponsors at baptism and greater flexibility in the burial service. Ronald Jasper noted of that book, 'Few of these proposals would have enriched the services of the Prayer Book. Liturgical precedents were frequently ignored, and with the exception of controversial points, such as the Athanasian Creed and the Ornaments Rubric, the changes were trifling.'[94] It was probably just as well that these proposals came to nothing.

NINETEENTH-CENTURY PRAYER BOOK REVISIONS

In Ireland fear of an assertive Roman Catholic Church and the reaction to disestablishment led the Church of Ireland to limit and outlaw the ritualist implications of Tractarianism. The canons were revised to exclude a cross on or behind the Holy Table, and to prohibit the lighting of candles for services unless to provide light, the use of incense, making the sign of the cross, as well as bowing before the Holy Table. It was also forbidden for the officiant to turn his back to the people while saying prayers and to carry banners or a cross in procession.[95] The Evangelical party wanted changes such as removal of the absolution from the Visitation to the Sick, and the more liberal factions of the Church wanted to remove the Athanasian Creed. After considerable heated debate, a new Book of Common Prayer was issued in 1878. Richard Clarke wrote:

> At the end of all the turmoil, little was done to the received text of the Prayer Book. The special absolution to the Office for the Visitation to the Sick, which included a direct translation of the form for absolving used in the confessional, *Ego te absolvo*, was removed. The Athanasian Creed was left unaltered but no directions were given as to when it should be used, if ever.[96]

---

94 R. C. D. Jasper, *Prayer Book Revision in England 1800–1900* (London: SPCK 1954), p. 126.

95 These canons are bound with the 1878 Book of Common Prayer. <www.books.google.com/books?id=_cMUAAAAQAAJ&printsec=frontcover&source=gbs_ge_summary_r&cad=0#v=onepage&q&f=false> (accessed 22 November 2016).

96 Richard Clarke, 'The 1878 Book of Common Prayer' in Michael Kennedy et al. (eds), *The Prayer Books of the Church of Ireland 1551–2004* (Dublin: The Columba Press 2004), pp. 18–25, p. 24.

Brian Mayne has noted that the Preface had been described as an elaborate fudge, setting out the positions of all the protagonists and apologizing to each in turn that they might not have got their own way entirely.[97] It could, however, be argued that it was framed in the spirit of that of 1662. It concluded:

> And now, if some shall complain that these changes are not enough, and that we should have taken this opportunity of making this Book as perfect in all respects as they think it might be made, or if others say that these changes have been unnecessary or excessive, and that what was already excellent has been impaired by doing that which, in their opinion, might well have been left undone, let them, on the one side and the other, consider that men's judgments of perfection are very various, and that what is imperfect, with peace, is often better than what is otherwise excellent, without it.[98]

The Protestant Episcopal Church in the USA revised its 1789/90 Prayer Book in 1892. In this Church, there was already a High Church tradition and much of the teaching of the Tractarians was received with less concern than in Ireland. The first effects of the Tracts in the Episcopal Church are said to be traced to General Theological Seminary, New York, among faculty and students, particularly when three students went with the High Church missionary Bishop, Jackson Kemper, and were later in 1841 to found Nashotah House Seminary.[99] Certainly the General Theological Seminary was regarded as harbouring crypto-papists.

The Tracts were attacked by Bishop Charles McIlvaine of Ohio and William Meade, Assistant Bishop of Virginia, but they were defended by Bishop Thomas Brownell of Connecticut and the Revd Samuel Seabury, grandson of Bishop Seabury. Bishop Doane of New Jersey was also a supporter. He had brought out the first American edition

---

97 Brian Mayne, 'Ireland' in Charles Hefling and Cynthia Shattuck (eds), *The Oxford Guide to the Book of Common Prayer: A Worldwide Survey* (Oxford: Oxford University Press 2006), pp. 202–8, p. 205.

98 <www.books.google.com/books?id=_cMUAAAAQAAJ&printsec=frontcover& source=gbs_ge_summary_r&cad=0#v=onepage&q&f=false> (accessed 2 November 2016).

99 The following section is reliant upon George E. DeMille, *The Catholic Movement in the American Episcopal Church* (Philadelphia, PA: Church Historical Society 1941, second enlarged edn 1951). For more recent challenges to some of DeMille and other older works, see Larry Crockett, 'Oxford Movement and the 19th-Century Episcopal Church: Anglo-Catholic Ecclesiology and the American Experience', *Quodlibet Online Journal* 1 (1999), no pagination. See also Cody C. Unterseher, *American Sarum* (Bronxville, NY: Christ Church Press 2010), pp. 99–110.

of Keble's *The Christian Year* and maintained correspondence with the English leaders. In 1843 we find a General Theological Seminary graduate, Arthur Carey, being presented for the diaconate, and ordination being postponed because of Evangelical objections. The case was investigated, and even though two clergymen verbally objected at the actual ordination, the bishop overruled them. But what was under scrutiny was Carey's theological beliefs rather than liturgical ceremonial.

Ceremonial varied, and in many places clergy apparently wore clerical dress or a black gown for services. As late as 1840, the use of the surplice for any service in the Episcopal Church was far from universal. Indeed, it is estimated that in 1837 there were not half a dozen surplices in the whole diocese of Ohio. Yet already in 1827 William Augustus Muhlenberg, in the school chapel at Flushing, Long Island, used candles, had a vested choir and at Christmas placed on the Holy Table a picture of the Virgin and Child – but this was a Lutheran background coming out rather than an anticipation of the Ritualist movement. In 1843 the Revd Frederick Pollard, a graduate of General Theological Seminary, came to Trinity Church, Nantucket, Connecticut. Here he pulled down the three-decker pulpit, built an altar, raised above the level of the church floor and backed by a reredos, and put on it two candlesticks and a picture of the Madonna and Child. He read the Epistle and Gospel from each side of the altar. The daily office was read from a faldstool, facing the altar. There was a credence table; wafer bread was used; and the priest was assisted by a server who was not robed.

With John Ireland Tucker, Gregorian chant and Merbeck were introduced into the Episcopal Church. In 1848 the New York Ecclesiological Society was founded, and promoted in the USA what the Camden Society did in England. The father of Gothic architecture in the United States was Richard Upjohn, who found the opportunity when Trinity Church, New York, was rebuilt in 1839. He persuaded the church to adopt his plan, which was designed to allow developed Catholic ceremonial. The history of Grace Church, Newark, is an epitome of ritualistic advance. It was founded in 1837 under George Chapman, who was a supporter of the Tractarian writings. He introduced a weekly Communion, and the recitation in church of the daily office; in 1866 it had a vested choir; and in 1871 altar lights. By 1879 it had a daily Communion and regular confession, and, by 1890, Benediction of the Blessed Sacrament. St Albans Church, New York, under Charles Morrill in 1865, had vestments, incense and servers. In 1870 Thomas McKee Brown founded St Mary the Virgin, New York, which represented the epitome of the Anglo-Catholic revival. Bishop Hopkins had defended the use of vestments in his 1866 book, *The Law of Ritualism*. There were indeed ritual controversies, and some bishops tried to stamp out this creeping popery, but ultimately without success. It was less bloody than in England because State legislation was not involved. But at the General Convention of 1871 there was a recommendation to ban vestments, incense, crucifixes, candles, the mixed chalice and elevation. It failed, though elevation of the sacrament was banned. Part of the problem and solution was that the American Prayer Book did not have the ornaments rubric. It neither allowed post-reformation ceremonial, nor did it forbid it. In 1895 the *New York Sun* could report: 'Ritualism in New York as elsewhere has advanced usually by these well-recognized steps; the surplice, unlighted tapers, lighted tapers, plain vestments, colored vestments, high mass, and finally the confessional.'[100]

However, for all the apparent ease of entry of Tractarianism and ritualism into the American Church, it was hardly reflected in the 1892 Prayer Book, which, like the Irish Book, was something of a compromise. As elsewhere, Evangelicals and liberals vied for specific agendas. A firm proposal for revision was introduced at the 1880 General Convention by William Reed Huntingdon, who may be regarded as a Broad or Liberal Churchman. The object was to gain flexibility of use, enrichment of resources and adaptations to take account of the changes in culture and society. A Book Annexed was introduced at the general Convention of 1883, but Evangelicals and High Churchmen were unenthusiastic, and even more opposition was expressed in 1886. Of the 1892 resulting liturgy, Lesley Northup has commented:

> It was not exactly the book anyone wanted – too conservative for some, too radical for others, disappointingly inconsistent for many. But revisionary exhaustion and sheer timidity had ultimately triumphed, and – for better or for worse – the prayer book had been revised.[101]

Among the alterations and changes were the inclusion of the feast of the Transfiguration, restoration of the Nunc Dimittis, Magnificat and the previously omitted portions of the Benedictus, new collects and prayers, the Kyrie and ten new selections of psalms. Increased flexibility

---

100 DeMille, *The Catholic Movement*, p. 126.
101 Lesley Armstrong Northup, *The 1892 Book of Common Prayer* (Lewiston, NY: Edwin Mellen Press 1993), p. 161. See also the section in Thaddaeus A. Schnitker, *The Church's Worship: The 1979 American Book of Common Prayer in a Historical Perspective* (Frankfurt am main: Peter Lang 1989).

was introduced as regards hymns and metrical psalmody and alternative forms. George DeMille felt that the Book expressed a more Catholic feeling, but Northup more accurately noted that in comparison with 1789, its content was slightly richer, its style remained Tudor and its tone was distinctly conservative.[102]

Not all liked the direction in which either the Protestant Episcopal Church or the Church of England seemed to be heading.[103] Alarmed by Tractarianism, the American Bishop George Cummins, Assistant Bishop of Kentucky, seceded from the Episcopal Church to found the Reformed Episcopal Church. In 1874 he issued *The Book of Common Prayer of the Reformed Episcopal Church*, published in Philadelphia. It was more in line with the 1662 Prayer Book than that of 1789. In 1876 another bishop of this Church, Dr Edward Cridge, journeyed to England to consecrate Benjamin Price as Bishop of the Free Church of England. That Church can be traced to James Shore, who was refused a licence by Bishop Phillpotts to minister at Bridgetown Chapel-of-Ease, Totnes, used by the tenants of the Duke of Somerset. For a while Shore co-operated with the Countess of Huntingdon's Connexion, though this link ceased with Price's consecration. Some clergy of the Free Church of England used the 1873 *Book of Common Prayer Revised* of Lord Ebury's group, and others used *The Book of Common Prayer revised according to the use of the Free Church of England* (1876). Lord Ebury's group petitioned the American Reformed Episcopal Church to consecrate Dr Huband Gregg as bishop, and on his return from the United States he headed the Reformed Episcopal Church of the United Kingdom. A split occurred and another group was styled the Reformed Church of England. In 1879 Gregg published *The Book of Common Prayer according to the use of the Reformed Episcopal Church in the United Kingdom, otherwise called the Reformed Church of England*. What these share in common is a conservative revision of the 1662 Book of Common Prayer, with an emphasis on making the book more acceptable to Dissenters and unacceptable to Anglo-Catholics.

AND ENGLAND INTO THE TWENTIETH CENTURY

An important official move for the Church of England came in 1904, when the Royal Commission on Ecclesiastical Discipline was appointed

---

102 DeMille, *The Catholic Movement*, p. 196; Northup, *The 1892 Book of Common Prayer*, p. 166.
103 Peaston, *The Prayer Book Tradition in the Free Churches*, pp. 70–87; Fenwick, *The Free Church of England*, pp. 225–43.

to inquire into alleged breaches of the law. The evidence taken by the Commission was extremely wide and included breaches such as the omission of the creed in Westminster Abbey. Typical of Anglo-Catholic services was that of Verwood, Dorset. Morning Prayer was abbreviated by omissions. The visitor reported on numerous illegalities and observed the many children present at the Communion, 'the English Prayer Book they do not know'.[104] At St Saviour's, Hitchin, it was reported concerning the 10 a.m. service:

> The clergyman wore an alb, green chasuble, girdle, maniple, and stole, and was attended by two servers. There were two lighted candles on the Holy Table, and two large brass standards lighted in the chancel . . . A wafer was used instead of ordinary bread. Both during and after consecration the clergyman elevated the paten and chalice.[105]

It was clear that the rite was augmented with material from elsewhere. In reply, the Vicar, George Gainsford, noted that he had been in the parish forty years, and had always used vestments in accordance with the ornaments rubric. As for interpolations, the use of any hymn was interpolation and he denied many of the claims of the 'nameless spy'.[106]

Thus it was that the report in 1906 came to make reference to the Prayer Book as being too narrow for the religious life of this present generation. It was not the liturgy that had changed, but English culture.[107] The impact of the Romantic Movement as well as continued industrialization and nineteenth-century technology meant that Queen Victoria had been born in one world and died in another. Some Evangelicals and Broad Churchmen, as well as Anglo-Catholics, omitted things from the Prayer Book, or substituted unauthorized material in worship – 1906 was a world apart from when John Skinner had 'read prayers as usual'. Although no revised liturgy was authorized in the nineteenth century, the flood of liturgical revision that came in the late twentieth century was set in motion by the Victorian assaults on the Prayer Book,

104 *Minutes of Evidence*, p. 251: <www.catalog.hathitrust.org/Record/011723646> (accessed 14 June 2017).
105 *Minutes of Evidence*, p. 261.
106 *Minutes of Evidence*, p. 262.
107 For the discussion of Tractarianism and the Ecclesiologists in a broader cultural context, see Michael Hall, 'What do Victorian Churches Mean? Symbolism and Sacramentalism in Anglican Church Architecture 1850–1870', *Journal of the Society of Architectural Historians* 59.1 (2000), pp. 78–95. See also Janes, *Victorian Reformation*.

both on its textual limitations and on its ritual and musical performance. What could be deemed an 'excellent liturgy' had, by the end
of the nineteenth century, become 'too narrow for the religious life'
and the liturgical appetite of a good many in the Church of England.[108]
Yet the Church of England would have to wait until the second half
of the twentieth century for that appetite to begin to be officially
addressed, under a different Queen Elizabeth.

---

108 It is interesting that Walter Frere's correspondence from 1906 to 1907 changes from
concern for rubrical change to the need for proper liturgical revision. *Walter Howard
Frere: His Correspondence on Liturgical Revision and Construction*, ed. R. C. D. Jasper
(London: SPCK 1954), pp. 5–25.

Postscript

The Royal Commission Report of 1906 paved the way for the 1662 Book of Common Prayer to lose its monopoly as the sole legal form of regular worship in the Church of England. The rather drawn-out and acrimonious process of revision that the report set in motion resulted in the stillbirth of the 1927 and 1928 Proposed Book of Common Prayer.[1] With this revised version failing to gain Parliamentary approval, the 1662 Prayer Book was left as the sole legal liturgy. The bishops announced that 'during the present emergency and until further order be taken' they would not regard as inconsistent with loyalty to the principles of the Church of England the use of such additions or deviations as fell within the limits of the 1928 proposals. Parts of 1928 appeared in the 1935 publication, *The Churchpeople's Prayer Book and the Sacraments of the Church* and in the successful *The Shorter Prayer Book* (1947). This latter was in use at All Saint's, Cressing, Essex, where I was an altar server in the 1960s, though the altar book used by the Vicar, the Revd Arthur Alastair Malcolm Sandeman, was *The Altar Missal* (1936) from the Society of St John the Evangelist. With the founding of a Liturgical Commission in 1955, there eventually flowed the experimental texts of Series 1, Series 2 and Series 3, culminating in *The Alternative Service Book 1980* (ASB). It evoked a Pastoral Letter from the Archbishops of Canterbury and York, which the clergy were asked to regard as confidential until a certain date. The late Douglas Webb of Wilburton, known best for his scholarly work on the East Syrian liturgies, remarked in an unpublished paper that it was a letter of such inconsequence that

---

1 Donald Gray, *The 1927–28 Prayer Book Crisis. 1: Ritual, Royal Commissions, and Reply to the Royal Letters of Business*, Alcuin/GROW Joint Liturgical Study 60 (Norwich: SCM-Canterbury Press 2005); *The 1927–28 Prayer Book Crisis. 2: The cul-de-sac of the 'Deposited Book' . . . until further order be taken*, Alcuin/GROW Joint Liturgical Study 61 (Norwich: SCM-Canterbury Press 2006); Bryan D. Spinks, 'The Prayer Book "Crisis" in England' in Charles Hefling and Cynthia Shattuck (eds), *The Oxford Guide to The Book of Common Prayer* (Oxford: Oxford University Press 2006), pp. 239–43.

it could have remained confidential for ever without any great loss. The *Daily Telegraph* extolled the literary merits of 1662 over what it regarded as the banal and thin language of the ASB, failing perhaps to notice that this was because the ASB was written in *Daily Telegraph*-style language. For those in the Anglo-Catholic and Anglo-Papalist tradition, Rome had its own new rites stemming from the Second Vatican Council reforms which satisfied more those particular appetites. In 1986 came the *Services for Lent, Holy Week and Easter*. I had the privilege of serving on the Liturgical Commission as a member from 1986 to 1995, and thereafter as a consultant until 2000, helping to prepare *Patterns for Worship* and *Common Worship* in its several volumes. The 1662 Book of Common Prayer still holds sway in cathedrals and collegiate churches for Morning and Evening Prayer, enriched with several centuries of wonderful music, proving how successful, even if somewhat monastic in character, those offices were and are. For other services, though, the newest rites hold sway in most parish churches, as indeed they should. What is surprising is that the 1662 revision remained so long without any further revision. This had more to do with the lack of ecclesiastical machinery to allow for such an undertaking than any literary merit the Book is deemed to possess. The Book of Common Prayer no longer holds the position in the Church of England that it had from 1559 until the nineteenth-century erosion. With the choice of so many alternative new services, there is no concern to remove the 1662 Book from the statute books and so perhaps, like the poor, it will always be with us.

Appendix
A Supply of Prayer for Ships, 1645

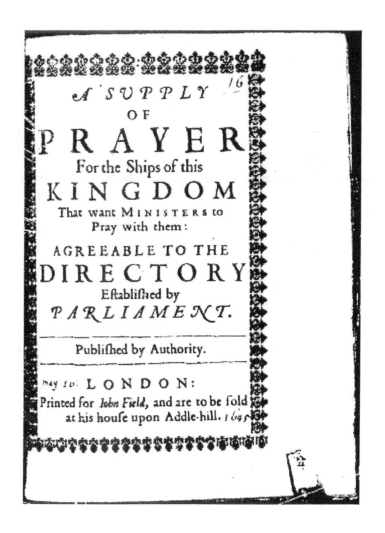

A SUPPLY
OF
PRAYER
For the Ships of this
KINGDOM
That want MINISTERS to
Pray with them:

AGREEABLE TO THE
DIRECTORY
Established by
PARLIAMENT.

Published by Authority.

May 10. LONDON:
Printed for *John Field,* and are to be sold
at his house upon Addle-hill. 1645

A Reason of this Work.

WHereas there are thousands of ships belonging to this Kingdom, which have not Ministers with them to guide them in Prayer, and therefore either use the old Form of Common-Prayer, or no Prayer at all. The former whereof for many weighty Reasons hath been abolished, and the latter is likely to make them rather Heathens then Christians (the Lords day being left without any mark of Piety or Devotion) Therefore, to avoid these Inconveniences, It hath been thought fit to frame some Prayers, agreeing with the Directory established by Parliament; It being hoped, that it will be no grief of heart

A 2

(4)

to wise and full Christians, if the thirsty drink out of Cisterns, when themselves drink out of Fountains; But they will rather pity the wants of their needy Brethren, and out of Compassion innitiate him, who filleth the hungry with good things.

These Prayers being enlivened and sent up by the Spirit in him that prayeth, may be lively Prayers and acceptable to him who is a Spirit, and accepts of services in Spirit and Truth. And, in truth, though Prayers come never so new, even from the Spirit, in one that is a guide in Prayer, if the Spirit do not quicken and enliven that Prayer in the Hearer that follows him, it is to him but a dead Form, and a very carcase of Prayer.

The

(5)

The Company being assembled, they may thus begin with Prayer:

O Lord, in all reverence and humility, we acknowledge thy incomprehensible Greatnesse and Majesty, in whose presence we do now in a speciall manner appear, and our own vilenesse and unworthinesse, to approach so neer thee, with our utter inability of our selves, to such a holy day. And we humbly beseech thee for pardon, assistance, and acceptance, in the whole service now to be petitioned, and for a Blessing on the particular portions of thy Word now to be read, and all in the Name and Mediation of the Lord Jesus Christ, in whose name and words wee pray unto thee saying,

Our Father, &c.

After this, some Psalms and Chapters being read out of both Testaments (but none out of those Books which are commonly called Apocrypha) and a Psalm being sung, a Prayer may follow in this manner:

O Great and gracious Lord, we acknowledge before thee our sinfulnesse, first, by reason of Originall gainſt ſin, which (beſides the guilt of it, which make us lyable to eternall damnation) is the ſeed of all rebellion, and hath depraved and poyſoned all the faculties and powers of ſoul and body, and doth defile our beſt actions, and (were it not reſtrained, or over-born) would break forth into innumerable Tranſgreſſions, and the greateſt Rebellions againſt the Lord, that ever were committed by the vileſt of the ſons of men. And next, we acknowledge the guilt of Actuall ſins, our own ſins, the ſins of Magiſtrates, Miniſters, and of the whole Nation, unto which we are many wayes acceſſary. Which ſins of ours receive many fearfull aggravations, we having broken all the Commandements of the holy, juſt, and good Law of God, doing that which is forbidden, and leaving undone what is enjoyned, and that not onely out of ignorance and infirmity, but alſo more preſumptuouſly, againſt the light of our mindes, checks of our conſciences, and motions of thy holy Spirit to the contrary, ſo that we have no cloak for our ſins; yet we have not onely deſpiſed the riches of Gods goodneſſe, forbearance, and long-ſuffering, which ſhould leade us to Repentance, and Holineſſe, but have ſtood out againſt many invitations, and offers of Grace in the Goſpel, not endeavouring as we ought, to receive Chriſt into our hearts by Faith, or to walk worthy of him in our lives. We bewail our blindneſſe of minde, hardneſſe of heart, unbelief, impenitency, ſecurity, lukewarmneſſe, barrenneſſe, our not endeavouring after Mortification, and newneſſe of life, nor after the exerciſe of Godlineſſe in the power thereof; and that the beſt of us have not ſo ſtedfaſtly walked

walked with God, kept our Garments ſo unſpotted, nor been ſo zealous of thy glory, and the good of others as wee ought, notwithſtanding the manifold and great mercies of thee our God, the love of Chriſt, the light of the Goſpel, and Reformation of Religion, our own Purpoſes, Promiſes, Vows, Solemn Covenant, and other ſpeciall obligations to the contrary. We acknowledge and confeſſe, that as we are convinced of our guilt, ſo out of a deep ſenſe thereof, we judge our ſelves unworthy of the ſmalleſt benefits, moſt worthy of thy fierceſt wrath, and of all the curſes of the Law, and heavieſt judgements inflicted upon the moſt Rebellious ſinners; and that thou mighteſt moſt juſtly take thy Kingdom and Goſpel from us, plague us with all ſorts of Spirituall and Temporall judgements in this life, and after caſt us into utter darkneſſe, in the Lake that burneth with Fire and Brimſtone, where is weeping and gnaſhing of Teeth for evermore. Notwithſtanding all which, we draw neer to the Throne of Grace, encouraging our ſelves, with hope of a gracious anſwer of our Prayers, in the Riches and All-ſufficiency of that onely one Oblation, the ſatisfaction and Interceſſion of the Lord Jeſus Chriſt, at the right hand of his Father, and our Father, and in confidence of the exceeding great and precious promiſes of Mercy and Grace in the new Covenant, through the ſame Mediator thereof. And we pray thee, for his ſake, to take away thy heavie wrath and curſe from us, which we are not able to avoid or bear, and humbly and earneſtly beſeech thee, out of thy free Grace and Mercy, to grant unto us the full Remiſſion of all our ſins, sies, and that onely for the bitter sufferings, and precious merits of that our onely Saviour Jesus Christ. O that the Lord would vouchsafe to shed abroad his love in our hearts by the holy Ghost, to seal unto us our Pardon and Reconciliation, the full assurance of our Pardon and Reconciliation, That he would comfort all that mourn in Zion, speak peace to the wounded and troubled spirits, and binde up the broken hearted. And as for secure and presumptuous sinners, Lord open their eyes, convince their consciences, and turn them from darknesse unto light, and from the power of Satan unto God, that they also may receive forgivenesse of sin, and an inheritance among them that are sanctified by Faith in Christ Jesus. With remission of sins through the blood of Christ, we pray thee also to give us Sanctification by his Spirit, Mortification of sin dwelling in us, and many times tyrannizing over us; the quickning of our dead Spirits with the life of God in Christ, Grace to fit and enable us for all duties of conversation and callings towards God and Man, strength against temptations, the sanctified use of Blessings and Crosses, and perseverance in Faith and Obedience to our lives end, through Jesus Christ our Lord, *Amen.*

A Prayer

O Lord, who doest gather to thy self a Church out of all Nations, we beseech thee, to this end to Propagate thy Gospel and the Kingdom of Christ Jesus to all Nations, convert the Jews, fill up the fulnesse of the Gentiles, hasten the fall of Antichrist, and the second coming of our Lord; Grant deliverance to the distressed Churches abroad from the Tyranny of the Antichristian Faction, and from the cruell oppressions and blasphemies of the Turke: We pray thee send thy Blessing upon all the Reformed Churches, especially upon the Churches and Kingdoms of *England, Scotland,* and *Ireland,* now more strictly, and Religiously united in the Solemne League and Covenant: We pray thee for our Plantations in the remote parts of the world, more particularly for that Church and Kingdom whereof we are Members, that therein God would establish Peace and Truth, the Purity of all his Ordinances, and the power of godlinesse; prevent and remove Heresie, Schisme, Prophanenesse, Superstition, security, and unfruitfulnesse under the means of Grace, heal our rents and divisions, and preserve us from breach of our Solemn Covenant. We pray thee for all in Authority, especially for the Kings Majesty, that God would make him rich in Blessings, both in his Petition and Government, Establish his Throne in Religion and Righteousnesse; save him from evil Councell, and make him a blessed and glorious Instrument for the conservation and propagation of the Gospel, for the incouragement and protection of them that do well, the terrour of all that do evil, and the great good of the Church of Christ, and of these United Kingdoms. We pray thee convert

convert the Queen, give a Religious Education to the Prince, and the rest of the Royall Seed; comfort their afflicted Queen of *Bohemia*, Sister to our Soveraign: We pray thee for the Restitution and Establishment of the illustrious Prince, The Elector Palatine of the *Rhine*, to all his Dominions and Dignities: Blesse the High Court of Parliament, the Nobility, the subordinate Judges and Magistrates, the Gentry, and all the Commonalty: Blesse all Pastors and Teachers, O Lord, fill them with thy spirit, and make them exemplarily holy, sober, just, peaceable, and gracious in their lives; found, faithfull, and powerfull in their Ministry, and follow all their labours with abundance of successe and blessing. And give unto all thy People, Pastors according to thy own heart: Blesse the Universities, and all Schools, and Religious Seminaries of Church and Common-wealth, that they may flourish more and more in Learning and Piety. Powre out a blessing upon the Ministry of the Word, Sacraments, and Discipline; give thy mercy and consolation, to the afflicted under any inward or outward distresse, Lord, give various seasonable Weather, and Fruitfull Seasons: Lord, turne away thy Judgements, that we feel or fear or are liable unto. With all outward means of salvation, be graciously pleased to powre out the spirit of Grace into our hearts; causing us to attaine such a measure of the Excellency of the knowledge of Christ Jesus our Lord, and in sum of the things which belong to our Peace, that we may account all things but as dung in comparison of him, and that we tasting the first fruits of the glory that is to be revealed, may long for a more full and perfect Communion with him, that where he is we may be also, and enjoy the fulnesse of those joyes and pleasures which are at thy

the Right hand for evermore; and all this through the same Chief Jesus, our onely Mediator and Advocate, Amen.

After this Prayer, a Psalm may be sung, and the conclusion may be with a Thanksgiving and Blessing.

The Thanksgiving.

WE give thee thanks, most gracious Father, the Fountain of every good and perfect gift, for all thy blessings, both Spirituall and Temporall; especially, for thy great love, in sending thy Son Christ Jesus unto us; for the Communication of thy holy spirit, for the sight and liberty of thy glorious Gospel, and the rich heavenly blessings revealed therein, as namely, our Election, Vocation, Adoption, Justification, Sanctification, and hope of glory; for the admirable goodnesse of God in freeing the land from Antichristian darknesse and Tyranny, and for all other Nationall deliverances: We Blesse thee for the Reformation of our Religion, our continuall preservation, and for many other Temporall blessings. We pray thee for the continuance of all thy favours and blessings, and particularly of thy Gospel, and all the Ordinances thereof, in their purity, power, and liberty: We pray thee make thy word powerfull, that it may abide in our hearts, and bring forth fruit in our live, and conversation. We beseech thee fit and prepare us for death, and judgement, and that we may watch for the coming of our Lord Jesus Christ. We intreat thee forgive the iniquity of our holy things, and accept of our Spirituall sacrifices, through the merit and mediation of our great High Priest and Saviour, the Lord Christ Jesus, Amen.

Prayer

12

Prayer for a Blessing.

THE Lord bless us, and keep us; the Lord make his face to shine upon us, and be gracious unto us; the Lord lift up his countenance upon us, and give us his Peace. And the very God of Peace, sanctifie us wholly, that our whole spirit, soul, and body, may be preserved blamelesse unto the coming of our Lord Iesus Christ And the grace of our Lord Iesus Christ, and the love of God the Father, and the Communion of the Holy Ghost be with us all, *Amen.*

A Prayer particularly fitted for those that travel upon the Seas.

O Lord, who art the hope of the ends of the Earth, and of those that are upon the wide Sea, by whole Providence men go down to the Sea in Ships, and follow businesse in great Waters, we pray thee to take both Ship and persons under thy protection and preservation, and let a blessing come from thee upon our businesses and endeavours. And, Lord, though we by our sins have deserved rather curses then blessings, yet we pray thee to deal with us, not according to our sins and our own deservings, but according to thy infinite free mercy, and the merits of thy son Christ Jesus, which are of an infinite value. Behold us in him, we beseech thee, in whom thou art well pleased, and in him be well pleased with us. And, Lord, we pray thee that he may be unto us not onely justification from the guilt of sin, but sanctifi-cation deliver us from the power and service of sin, that

that we may be partakers of his Holinesse, without which no man shall see thee. And, Lord, while we are upon the Sea, cause us to take notice of thy great works, for that hast made the Sea, and therein creatures innumerable, both small and great; And while wee behold things carried by thee, let our hearts be lifted up to thee who hast created them, to worship thee, to love thee, and to serve thee; by whom, and for whom all things were created. Keep us, Lord, from storms and tempests, and if they shall arise, let thy word come forth, and turn the storm into a calm, make the Waters still, and bring us in good season, to the Haven of our desires. In the mean time, preserve us also from Sea-thieves, Enemies, and other dangers to which our Voyages are subject; And, Lord, when thou shalt preserve us, and bring us home in safty, give us grace to be truly and really thankfull to thee, and to expresse our Thankfulnesse in a holy life and conversation; that we may serve, and please thee, who preservest us. And let not thy often preservations of us, make us the lesse sensible of them, but rather the more thankfull to thee for them; For, Lord we confesse, such is the corruption of our nature, that when we often passe through dangers, and escape them, we take lesse notice of thy gracious providence and preservation in them; whereas we should be the more thankfull to thee, the more thou multipliest thy favours upon us. But, Lord yet more, upon our returns to return to folly and sin, and that we, whom thou preservest, should offend thee by sinfull courses, in stead of serving thee, and bring thankfull to thee; For, then mayst thou justly come upon us by thy judgements, in an hour which we think not on, and let in the Seas and other dangers upon us, to swallow us up and devoure us, and after give us our portion in a

L et

14

Lake of Fire that burneth for evermore. But, Lord, we pray thee to guide us ever by thy grace, and not to leave us to our selves and our own corruptions, but through all the passages of this our pilgrimage, both upon Sea and Land, leade us by thy good Spirit, and bring us at last to the true Haven of Blessednesse and place of rest, where in thy presence, where is fulnesse of joy, and where are pleasures for evermore. Hear us, O Lord, and accept our persons and prayers, through thy beloved Son Christ Jesus, who, sitting at thy right hand, makes intercession for us, to whom with the Almighty Father, and the most blessed and holy Spirit, be all honour, service and praise, from this time forth for evermore, *Amen.*

A Prayer in a Storm.

O Lord, we acknowledge, that by thy own Providence and will, this storm is now come upon us; for thy Word hath taught us, that thou commandest and raisest the stormy Winds which lift up the waves of the Sea, so that they mount up to the Heaven, and go down againe to the Depths and the souls of men are melted because of trouble, and they are at their wits ends. And, Lord, we confesse that we have sins enough to draw down all thy stormes upon us, and too overwhelm us with all thy waves: But Lord, we beseech thee to make our hearts to search themselves, as for all sins, so for those especially which may draw down this great Tempest upon us; and let us cast out these sins as the Marriners cast our *Jonas,* and let the wind and Sea cease from their raging. And, Lord, we pray thee that we may so cast them out, that we may never take them in again, lest greater storms overtake us.

For

For we acknowledge, that where sins, there must storms be expected; Storms and Tempests, Fire and Brimstone are the portion of sinners: grant us also such grace, that we may not only have our sins and cast them out, because they are so followed with storms and Judgements; but because they are odious in themselves, being contrary to thy Righteous Law, and to thee who art the Fountain and fule of Righteousnesse. And, Lord, let us also take thy Son Christ Jesus into our souls to sanctifie them, and raien in them, remembring also that Christ Jesus makes a Calm in the souls where he Raignes, for being justified by him, we have Peace with God; and he also when he was here below, being in the Ship, made a calm there also, and commanded the winds to be still: Lord, we pray thee, grant at this time both these calms unto us; for as my Word told us, that when thou commandest, a storm ariseth, so it also sheweth us, that when men cry to thee in their trouble, thou bringest them out of their distresse, thou makest the storm a calm, and the waves of the Sea are still; then are men glad because they be quiet, and thou bringest them to their desired Haven. Lord, we beseech thee, let it be now to thy servants according to this thy Word, and then let that also be done which justly followeth: Let us Praise the Lord for his goodnesse, and his wonderfull workes to the sons of men: Let us Exalt thee in the Congregation of the People, and Praise thee in the Assembly of the Elders: And if the Heathen Marriners which carried *Jonah,* being delivered from the storm, did fear the Lord exceedingly, and offered Sacrifice to the Lord, and made Vows; Let us much more who have the light of the Gospel in greater measure before us, fear them, fear thee greatly, and offer to thee the Sacrifices of Praise, and make Vows of better Obedience:

And

And, Lord, having made such Vows, assist us by thy grace that we may perform them ; and cause us all our lives to carry with us, and in us, the same thoughts and resolutions of holinesse and good Conversation, which we have when we are in a storm, and not obey thee worse after deliverances, then we resolved to do in dangers. And, Lord, howsoever thou shalt please to dispose of us, we do here cast our selves down under thy Mighty hand ; We submit our selves to thee, as the clay to the Potter, to do with us what is good in thy sight ; for thou hast promised that all shall turn to good to those whom thou hast chosen : And hast further shewed us, that neither life nor death can separate us from thy love that is in Christ Jesus ; Let it be so unto thy servants, let thy love alwayes be towards us in Christ Jesus the Son of thy Love : Whatsoever Iudgements fall on our bodies, let our souls be saved by the Lord Jesus ; Let us so be knit unto him by a lively Faith, that we may be partakers of him , and in him , of life Eternall: And having a sure hope and confidence hereof, let us desire to be dissolved and to be with Christ, which is best of all ; and at our dissolution, speak with assurance to be heard , Lord Iesus Receive our Spirits : Hear us, O Lord, and grant us our Petitions, and whatsoever thy wisdom knows to be best for us, which is far beyond all that we can ask or think, and all for the sake of thy Son and our blessed Saviour, through whom alone we and our Prayers have accesse unto thee ; to whom with thy G orious self, and most Holy Spirit, be all Honour and Glory, Praise and Thanksgiving, Service and Obedience, from this time forth, and for evermore, *Amen*.

F I N I S.

Bibliography

A Survey of the Book of Common Prayer By Way of 197 Quares grounded upon 58 places, London 1610.

Adamson, John, 'The Kingdom of England and Great Britain: The Tudor and Stuart Courts 1509–1714' in Adamson, John (ed.), *The Princely Courts of Europe. Ritual, Politics and Culture under the Ancien Régime 1500–1750*, Weidenfeld and Nicolson, London 1999, pp. 95–117.

An Abridgement of that Booke which the Ministers of the Lincolne Diocesse Delivered to his Majestie upon the first of December 1605, London 1617.

Andrewes, Lancelot, *Ninety-Six Sermons by the Right Honourable and Reverend Father in God, Lancelot Andrewes*, Vol. IV, John Henry Parker, Oxford 1841.

Andrews, C. Bruyn (ed.), *The Torrington Diaries: Containing the Tours through England and Wales of the Hon, John Byng (later Fifth Viscount Torrington) between the Years 1781 and 1794*, 4 vols, Henry Holt and Company, New York 1936.

Apthorp, East, *The Excellence of the Liturgy of the Church of England: A Sermon at the Church of St. Mary-le-Bow, 1778*, London 1778.

Arber, E. (ed.), *A Brieff Discours of the Troubles at Frankfort 1554–1558 A.D.*, Elliot Stock, London 1908.

Armstrong, Herbert B. J. (ed.), *Armstrong's Norfolk Diary: Further Passages from the Diary of the Reverend Benjamin John Armstrong*, Hodder and Stoughton, London 1963.

Armstrong, Herbert B. J. (ed.), *A Norfolk Diary: Passages from the Diary of the Rev. Benjamin John Armstrong*, George Harrap and Company Ltd, London 1949.

Ashbee, Andrew and Harley, John (eds), *The Cheque Books of the Chapel Royal*, 2 vols, Ashgate, Aldershot 2000.

Atherstone, Andrew, *Charles Simeon on the Excellency of the Liturgy*, Alcuin Club/GROW Joint Liturgical Study 72, Hymns Ancient and Modern, Norwich 2011.

Ayres, Jack (ed.), *Paupers and Pig Killers: The Diary of William Holland, a Somerset Parson, 1799–1818*, Alan Sutton Publishing, Gloucester 1984.

Baillie, Robert, *A Large Supplement of the Canterburian Self-Conviction*, 1641.

Balcanquhal, Walter and Charles I, *A Large Declaration concerning the late Tumults in Scotland*, 1639.

Baldwin, David, *The Chapel Royal: Ancient and Modern*, Duckworth, London 1990.

Baring-Gould, Sabine, *The Church Revival: Thoughts Theron and Reminiscences*, Methuen, London 1914.

Barrett, Philip, *Barchester: English Cathedral Life in the Nineteenth Century*, SPCK, London 1993.

Beeson, Trevor, *The Church's Folk Songs from Hymns Ancient and Modern to Common Praise 1861–2011*, Canterbury Press, Norwich 2011.

Bentley, James, *Ritualism and Politics in Victorian Britain*, Oxford University Press, Oxford 1978.

Beresford, John (ed.), *The Diary of a Country Parson: The Reverend James Woodforde 1758–1802*, 3 vols, Oxford University Press, Oxford 1924–27.

Berger, Teresa, *Liturgie-Spiegel der Kirche. Eine systematische-theologische Analyse des liturgischen Gedankenguts im Traktarianismus*, Forschungen zur Systematischen und ökumenischen Theologie 52, Vandenhoeck and Ruprecht, Göttingen 1986.

Birt, H. N., *The Elizabethan Religious Settlement: A Study of Contemporary Documents*, George Bell and Sons, London 1907.

Bisse, Thomas, *Decency and order in Public Worship Recommended in Three Discourses, Preached in the Cathedral Church of Hereford*, London 1723.

Booty, John E., *The Book of Common Prayer 1559*, reprint, University of Virginia, Charlottesville 2005.

Bowers, Rick, 'James VI, Prince Henry, and *A True Reportarie* of Baptism at Stirling 1594', *Renaissance and Reformation* 29 (2005), pp. 3–21.

Bowers, Roger, 'Chapel and Choir, Liturgy and Music' in Massing, Jean Michel and Zeeman, Nicolette, *King's College Chapel 1515–2015: Art, Music and Religion in Cambridge*, Harvey Miller Publishers, London 2014, pp. 259–83.

Bowers, Roger, 'The Chapel Royal, the first Edwardian Prayer Book, and Elizabeth's Settlement of Religion, 1559', *The Historical Journal* 43/2 (2000), pp. 317–44.

Box, Charles, *Church Music in the Metropolis*, William Reeves, London 1884.

Braddock, Andrew, *The Role of the Book of Common Prayer in the Formation of Modern Anglican Identity: A Study of English Parochial Worship, 1750–1850*, Edwin Mellen Press, Lewiston, NY 2010.

Brandwood, Geoffrey K., '"Mummeries of a Popish Character" – the Camdenians and Early Christian Worship' in Webster, C. and Elliott, J., *'A Church as it Should Be': The Cambridge Camden Society and Its Influence*, Shaun Tyas, Donington 2000, pp. 62–97.

Brightman, F. E., *The English Rite*, 2 vols, Rivingtons, London 1915.

Bromwich, D. (ed.), *The Diary & Memoires of John Allen Giles*, Somerset Record Office, Taunton 2000.

Brown, R. and Bentinck, G. C., *Calendar of State Papers Venetian VII* (1558–80), Her Majesty's Stationery Office, London 1890.

Browning, Andrew (ed.), *English Historical Documents, 1660–1714*, Taylor and Francis, London and New York 2006.

Broxap, Henry, *A Biography of Thomas Deacon*, Manchester University Press, Manchester 1911.

Broxap, Henry, *The Later Non-Jurors*, Cambridge University Press, Cambridge 1924.

Buchanan, Colin, *The Hampton Court Conference and the 1604 Book of Common Prayer with Related Documents, Introduction and Annotation*, Alcuin/GROW Liturgical Study 68, Hymns Ancient and Modern, Norwich 2009.

Buchanan, Colin, *The Savoy Conference Revisited*, Alcuin/GROW Joint Liturgical Study 54, Grove Books, Cambridge 2002.

Buckeridge, John, *A Sermon Preached before his Maiestie at Whitehall, March 22 1617*, London 1618.

Bumpus, John S., *A History of English Cathedral Music 1549–1889*, Gregg International Reprint, Westmead 1972.

Butler, Janet et al. (eds), *Hymns Ancient & Modern and Henry Williams Baker*, The Leominster History Study Group, Leominster 2013.

Buxton, Richard, *Eucharist and Institution Narrative*, SPCK, London 1976.

Cardwell, Edward (ed.), *Synodalia: A Collection of Articles of Religion, Canons, and Proceedings of Convocations in the Province of Canterbury. From the Year 1547 to the Year 1717*, Oxford University Press, Oxford 1842.

Carlson, Leland H. (ed.), *The Writings of John Greenwood and Henry Barrow 1592–1593*, George Allen and Unwin Ltd., London 1970.

Cheshunt Foundation Archives at Westminster College, Cambridge A4/5.25.

Chetham, John, *A Book of Psalmody*, London 1718.

Christie, James, *Some Accounts of Parish Clerks*, private printing 1893.

Christie, O. F. (ed.), *The Diary of the Revd. William Jones 1777–1821. Curate and Vicar of Broxbourne and the Hamlet of Hoddesdon 1781–1821*, Brentano's, London 1929.

Clarke, Richard, 'The 1878 Book of Common Prayer' in Kennedy, Michael et al., *The Prayer Books of the Church of Ireland 1551–2004*, The Columba Press, Dublin 2004.

Clarke, Samuel, *An Exposition of the Church-Catechism*, Dublin 1730.

Clay, William K. (ed.), *Liturgies and Occasional Forms Set Forth in the Reign of Queen Elizabeth*, Cambridge University Press, Cambridge 1847.

Clay, William K., *Private Prayers Put Forth by Authority during the Reign of Queen Elizabeth*, Cambridge University Press, Cambridge 1851.

Close, F., *The Restoration of Churches is the Restoration of Popery. A Sermon*, Hatchard, London 1844.

Constitutions and Canons Ecclesiastical Treated upon by the Archbishops of Canterbury and York, Robert Barker, London 1640.

Cooper, Trevor, '"Wise as serpents": The Form and Setting of Public Worship at Little Gidding in the 1630s' in Mears, Natalie and Ryrie, Alec (eds), *Worship in the Parish Church in Early Modern Britain*, Ashgate, Farnham 2013, pp. 197–219.

Cooper, Trevor (ed.), *The Journal of William Dowsing. Iconoclasm in East Anglia during the English Civil War*, Boydell, Woodbridge 2001.

Cooper, Trevor and Brown, Sarah (eds), *Pews, Benches and Chairs: Church Seating in English Churches from the Fourteenth Century to the Present*, Ecclesiological Society/Shaun Tyas, Donington 2011.

Corpus Christi College, Oxford, MS C/1/1/9.

Cowper, William, *The Workes of William Cowper*, London 1623.

Craig, John, 'Psalms, Groans and Dogwhippers: The Soundscape of Worship in the English Parish Church, 1547–1642' in Coster, Will and Spicer, Andrew (eds), *Sacred Space in Early Modern Europe*, Cambridge University Press, Cambridge 2005, pp. 104–23.

Craigie, James (ed.), *Basilicon Doron*, Blackwood, Edinburgh 1944.

Craven, J. B. (ed.), *Journals of the Episcopal Visitations of the Right Rev. Robert Forbes, MA*, Skeffington and Sons, Ltd, London 1923.

Cressy, David, *Bonfires and Bells. National Memory and the Protestant Calendar in Elizabethan and Stuart England*, University of California Press, Berkeley, CA 1989.

Cressy, David, *England on Edge: Crisis and Revolution 1640–1642*, Oxford University Press, Oxford 2006.

Crockett, Larry, 'Oxford Movement and the 19th Century Episcopal Church: Anglo-Catholic Ecclesiology and the American Experience', *Quodlibet Online Journal* 1 (1999), no pagination.

Crosby, Brian, '"The Sacrament it selfe is turned well neare into a theatricall stage play": Liturgical Innovations and Reactions in the 1620s' in *Conflict and Disaster at Durham: Four Talks Delivered to the Friends of Durham Cathedral 2001–02*, Friends of Durham Cathedral, Durham 2003.

Crowther, S., *A Sermon Preached at St. Mary-Le-Bow, by the Rev. S. Crowther, A.M. Vicar of Christ Church in the city of London on St. Mark's Day, April 25 1804*, J. Adlard, London 1804.

Cull, Richard, *Garrick's Mode of Reading the Liturgy of the Church of England*, John Parker, London 1840.

Cuming, G. J., *The Durham Book*, Oxford University Press for the University of Durham, 1961, and Alcuin Club, 1975.

Cuming, G. J., 'Two Fragments of a Lost Liturgy?', *Studies in Church History* 3, E. J. Brill, London 1966, pp. 247–53.

Dalby, Mark, *Anglican Missals and Their Canons: 1549, Interim Rite and Roman*, Alcuin/GROW Joint Liturgical Study 41, Grove Books, Cambridge 1998.

Davenport, John, *The triall of the English liturgie*, 1638.

Davies, Julian, *The Caroline Captivity of the Church: Charles I and the Remoulding of Anglicanism*, Clarendon Press, Oxford 1992.

Dearnley, Christopher, *English Church Music 1650–1750*, Barry and Jenkins, London 1970.

Defoe, Daniel, *A Tour Thro' the whole Island of Great Britain*, London 1762.

DeMille, George E., *The Catholic Movement in the American Episcopal Church*, Church Historical Society, Philadelphia, PA 1941.

Ditchfield, P. H., *The Parish Clerk*, Createspace Independent Publishing Platform USA, 2014.

Dixon, Philip, *Nice and Hot Disputes: The Doctrine of the Trinity in the Seventeenth Century*, T & T Clark, London 2003.

Doelman, James, *King James I and the Religious Culture of England*, D. S. Brewer, Cambridge 2000.

Donaldson, Gordon, 'A Scottish Liturgy of the Reign of James VI' in *Miscellany of the Scottish History Society* 10 (1965), pp. 89–117.

Donaldson, Gordon, *The Making of the Scottish Prayer Book of 1637*, Edinburgh University Press, Edinburgh 1954.

Drain, Susan, *The Anglican Church in Nineteenth Century Britain: Hymns Ancient and Modern (1860–1875)*, Edwin Mellen Press, Lewiston, NY 1989.

Du Prey, Pierre de la Ruffinière, *Hawksmoor's London Churches: Architecture and Theology*, University of Chicago Press, Chicago, IL 2000.

Duffy, Eamon, *Fires of Faith: Catholic England under Mary Tudor*, Yale University Press, New Haven, CT 2009.

Duffy, Eamon, *The Voices of Morebath: Reformation and Rebellion in an English Village*, Yale University Press, New Haven, CT 2001.

Dugdale, William, *The History of St. Paul's Cathedral in London*, Thomas Warren, London 1658.

Duguid, Timothy, *Metrical Psalms in Print and Practice: English 'Singing Psalms' and Scottish 'Psalm Buiks', c.1547–1640*, Ashgate, Farnham 2014.

Duguid, Timothy, 'Sing a New Song: English and Scottish Metrical Psalmody from 1549–1640', PhD Thesis, Edinburgh University 2011.

Earl of Bessborough, The (ed.), *Lady Charlotte Guest: Extracts from Her Journal 1833–1852*, John Murray, London 1950.

Ellsworth, L. E., *Charles Lowder and the Ritualist Movement*, Darton, Longman and Todd, London 1982.

Essex Standard, 1 February 1845.

Fawcett, Timothy J., *The Liturgy of Comprehension 1689*, Mayhew-McCrimmon, Southend on Sea 1973.

Felton, Gayle Carlton, *This Gift of Water: The Practice and Theology of Baptism among Methodists in America*, Abingdon Press, Nashville, TN 1992.

Fenwick, John, *The Free Church of England*, T & T Clark, London 2004.

Ferguson, J. P., *Dr. Samuel Clarke: An Eighteenth Century Heretic*, The Roundwood Press, Kineton, 1976.

Ferrell, Lori Anne, *Government by Polemic: James I, the King's Preachers, and the Rhetorics of Conformity, 1603–1625*, Stanford University Press, Palo Alto, CA 1998.

Fincham, Kenneth, '"According to Ancient Custom": The Return of Altars in the Restoration Church of England', *Transactions of the Royal Historical Society* 13 (2003), pp. 29–54.

Fincham, Kenneth, *Prelate as Pastor: The Episcopate of James I*, Clarendon Press, Oxford 1990.

Fincham, Kenneth, 'The Restoration of Altars in the 1630s', *Historical Journal* 44 (2002), pp. 919–40.

Fincham, Kenneth and Tyacke, Nicholas, *Altars Restored: The Changing Face of English Religious Worship, 1547–c.1700*, Oxford University Press, Oxford 2007.

Firth, C. H. and Rait, R. S. (eds), *Acts and Ordinances of the Interregnum 1642–1660*, 3 vols, His Majesty's Stationery Office, London 1911.

Force, James E., *William Whiston: Honest Newtonian*, Cambridge University Press, Cambridge 1985.

Force, James E. and Popkin, Richard, *Essays on the Context, Nature and Influence of Isaac Newton's Theology*, Kluwer Academic, Dordrecht 1990.

Fowler, J. T. (ed.), *Life and Letters of the Rev. John Bacchus Dykes*, John Murray, London 1897.

Frere, W. H. and Douglas, C. E., *Puritan Manifestoes*, SPCK, London 1907.

Gammon, Vic, 'The Performance Style of West Gallery Music' in Turner, Christopher (ed.), *Georgian Psalmody 1: The West Gallery Tradition*, SG Publishing, Corby Glen 1997, pp. 43–51.

Gatens, William J., *Victorian Cathedral Music in Theory and Practice*, Cambridge University Press, Cambridge 1986.

Gee, Henry, *The Elizabethan Clergy and the Settlement of Religion*, Clarendon Press, Oxford 1898.

Gee, Henry and Hardy, William John, *Documents Illustrative of English Church History*, MacMillan, London 1914.

Gerrish, Brian, 'The Lord's Supper in the Reformed Confessions' in McKim, Donald K. (ed.), *Major Themes in the Reformed Tradition*, Eerdmans, Grand Rapids, MI 1992, pp. 245–58.

Gibson, William, *Religion and the Enlightenment 1600–1800: Conflict and the Rise of Civic Humanism in Taunton*, Peter Lang, Bern 2007.

Gillespie, George, *A dispute against the English-popish ceremonies, obtruded upon the Church of Scotland*, Edinburgh 1637.

Goodman, Florence Remington (ed.), *The Diary of John Young S.T.P. Dean of Winchester 1616 to the Commonwealth*, SPCK, London 1928.

Graber, Gary, *Ritual Legislation in the Victorian Church of England. Antecedents and Passage of the Public Worship Regulation Act, 1874*, Edwin Mellen Press, Lewiston, NY 1993.

Gray, Donald, 'Liturgy, 1714–2004' in Keene, Derek, Burns, Arthur and Saint, Andrew (eds), *St. Paul's: The Cathedral Church of London 604–2004*, Yale University Press, New Haven, CT 2004, pp. 352–62.

Gray, Donald, *The 1927–28 Prayer Book Crisis. 1: Ritual, Royal Commissions and Reply to the Royal Letters of Business*, Alcuin/Grow Joint Liturgical Study 60, SCM-Canterbury Press, Norwich 2005.

Gray, Donald, *The 1927–28 Prayer Book Crisis. 2: The Cul-de-sac of the 'Deposited Book'. . . until further order to be taken*, Alcuin/Grow Joint Liturgical Study 61, SCM-Canterbury Press, Norwich 2006.

Gray, E., *Papers and Diaries of a York Family 1764–1839*, Sheldon Press, London 1927.

Green, I. M., *The Re-Establishment of the Church of England 1660–1663*, Oxford University Press, Oxford 1978.

Green, Ian, '"Puritan Prayer Books" and "'Genevan Bible": An Episode in Elizabethan Publishing', *Transactions of the Cambridge Bibliographical Society* 11 (1998), pp. 313–49.

Grisbrooke, W. Jardine, *Anglican Liturgies of the Seventeenth and Eighteenth Centuries*, SPCK, London 1958.

Gyford, Janet, *A History of Witham*, Janet Gyford, Witham 2005.

Hall, Elias, *The psalm-singer's compleat companion*, London 1706.

Hall, Michael, 'What do Victorian Churches Mean? Symbolism and Sacramentalism in Anglican Church Architecture 1850–1870', *Journal of the Society of Architectural Historians* 59.1 (2000), pp. 78–95.

Hall, Stuart G., 'Patristics and Reform: Thomas Rattray and *The Ancient Liturgy of the Church of Jerusalem*' in Swanson, R. N. (ed.), *Continuity and Change in Christian Worship*, Boydell and Brewer, Woodbridge 1999, pp. 240–60.

Hannah, Gavin (ed.), *The Deserted Village: The Diary of an Oxfordshire Rector James Newton of Nuneham Courtenay 1736-86*, Alan Sutton, Dover 1992.

Hart, Richard, *Parish Churches Turn'd into Conventicles . . . in Particular, by Reading the Communion Service, or any Part Thereof at the Desk*, London 1683.

Hatchett, Marion J., *The Making of the First American Book of Common Prayer*, Seabury Press, New York 1982.

Haugaard, William P., *Elizabeth and the English Reformation*, Cambridge University Press, Cambridge 1968.

Hawkes, Francis L. and Perry, William Stevens, *Documentary History of the Protestant Episcopal Church in the United States of America: Connecticut*, 2 vols, J. Pott, New York 1863–64.

Henderson, G. D. and Porter, H. H. (eds), *James Gordon's Diary 1692–1710*, Spalding Club, Aberdeen 1949.

Herring, George, *The Oxford Movement in Practice: The Tractarian Parochial World from the 1830s to the 1870s*, Oxford University Press, Oxford 2016.

Heylyn, Peter, *Cyprianus Anglicus or the Life and Death of the Most Reverend and Renowned Prelate William, by Divine Providence, Lord Archbishop of Canterbury . . .*, London 1671.

Hieron, Samuel, *A short dialogue proving that the ceremonies and some other corruptions now in question are defended, by none other arguments then such as the papists have heretofore used*, London 1605.

Higgott, Gordon, 'The Fabric to 1670' in Keene, Derek, Burns, Arthur and Saint, Andrew (eds), *St. Paul's: The Cathedral Church of London 604–2004*, Yale University Press, New Haven, CT 2004, pp. 171–89.

Hoak, Dale, 'The Coronations of Edward VI, Mary I, and Elizabeth I, and the Transformation of the Tudor Monarchy' in Knighton, C. S. and Mortimer, Richard (eds), *Westminster Abbey Reformed 1540–1640*, Ashgate, Aldershot 2003, pp. 114–51.

Holinshed, Raphael, *The Chronicles of England, Ireland and Scotland*, Johnson et al., London 1807.

Holland, Bernard G., *Baptism in Early Methodism*, Epworth Press, London 1970.

Hooker, Richard, *Lawes of Ecclesiastical Polity, Book V*, Keeble edn, Clarendon Press, Oxford 1865.

Hunt, Arnold, 'Laurence Chaderton and the Hampton Court Conference' in Wabuda, Susan and Litzenberger, Caroline (eds), *Belief and Practice in Reformation England*, Ashgate, Aldershot 1998, pp. 207–28.

Jacobson, William (ed.), *Fragmentary Illustrations of the History of the Book of Common Prayer*, John Murray, London 1874.

James, J. F. and Bettey, J. H. (eds), *Farming in Dorset: Diary of James Warne, 1758, Letters of George Boswell, 1787–1805*, Dorset Record Society, Dorchester 1993.

Janes, Dominic, *Victorian Reformation: The Fight over Idolatry in the Church of England 1840–1860*, Oxford University Press, New York 2009.

Jasper, R. C. D., *Prayer Book Revision in England 1800–1900*, SPCK, London 1954.

Jasper, R. C. D. (ed.), *Walter Howard Frere: His Correspondence on Liturgical Revision and Construction*, SPCK, London 1954.

Jeanes, Gordon, *Signs of God's Promise: Thomas Cranmer's Sacramental Theology and the Book of Common Prayer*, T & T Clark, London 2008.

Jebb, John, *The Choral Service of the United Church of England and Ireland: Being an Enquiry into the Liturgical System of the Cathedral and Collegiate Foundations of the Anglican Communion*, John Parker, London 1843.

Jesus College Cambridge Archives A/C.1.3.

Johnson, John, *The Unbloody Sacrifice and Altar, unvail'd and Supported*, Part 1, London 1714.

Jones, Norman, *Faith by Statute: Parliament and the Settlement of Religion 1559*, Royal Historical Society, London 1968.

Judge, Roy, 'May Morning and Magdalen College, Oxford', *Folklore* 97 (1986), pp. 15–40.

Kim, Joong-Lak, 'Firing in Unison? The Scottish Canons of 1636 and the English Canons of 1640', *Records of the Scottish Church History Society* 28 (1998), pp. 58–77.

Kim, Joong-Lak, 'The Scottish-English-Romish Book: The Character of the Scottish Prayer Book of 1637' in Braddock, Michael J. and Smith, David L., *The Experience of Revolution in Stuart Britain and Ireland*, Cambridge University Press, Cambridge 2011.

King, Archdale A., *Liturgies of the Past*, Longmans, London 1959.

Kirk, Robert, *Sermons, Conferences . . . with a Description of London. Ann 1689*, University of Edinburgh Department of Manuscripts, La.III.545.

Lake, Peter, 'The Laudian Style: Order, Uniformity and the Pursuit of the Beauty of Holiness in the 1630s' in Fincham, Kenneth (ed.), *The Early Stuart Church, 1604–1642*, Stanford University Press, Palo Alto, CA 1993, pp. 161–85.

Lambeth Palace Library MS 9333.8.

Lane, Calvin, *The Laudians and the Elizabethan Church*, Pickering and Chatto, London 2013.

Laud, William, *The Works of the Most Reverend Father in God, William Laud, DD*, John Henry Parker, Oxford 1853.

Le Huray, Peter, *Music and Reformation in England 1549–1660*, Herbert Jenkins Ltd, London 1967.

Leaver, Robin A., *Goostly Psalmes and Spirituall Songes: English Metrical Psalms from Coverdale to Utenhove 1535–1566*, Oxford University Press, Oxford 1991.

Leaver, Robin A., 'Liturgical Music as Homily and Hermeneutic' in Leaver, Robin A. and Zimmerman, Joyce Ann (eds), *Liturgy and Music: Lifetime Learning*, Liturgical Press, Collegeville, MN 1998, pp. 340–59.

Leech, Joseph, *The Bristol Church Goer: His Visits to Bitton,&c.*, John Riddler, Bristol 1849.

Leech, Joseph, *The Church-goer: Rural Rides*, 3rd edn, John Ridler, Bristol 1851.

Leech, Joseph, *Rural Rides of the Bristol Churchgoer*, ed. Alan Sutton, Nonsuch Publishing Ltd, Stroud 2004.

Legg, J. Wickham, *English Church Life from the Restoration to the Tractarian Movement*, Longmans, Green and Co., London 1914.

Lindsay, David (ed.), *Funerals of a Right Reverend Father in God: Patrick Forbes of Corse, Bishop of Aberdene*, Aberdeen 1635.

Lowe, Edward, *A Review of some short Directions for the performance of Cathedral Service*, London 1664.

McCall, Fiona, *Baal's Priests: The Loyalist Clergy and the English Revolution*, Ashgate, Farnham 2013.

McCart, Thomas K., *The Matter and Manner of Praise: The Controversial Evolution of Hymnody in the Church of England 1760–1820*, Scarecrow Press, Lanham, MD 1998.

MacCulloch, Diarmaid, 'Putting the English Reformation on the Map', *Transactions of the Royal Historical Society* 15, Royal Historical Society, London 2005, pp. 75–95.

MacCulloch, Diarmaid, 'Richard Hooker's Reputation', *English Historical Review* 117 (2002), pp. 773–812.

MacCulloch, Diarmaid, *The Later Reformation in England, 1547–1603*, Palgrave, Basingstoke 2001.

MacCulloch, Diarmaid, *Thomas Cranmer: A Life*, Yale University Press, New Haven, CT 1996.

McCullough, Peter, 'Absent Presence: Lancelot Andrewes and 1662' in Platten, Stephen and Woods, Christopher (eds), *Comfortable Words: Polity, Piety and the Book of Common Prayer*, SCM Press, London 2012, pp. 49–68.

Macfarlane, A. (ed.), *The Diary of Ralph Josselin 1616–1683*, Oxford University Press for the British Academy, Oxford 1976.

MacKechnie, 'James VI's Architects and their Architecture' in Goodare, Julian and Lynch, Michael (eds), *The Reign of James VI*, Birlinn Ltd, Edinburgh 2008, pp. 154–69.

Maltby, Judith, '"Extravagancies and Impertinences": Set Forms, Conceived and Extempore Prayer in Revolutionary England' in Mears, Natalie and

Ryrie, Alec (eds), *Worship and the Parish Church in Early Modern Britain*, Ashgate, Farnham 2013, pp. 221–43.

Maltby, Judith, 'Petitions for Episcopacy and the Book of Common Prayer on the Eve of the Civil War 1641–1642' in Taylor, Stephen (ed.), *From Cranmer to Davidson: A Miscellany*, Church of England Record Society 7, Boydell and Brewer, Woodbridge 1999, pp. 105–67.

Maltby, Judith, *Prayer Book and People in Elizabethan and Early Stuart England*, Cambridge University Press, Cambridge 1998.

Marshall, Paul Victor, *One, Catholic and Apostolic: Samuel Seabury and the Early Episcopal Church*, Church Publishing, New York 2004.

Marwick, J. D. (ed.), *Extracts from the Records of the Burgh of Edinburgh*, Vol. 8, Scottish Burgh Records Society, Oliver and Boyd, Edinburgh 1869.

Maurice, Frederick Denison, *The Prayer-Book considered in Reference to the Roman System. Nineteen Sermons preached in the Chapel of Lincoln's Inn 1848*, Macmillan and Co., London 1893.

Mayne, Brian, 'Ireland' in Hefling, Charles and Shattuck, Cynthia (eds), *The Oxford Guide to the Book of Common Prayer: A Worldwide Survey*, Oxford University Press, Oxford 2006, pp. 202–8.

Mears, Natalie, Raffe, Alasdair, Taylor, Stephen and Williamson, Philip (with Lucy Bates) (eds), *National Prayers: Special Worship Since the Reformation. Vol. 1: Special Prayers, Fasts and Thanksgivings in the British Isles 1533–1688*, The Church of England Record Society and Boydell Press, Woodbridge 2013.

Meikle, Henry W. (ed.), *The Works of William Fowler*, Vol. 2, Blackwood, Edinburgh 1936.

Members of the Ecclesiological Late Cambridge Camden Society, *Hierurgia Anglicana, or Documents and extracts illustrative of the Ritual of the Church of England*, Rivington, London 1848.

Merritt, J. F., 'The Cradle of Laudianism? Westminster Abbey, 1558–1630', *Journal of Ecclesiastical History* 52 (2001), pp. 623–46.

Milert, William van, *The Excellency of the Liturgy, and the Advantage of being educated in the Doctrine and principles of the Church of England*, London 1797.

Milton, Anthony, '"Anglicanism" by Stealth: The Career and Influence of John Overall' in Fincham, Kenneth and Milton, Anthony (eds), *Religious Politics in Post-Reformation England*, Boydell Press, Woodbridge 2006, pp. 159–76.

Minutes of the Methodist Conference, Vol. 1, Conference Office, London 1812.

Mitchell, Leonel L., 'The Influence of the Rediscovery of the *Apostolic Constitutions* on the Nonjurors', *Ecclesia Orans* 13 (1996), pp. 207–21.

Nelson, Bernadette, 'Ritual and Ceremony in the Spanish Royal Chapel, c.1559–c.1561', *Early Music History* 19 (2000), pp. 105–200.

Nichols, John, *The Progresses, Processions, and Magnificent Festivities, of King James the First*, Vol. 3, J. B. Nichols, London 1828.

Nichols, John Gough (ed.), *The Diary of Henry Machyn: Citizen and Merchant-Taylor of London, from AD 1550–AD 1563*, Camden Society, London 1848.

Noone, Michael, *Music and Musicians in the Escorial Liturgy under the Hapsburgs, 1563–1700*, University of Rochester Press, Woodbridge 1998.

Northup, Lesley Armstrong, *The 1892 Book of Common Prayer*, Edward Mellen Press, Lewiston, NY 1993.

O. U., *Parish-Churches no Conventicles*, London 1683.

The Parish Choir 1, John Ollivier, London 1846.

Parry, Graham, *The Arts of the Anglican Counter-Reformation: Glory, Laud and Honour*, Boydell Press, Woodbridge 2006.

Patrick, John, *A Century of Select Psalms, and Portions of the Psalms of David, Especially those of praise. Turned into Meter, and fitted to the usual Tunes in Parish Churches, For use of the Charter-House, London*, London 1679.

Pearse, E., *The Conformist's Plea for the Nonconformists*, Jonathan Robinson, London 1681.

Peaston, A. Elliott, *The Prayer Book Reform Movement in the XVIIIth Century*, Blackwell, Oxford 1940.

Peaston, A. Elliott, *The Prayer Book Revisions of the Victorian Evangelicals*, APCK, Dublin 1963.

Peaston, A. Elliott, *The Prayer Book Tradition in the Free Churches*, James Clarke, London 1964.

Pebworth, Ted-Larry, 'An Anglican Family Worship Service of the Interregnum: A Cancelled Early Text and a New Edition of Owen Felltham's "A Form of Prayer"', *English Literary Renaissance* 16 (1986), pp. 206–33.

Peterhouse MS. Consecration of St. Pet. Collg Chap. AD 1632.

Pfizenmaier, Thomas C., *The Trinitarian Theology of Dr. Samuel Clarke (1675–1729): Context, Sources, and Controversy*, E. J. Brill, Leiden 1997.

Phillips, Peter, *English Sacred Music 1549–1649*, Gimell, Oxford 1991.

Plomer, William (ed.), *Kilvert's Diary 1870–1879: Selections from the Diary of the Rev. Francis Kilvert*, The Macmillan Company, New York 1947.

Port, M. H., *Six Hundred New Churches: The Church Building Commission 1818–1856*, Spire Books, Reading 2006.

Prynne, William, *A briefe Survey and censure of Mr. Cozens His Couzening Devotions*, London 1628.

Prynne, William, *Canterburies Doom*, London 1646.

Prynne, William, *Wren's Anatomy. Discovering His notorious pranks, and shamfull wickednesse; with some of his most lewd facts, and infamous deeds; both in his government of Peter-house Colledge, and domineering in three Bishopricks, to his perpetuall shame and infamy*, London 1641.

Quitslund, Beth, *The Reformation in Rhyme: Sternhold, Hopkins and the English Metrical Psalter, 1547–1603*, Ashgate, Aldershot 2008.

R. T., *De Templis*, R. Bisho, London 1638.

Rainbow, Bernarr, *The Choral Revival in the Anglican Church (1839–1872)*, Oxford University Press, New York 1970.

Raines, F. R. (ed.), *The Journal of Nicholas Assheton*, Chetham Society Publication, Vol. 14, Manchester 1848.

Ratcliff, E. C., 'The English Usage of Eucharistic Consecration 1548–1662 – II', *Theology* 60 (1957), pp. 273–80.

Raymer, Victoria, 'Durham House and the Emergence of Laudian Piety', PhD dissertation, Harvard University 1981.

Read, Sophie, *Eucharist and the Poetic Imagination in Early Modern England*, Cambridge University Press, Cambridge 2013.

Report of the Royal Commission on Ecclesiastical Discipline 1906, http://anglican-history.org/pwra/rced11.html (accessed 20 January 2012).

Rimbault, Edward Francis, *The Old Cheque-book, or Book of remembrance, of the Chapel Royal, from 1561–1744*, Camden Society, London 1872.

Robbins, Caroline (ed.), *The Diary of John Milward, Esq, member of Parliament for Derbyshire September, 1666 to May 1668*, Cambridge University Press, Cambridge 1938.

Roe, G. and Hutchings, A., *J. B. Dykes (1823–1876): Priest and Musician*, St Oswald's Parochial Church Council, Durham 1976.

Rogers, Charles, *History of the Chapel Royal in Scotland*, The Grampian Club, Edinburgh 1882.

Rogers, Thomas, *Lectures Delivered in the Parish Church of Wakefield in the Year 1802 on that part of the Liturgy of the Church of England contained in the Morning Prayer*, Longman, Hurst, Rees and Orme, London 1816.

Rosendale, Timothy, *Liturgy and Literature in the Making of Protestant England*, Cambridge University Press, Cambridge 2007.

Rowe, Lesley A., *The Life and Times of Arthur Hildersham: Prince among Puritans*, Reformation Heritage Books, Grand Rapids, MI 2013.

St John's College Oxford Archive 1.A.16 1.A.19.

Schnitker, Thaddaeus A., *The Church's Worship: The 1979 American Book of Common Prayer in a Historical Perspective*, Peter Lang, Frankfurt am Main 1989.

Segger, Glen J., *Richard Baxter's Reformed Liturgy: A Puritan Alternative to the Book of Common Prayer*, Ashgate, Farnham 2014.

Sharp, Thomas, *The Rubrick in the Book of Common Prayer*, London 1753.

Shaw, Douglas, 'St. Giles' Church and Charles I's Coronation Visit to Scotland', *Historical Research* 77 (2004), pp. 481–502.

Shuckford, Samuel, *The Use of a Liturgy, and the Excellency of the Liturgy of the Church of England Considered, in a Sermon*, London 1752.

Simeon, Charles, *The Excellency of the Liturgy, in Four Discourses. Preached Before the University of Cambridge, in November 1811*, J. Smith, Cambridge 1812.

Skinner, John, *Journal of a Somerset Rector 1803–1834*, ed. Coombs, Howard and Peter, Oxford University Press, Oxford 1984.

Smart, Peter, *A Sermon Preached in the Cathedrall Church of Durham, July 7 1628*, 1640 edn.

Smith, Alan, 'Elizabethan Church Music at Ludlow', *Music and Letters* 49/2 (1968), pp. 108–21.

Smith, James David, *The Eucharistic Doctrine of the Later Nonjurors*, Alcuin Club/GROW Joint Liturgical Study 46, Grove Books, Cambridge 2000.

Spalding, John, *The History of the Troubles and Memorable Transactions in Scotland 1624–1645*, Vol. 1, Aberdeen 1791.

Spicer, Andrew, '"Laudianism" in Scotland? St. Giles' Cathedral, Edinburgh, 1633–39: A Reappraisal', *Architectural History* 46 (2003), pp. 95–108.

Spinks, Bryan D., 'Brief and Perspicuous Text; Plain and Pertinent Doctrine: Behind "Of the Preaching of the Word" in the Westminster Directory' in Dudley, Martin (ed.), *Like a Two-edged Sword*, Canterbury Press, Norwich 1995, pp. 91–111.

Spinks, Bryan D., *Do This in Remembrance of Me: The Eucharist from the Early Church to the Present Day*, SCM Press, London 2013.

Spinks, Bryan D., 'Durham House and the Chapels Royal: Their Liturgical Impact on the Church of Scotland', *Scottish Journal of Theology* 67 (2014), pp. 379–99.

Spinks, Bryan D., *Freedom or Order? The Eucharistic Liturgy in English Congregationalism 1645–1980*, Pickwick Publications, Allison Park, PA 1984.

Spinks, Bryan D., *From the Lord and 'The Best Reformed Churches': A Study of the Eucharistic Liturgy in the English Puritan and Separatist Traditions 1550–1633*, CLV Edizioni Liturgiche, Rome 1984.

Spinks, Bryan D., *Liturgy in the Age of Reason: Worship and Sacraments in England and Scotland 1662–c.1800*, Ashgate, Farnham 2008.

Spinks, Bryan D., 'Not so Common Prayer: The Third Service' in Perham, Michael (ed.), *The Renewal of Common Prayer: Unity and Diversity in Church of England Worship*, SPCK, London 1993, pp. 55–67.

Spinks, Bryan D., 'On the Wrong Side of History? Reimagining William Whittingham, Dean of Durham, 1563–1579' in Berger, Teresa and Spinks, Bryan D. (eds), *Liturgy's Imagined Past/s: Methodologies and Material in the Writing of Liturgical History Today*, Liturgical Press, Collegeville, MN 2016, pp. 205–29.

Spinks, Bryan D., *Reformation and Modern Rituals and Theologies of Baptism: From Luther to Contemporary Practices*, Ashgate, Aldershot 2006.

Spinks, Bryan D., *Sacraments, Ceremonies and the Stuart Divines: Sacramental Theology and Liturgy in England and Scotland 1603–1662*, Ashgate, Aldershot 2002.

Spinks, Bryan D., 'The Prayer Book "Crisis" in England' in Hefling, Charles and Shattuck, Cynthia (eds), *The Oxford Guide to the Book of Common Prayer*, Oxford University Press, Oxford 2006, pp. 239–43.

Spinks, Bryan D., 'The Transition from "Excellent Liturgy" to being "Too Narrow for the Religious Life of the Present Generation": The Book of Common Prayer in the Nineteenth Century' in Platten, Stephen and Woods, Christopher (eds), *Comfortable Words: Piety and the Book of Common Prayer*, SCM Press, London 2012, pp. 98–120.

Spinks, Bryan D., 'Treasures Old and New: A Look at Some of Thomas Cranmer's Methods of Liturgical Compilation' in Ayris, P. and Selwyn, D. (eds), *Thomas Cranmer: Churchman and Scholar*, Boydell and Brewer Ltd, Woodbridge 1993, pp. 175–88.

Spinks, Bryan D., *Two Faces of Elizabethan Anglican Theology: Sacraments and Salvation in the Thought of William Perkins and Richard Hooker*, Scarecrow Press, Lanham, MD 1999.

Spinks, Bryan D., 'What was wrong with Mr. Cosin's Couzening Devotions? Deconstructing an Episode in Seventeenth-Century Anglican "Liturgical Hagiography"', *Worship* 74 (2000), pp. 308–29.

Spratt, Thomas, *History of the Royal Society*, London 1667.

Sprott, G. W., *Scottish Liturgies in the Reign of James VI*, Blackwood, Edinburgh and London, 1901.

Stanwood, P. G. (ed.), *John Cosin: A Collection of Private Devotions*, Oxford University Press, Oxford 1967.

Stebbing, Henry, *A Sermon Preached at the Parish Church of St. Mary-le-Bow, on St. Mark's Day, 1760*, London 1760.

Stevenson, Kenneth, *Liturgy and Interpretation*, SCM Press, London 2011.

Strype, John, *Annals of the Reformation*, Clarendon Press, Oxford 1824.

Strype, John, *The Life and Acts of Matthew Parker*, printed for John Wyat, London 1711.

Swift, Daniel, *Shakespeare's Common Prayers: The Book of Common Prayer and the Elizabethan Age*, Oxford University Press, New York 2013.

Symondson, A., 'Theology, Worship and the Late Victorian Church' in Brooks, C. and Saint, A. (eds), *The Victorian Church: Architecture and Society*, Manchester University Press, Manchester 1995.

Taylor, Jeremy, *The Works of the Right Rev. Jeremy Taylor*, Vol. 3, Longman, London 1889.

Temperley, Nicholas, 'Present at the Birth' in Turner, Christopher (ed.), *Georgian Psalmody 1: The Gallery Tradition*, SG Publishing, Corby Glen 1997, pp. 1–7.

Temperley, Nicholas, *The Music of the English Parish Church*, Vol. 1, Cambridge University Press, Cambridge 1979.

Thomann, Günther, *John Ernest Grabe's Liturgies: Two Unknown Anglican Liturgies of the Seventeenth Century*, privately printed, Nürnberg 1989.

Thomann, Günther, *Studies in Church History*, privately printed, Stoke on Trent 1995.

Thomas, J. E., *Sabine Baring-Gould: The Life and Work of a Victorian*, Fonthill Media, Stroud 2015.

Thompson, Bard, *Liturgies of the Western Church*, World Publishing Company, New York 1962.

Thompson, T. (ed.), *Melville of Halhill, Memoirs of His Own Life*, Bannatyne Club, Edinburgh 1827.

Thurley, Simon, 'The Stuart Kings, Oliver Cromwell and the Chapel Royal 1618–1685', *Architectural History* 45 (2002), pp. 238–74.

Towerson, Gabriel, *A Sermon concerning vocal and instrumental musick in the church, as it was delivered in the parish church of St. Andrew, Undershaft, May 31st, 1696*, London 1696.

Townsend, Dave, 'Processes of Transmission in the Country Psalmody Tradition' in Turner, Christopher (ed.), *Georgian Psalmody 1: The West Gallery Tradition*, SG Publishing, Corby Glen 1997, pp. 31–3.

Trott, Michael, *The Life of Richard Waldo Sibthorp*, Sussex Academic Press, Brighton 2005.

Turner, Christopher (ed.), *Georgian Psalmody 1: The West Gallery Tradition*, SG Publishing in Association with Anglia Polytechnic University, Corby Glen 1997.

Unterseher, Cody C., *American Sarum*, Christ Church Press, Bronxville, NY 2010.

Usher, Roland G., *The Reconstruction of the English Church*, 2 vols, D. Appleton and Co., London 1910.

Wainwright, Arthur W. (ed.), *John Locke: A Paraphrase and Notes on the Epistles of St. Paul to the Galatians, 1 and 2 Corinthians, Romans, Ephesians*, 2 vols, Clarendon Press, Oxford 1987.

Watson, J. R., *The English Hymn: A Critical and Historical Study*, Clarendon Press, Oxford 1997.

Webster, Christopher, '"Absolutely Wretched": Camdenian Attitudes to the Late Georgian Church' in Webster, C. and Elliott, J. (eds), *'A Church as it Should Be': The Cambridge Camden Society and Its Influence*, Shaun Tyas, Donington 2000, pp. 1–21.

Wendeborn, F. A., *A View of England Towards the close of the Eighteenth Century by Fred. Aug. Wendeborn, LL.D.*, 2 vols, Dublin 1791.

Wenig, Scott A., *Straightening the Altars: The Ecclesiastical Vision and Pastoral Achievements of the Progressive Bishops under Elizabeth 1, 1559–1576*, Peter Lang, New York 2000.

Westerfield Tucker, Karen B., 'John Wesley's Prayer Book Revision: The Text in Context', *Proceedings of the Charles Wesley Society* 1 (1994), pp. 119–35.

Westminster Assembly Minutes, MS Dr Williams's Library, London, vol. 2.

Wheatley, Henry B. (ed.), *The Diary of Samuel Pepys*, Vol. I–III, G. Bell and Sons, New York 1923.

Whiston, William, *Historical Sketches of the Life of Dr. Samuel Clarke*, London 1730.

Whiston, William, *Memoirs of the Life and Writings of Mr. William Whiston*, London 1749.

Whiston, William, *Primitive Christianity Reviv'd*, London 1711.

White, James F., *John Wesley's Prayer Book: The Sunday Service of the Methodists in North America*, OSL Publications, Akron 1991.

White, Michael, *Isaac Newton: The Last Sorcerer*, Fourth Estate, London 1997.

Whiteford, Peter (ed.), *Vibrant Words: The Letters of Ursula Bethell*, Victoria University Press, Wellington, New Zealand 2005.

Williams, Isaac, *The Baptistery, or, the Way of Eternal Life*, John Henry Parker, Oxford 1842.

Willis, Jonathan, *Church Music and Protestantism in Post-Reformation England: Discourses, Sites and Identities*, Ashgate, Farnham 2010.

Willis, Robert and Clark, John, *The Architectural History of the University of Cambridge*, Vol. 1, Cambridge University Press 1886 (1988 reprint).

Witts, Francis E., *The Complete Diary of a Cotswold Parson. Vol. 2: The Curate and Rector*, Amberley Publishing, Chalfont 2008.

Wren, Matthew, *A Sermon Preached before the Kings Maiestie On Sunday the seventeenth of February last, at White-Hall*, Cambridge 1627.

Yates, Nigel, *Anglican Ritualism in Victorian Britain 1830–1910*, Oxford University Press, Oxford 1999.

Yates, Nigel, *Buildings, Faith, and Worship: The Liturgical Arrangement of Anglican Churches 1600–1900*, Oxford University Press, Oxford 1991.

Yates, Nigel, *The Anglican Revival in Victorian Portsmouth*, Grosvenor Press for Portsmouth City Council, Portsmouth 1983.

Yule, George, 'James VI and I: Furnishing the Churches in His Two Kingdoms' in Fletcher, Anthony and Roberts, Peter, *Religion, Culture and Society in Early Modern Britain: Essays in Honour of Patrick Collinson*, Cambridge University Press, Cambridge 2006, pp. 182–298.

The Zurich Letters, Comprising the Correspondence of Several English Bishops and Others, Parker Society, Cambridge 1842.

Index

Printed and bound by CPI Group (UK) Ltd, Croydon, CR0 4YY

25/03/2025

14647342-0003